Don Troiani's
SOLDIERS IN AMERICA
1754–1865

Don Troiani's

SOLDIERS IN AMERICA

1754–1865

Art by Don Troiani
Text by Earl J. Coates and James L. Kochan
Foreword by Brian Pohanka

Additional Contributors:
Rene Chartrand, Charles Cureton, Fred Gaede, Erik Goldstein

STACKPOLE
BOOKS

Published by
STACKPOLE BOOKS
5067 Ritter Road
Mechanicsburg, PA 17055

Printed in Hong Kong

10 9 8 7 6 5 4 3 2 1

FIRST EDITION

Library of Congress Cataloging-in-Publication Data

Troiani, Don.
    Don Troiani's soldiers in America 1754–1865 / art by Don
Troiani; text by Earl J. Coates and James L. Kochan; foreword by Brian
Pohanka; contributors, Rene Chartrand . . . [et al.].
        p.   cm.
    ISBN 0-8117-0519-6
    1. United States—History, Military—Pictorial works.
2. Soldiers—United States—Pictorial works. 3. Military supplies—
Pictorial works. I. Coates, Earl J. II. Kochan, James, 1958–   .
III. Title.
E181.T86   1998
355'.00973—dc21   98-11769
                                                     CIP

CONTENTS

The New Republic and Westward Expansion, 1790–1850

The Civil War, 1861–1865

FOREWORD

ORN IN NEW YORK CITY IN 1949 AND RAISED IN suburban Westchester County, Don Troiani admits to being captivated by military history "as long as I can remember."

"My first efforts at military art began as soon as I had crayons," he recalls. "I always wanted to draw soldiers and would not be swayed from it." His father, a successful commercial artist, encouraged his son's obvious talent. His mother, an antiques dealer, nurtured his curiosity about the artifacts and memorabilia of past generations. Thus a fusion of art and artifact—central to Don Troiani's creative process—was ingrained from his earliest youth.

By the time he began perfecting his skills at the Pennsylvania Academy of Fine Art and New York City's Art Students League, Troiani had already decided to make the field of military art his life's work. "America's history is filled with action, color and excitement," he says. "It is certainly a valid subject for an artist to pursue as long as it is approached in a thoughtful and thorough way."

Troiani's first venture into the field of limited-edition prints came in 1980, with his stirring depiction of Brig. Gen. George Armstrong Custer at the Battle of Gettysburg. Four years later he formed his own company, Historical Art Prints, to ensure the historical accuracy and quality control he deemed vital to the integrity of his chosen field. Stackpole Books' 1995 publication of *Don Troiani's Civil War,* which illustrated more than a hundred of the artist's selected works on the subject, provided a striking confirmation of the unparalleled talent that has seen him firmly established as America's preeminent painter of Civil War themes.

Though Troiani is primarily known for his Civil War art, and he concedes that, so far as the public is concerned, that bloodiest of American conflicts "is more popular than all the earlier periods put together," he also maintains a long-standing interest in Colonial and early-nineteenth-century military history. Throughout the 1970s much of his artwork centered on the American Revolution, appropriately coinciding with the nation's bicentennial. During those formative years of his artistic career Troiani painted more than one hundred watercolors of Revolutionary subjects for the National Park Service and a series of spirited battle scenes for *American Heritage* magazine. "That entire first century of American soldier life fascinates me," he explains. "People think of me as a Civil War artist, but I feel equally at home in the American Revolution or the War of 1812."

"I think of myself as a historian as much as an artist," Don Troiani says. "The illustrations in this book aren't just paintings; each figure is a visual document, an accurate historical reconstruction of an individual soldier of a specific unit at a specific time." Noting that diligent research in archival, museum, and private holdings is an absolute prerequisite to his craft, Troiani believes that for a historical artist to settle for less reveals a lack of interest—even disrespect—for the subject.

In Troiani's striving for authenticity he is forever on the lookout for primary documentation, which he defines as "information in its original context." He points to the fact that new data is constantly becoming available as historical societies catalog their holdings, and as letters, diaries, photographs, and artifacts turn up in private collections or family attics. The assembling and assimilation of that primary data was "absolutely vital" to the crafting of the illustrations in this volume, and Troiani is proud to note that in many cases, "this is very first time those soldiers have been represented accurately."

Research for a Troiani painting typically begins five or six years before the first brushstroke is put to canvas. His studio office contains hundreds of files on individual military units: their history, uniforms, and armament. At any one time, perhaps two dozen of these will be potential subjects for a painting, but Troiani will tackle the subject only when he feels his research is as complete as possible. "There are many paintings I would like to do, but don't have quite enough information to get it right," he explains. "I'd rather keep the file open indefinitely than paint by guesswork."

Another key ingredient in Troiani's art is his personal collection of militaria. "You can look at a picture of an artifact for days and still not know it," he says. "But examining it in your own hands reveals its texture, its substance, and how it works." His personal storehouse of uniforms, weapons, accoutrements ranks as one of the most extensive of its kind in the world. Many of these items are rare originals, and as a serious collector Troiani is quick to point out that some of the rarest are not necessarily the most expensive: "For me a surviving example of a British enlisted man's belt buckle is more desirable than some fancy sword presented to a famous general." Noting that "some of what were once the most common military items are now the most elusive," he cites the example of Civil War shoes: "Today there are several hundred presentation swords for every pair of Civil War shoes, and yet it was those brogans that were there marching and fighting the great battles like Gettysburg."

While most of the weapons in his paintings are originals, the fragile nature of century-old textiles required a military wardrobe of reproduction clothing, headgear, knapsacks, and other soldier trappings, specially reconstructed to Troiani's exacting specifications. In preparation for *Soldiers in America,* these meticulous recreations of period attire were used to garb a small army of models, who were themselves hand-picked by Troiani for their physical build, facial expression, and overall bearing. "I try to pick models who represent a character type of a particular era," he says. "I try to make each figure a portrait. They have to look like real people, not mannequins."

This creative synthesis of researching, collecting, and modeling is the same method used by the great French military artist Edouard Detaille (1848–1912), whom Troiani unabashedly refers to as his "idol." From vast canvasses of Napoleonic battle scenes to small pen-and-ink sketches of private soldiers, Detaille never wavered in his devotion to detail and accuracy. "His figures all look convincing because his models were dressed in the real thing," Troiani explains. "Detaille's approach is the only valid approach, and, like him, I aim to get as close to the real thing as possible. I am out to demolish misconceptions, to show the way soldiers really looked as opposed to how people think they looked."

Working in a genre more often characterized by artistic license than accuracy, Troiani's fixation on authenticity has been welcomed by military historians, many of whom are eager to share the results of their research. "Some of them have spent decades gathering material on a certain period, or a specific regiment," Troiani remarks. "It's pretty exciting for them when their work is translated into a pictorial reconstruction. It's as much fun for them to see as it is for me to paint it." So when it came time to prepare the text for *Soldiers in America,* Don Troiani was able to call upon several longtime historical advisors whose years of dedicated inquiry mark them as leaders in their field.

James L. Kochan dates his fascination with the material aspects of American military history to a 1963 visit to Fort George at Niagara-on-the-Lake, Canada. He was only five years old at the time, but his parents were quick to recognize and foster his burgeoning interest. Numerous family vacations to historic sites and his own forays into well-stocked local libraries continued to fuel the sparks of his youthful curiosity about the lives and times of Americans in the eighteenth and nineteenth centuries. An Ohio native, Kochan developed a particular interest in the struggle for control of the Great Lakes region, from the French and Indian War through the War of 1812. By the time he entered high school, he was already doing primary research in manuscript repositories and museums, pursuing his growing interest in period military clothing.

Graduating from Ohio's Miami University in 1980, Kochan was awarded a fellowship to pursue graduate work in early American history and historical archaeology at the College of William and Mary. During his academic years he published the first of his more than fifty scholarly articles on military uniforms and equipage. He was encouraged by the support and respect of leading specialists in the field, most notably the late artist/historian H. Charles McBarron, whom Kochan refers to as his "mentor." Further honing his own research skills, Kochan began to gain an understanding of the subtleties in cut and construction of military dress, and its evolution from the eighteenth to the mid-nineteenth centuries.

Over the next two decades Jim Kochan received many honors for his contributions to the study of early-American military history and material culture, as well as in museum management, including the Anne S. K. Brown Research Fellowship in military art, the prestigious Award of Merit from the American Association of State and Local History, and numerous National Park Service and U.S. Army awards and citations. A consultant to dozens of museums, historical organizations, and film projects, Kochan finds his present position as Director of Museum Collections for the Mount Vernon Ladies' Association—the custodians of George Washington's estate since 1858—ideally suited to his passion for eighteenth-century history. "It's an extremely challenging and exciting time to be at Mount Vernon," he notes, "as 1999 will mark the two-hundredth anniversary of Washington's death."

It was in 1983 that Kochan first corresponded with Don Troiani, whose artwork the zealous young historian had long admired. The two finally met in 1985, and two years later when Kochan assumed the position of supervisory curator at Morristown National Historic Park, New Jersey, their mutual interest in the Revolutionary War led to friendship and collaboration on a variety of projects. The two have worked together on numerous articles in scholarly journals as well as on limited-edition military prints, and served as the primary historical consultants for A&E Network's acclaimed documentary series *The American Revolution.* Their rapport is founded upon a common passion for research as a means of ensuring authenticity.

In his study of early-American militaria, Kochan employs not only the traditional tools of the academic historian, but brings to his work the detective skills of the archaeologist, the art historian, and the craftsman. Scouring museums, archives, and private collections throughout the United States, Canada, Great Britain, and the West Indies, he regularly travels with laptop computer and notebook at hand, as well as a camera, measuring devices, and drafting instruments. His research involves not only poring through long-forgotten manuscripts, but in documenting and preparing scaled pattern drafts of rare uniforms and equipment as well. Kochan's reproductions of uniforms, headgear, and accoutrements have been displayed in museum exhibits, featured in motion pictures, and are among Don Troiani's own substantial wardrobe of artistic props. Many were used in the preparation of this book.

Kochan believes an in-depth knowledge of material culture in general, and of clothing in particular, to be of vital importance in understanding past cultures and people. "Nothing is more personal than clothing. It tells you a lot about a person—about their society, their sense of nationality, their sense of affiliation with a regiment or a cause." Military garb "provides an invaluable sense of the common soldier," he declares, "no less than tactics and weaponry, the material, cut and style of clothing dictated how a soldier moved, how a regiment or army fought."

In crafting meticulous reconstructions of colonial and nineteenth-century uniforms, Jim Kochan invariably draws upon his own impressive collection of early tailoring manuals. "Revolutionary War and War of 1812 manuscripts provide detailed measurements of military clothing," he remarks, "and by marrying those to the tailoring methods and techniques of the time we come as close as we can to replicating the period construction." Of course, still more can be learned in cases where original examples have survived the ravages of time. Noting that "even the smallest fragment can provide invaluable clues," Kochan cites the example of a Revolutionary uniform illustrated in this volume. "We literally got down

to stitch counting," he recalls, "and determined the average number of stitches per inch needed to construct a Continental officer's uniform."

For Don Troiani there was no question that Kochan's expertise would be of incomparable value in the preparation of *Soldiers in America.* "I consider him the foremost authority on eighteenth- and early-nineteenth-century uniforms and equipage," Troiani says. "Jim's research is impeccable; he's always on the cutting edge of historical inquiry."

When it came to selecting an author for the Civil War sections of this book, Don Troiani unhesitatingly turned to his friend Jerry Coates, whom he characterizes as "the most thorough researcher of that war I have ever known."

"With Jerry, seeking out and cataloging new information from archival files is what a vacation would be for the average person," Troiani says.

A native of Ashland, Ohio, Earl J. "Jerry" Coates recalls being interested in the Civil War "as long as I can remember." In part, this was due to his family's involvement in the conflict. His great-uncle "was like a grandfather to me," Coates reflects, "and five of his uncles served in the Civil War. When I was in grade school we used to sit at the table and talk history." One of Coates's great-great-uncles— Nathan D. Hanson of the 1st Maine Heavy Artillery—was killed in action at the Battle of Petersburg. When Jerry was in junior high school his great-aunt presented him with the fallen soldier's carte-de-visite photograph and identity tag, and they remain among his most prized possessions, a tangible personal connection to that terrible war.

After attending Ashland College in his hometown, Coates graduated from Baltimore's Loyola College with a degree in American history. Following service in the U.S. Army, he accepted a position with the National Security Agency and moved to the Maryland suburbs of Washington, D.C. His decision to take the job, Coates reflects, "was in large part due to the fact that I'd be living close to primary research facilities like the National Archives." He retired from the government in 1994, and he takes pride in his nearly thirty-five years of service. Coates was instrumental in the establishment of the National Cryptologic Museum at Fort George G. Meade, and he served as the facility's first curator. In 1996 he received the Excellence in Federal Service Award for his work in the creation of the museum.

During his years in the Midwest, Jerry Coates had frequently obtained photocopies of Civil War records from the National Archives. But when he moved to the Washington area, he was able to peruse the Archives' vast holdings at his leisure, and he was soon spending at least one evening a week working his way through box after box of documents, many of them untouched since being filed away in the latter decades of the nineteenth century. "I felt like a little kid opening Christmas presents," he reflects. Initially seeking and compiling information on the Civil War's colorful Zouave regiments, Coates began to broaden his search to an exhaustive exploration of wartime records of the Quartermaster Department—the agency that oversaw the requisition and supply of Federal military attire.

"I decided that I was just simply going to look at all the Civil War Quartermaster records I could get my hands on," Coates recalls. And when he came across Record Group 92, Entry 2182—the "Miscellaneous Records" of the Quartermaster Department—he found that he had his work cut out for him. Filed chronologically in more than two hundred boxes, and taking up some two hundred feet of shelves, these official documents were an untapped gold mine of information, detailing in often-minute detail the specific articles of clothing issued to soldiers in Federal service. A quarter century after commencing his task, and still working steadily, Coates is confident he has reviewed "at least 90 percent of the records of the Quartermaster Department, and probably 100 percent of those that relate to Civil War era uniforms."

As he organized the fruits of his research into files on particular units, Coates broadened his search and began exploring other archival record groups. He soon realized that only a handful of historians had ever utilized the regimental books and papers that Union Army organizations were required to turn over to the government at the end of the Civil War. These dusty ledger books and official forms still bound with "red tape"—in some cases never untied since they were placed in storage a hundred or more years ago—provided minutiae on the issuance of uniforms, accoutrements, and weaponry to the Civil War fighting men. Another valuable resource were the official orders of the various brigades, divisions, and corps that made up the Northern armies. Arsenal records, ordnance records, treasury records, state claims—all were there, waiting to be explored by the diligent researcher. There was, he concluded, no need for writers or artists to "guess at" the historically correct garb of a Civil War serviceman. Coates discovered that by synthesizing this material, one could essentially trace the operations and assess the overall appearance of individual soldiers on a monthly, if not daily, basis.

Though there are fewer surviving Confederate records than the Northern documents that were maintained and preserved by the Federal government, they do exist in extensive numbers. "I realized about eight or nine years ago that the CSA records had been broken up," Coates recalls. "Southern ordnance and quartermaster records were assembled in individual personnel files for the various Confederate units." With typical zeal, he set about working his way through the microfilmed records of every Confederate military organiza-

tion, and, as in the case of their Yankee counterparts, unearthed a staggering array of descriptive detail.

"If you're real lucky," Coates remarks, "you'll hit something like the statement of effects for a deceased soldier, and in several cases with the Confederates it's just unbelievable that they listed every single item, down to the change in their pockets!" Similar accountings of personal effects exist for many Federals who perished from wounds or disease—generally located in the soldier's service or pension file. Coates cites the example of a Union officer, where, in addition to recording items of clothing and personal belongings, a hospital orderly took care to note the serial numbers on the man's revolver and pocket watch.

Jerry Coates has authored or coauthored several volumes and numerous articles and served as a consultant for Time-Life Books and the A&E Network's acclaimed documentary series *Civil War Journal*. He currently serves as president of the Friends of the National Park at Gettysburg (FNPG). But his interest in Civil War uniforms and firearms extends beyond the strictly academic. In 1970 he joined the North-South Skirmish Association (NSSA), a national organization of competitive marksmen using Civil War firearms. Eager to share his archival knowledge, Coates formed a committee to assist his fellow NSSA members with uniform research, and he helped to establish an annual award to be presented to the most authentically uniformed participant. After six years as the NSSA inspector general, and four years as deputy commander, in 1992 Coates was elected to a five-year term as national commander of the organization. His vast knowledge of nineteenth-century ordnance, firsthand experience in firing period muskets, carbines, and cannon, and knowledge of tactical drill gained in Civil War living history events, were of inestimable value in the preparation of this volume.

⁓

When asked what he thought was the most important factor that went into the crafting of *Soldiers in America,* Don Troiani emphatically responded, "Research! I can never overemphasize the role of research in military art, or in historical art of any kind, for that matter." Citing the invaluable expertise of Jim Kochan and Jerry Coates, along with contributing authors Rene Chartrand, Charles Cureton, Fred Gaede, and Erik Goldstein, Troiani concludes, "I look at us as a unique team, with a common passion for research and a commitment to authenticity. This book is the culmination of a lifetime of work for me, and for them. It's taken me forty-eight years to learn enough to do it right, and it may take me another forty-eight to do it perfectly. There is no end to learning. As soon as you stop learning, you're going downhill."

Brian C. Pohanka
Alexandria, Virginia

ACKNOWLEDGMENTS

To my buddies Jerry Coates and Jim Kochan, among the leading military uniform scholars in America, who spent countless hours slogging through this grueling project and suffering my relentless pestering with good humor, I give my heartfelt thanks and deepest gratitude.

To my lovely wife Donna and my family, who always support me in everything I do.

Special thanks to the contributing authors, equally noted leaders in their fields of study, who were always ready to help out, even at the last minute: Rene Chartrand, Dr. Charles Cureton, Fred Gaede, and Erik Goldstein. Also thanks to Tracey Studio, Southbury, Connecticut, for the black and white artifact photos, and all the fine folks at Stackpole Books, who have to be the easiest publishers on earth to work with.

And to my friends who generously assisted with this project: Larry Babits, DeWitt Bailey, Ray Baker, Bruce Bazelon, Herman Benninghoff, Joel Bohy, Christopher Bryant, Charles Childs, Norma Coates, Jo-Val Codling, Henry Cooke IV, Melissa Cronyn NPS, Caroline R. Cureton, William C. Davis, Dr. David Evans, Scott Ferriss, James C. Frasca, Joseph Fulginiti, William Gladstone, Randy Hackenburg, Holly Hageman, Steven Hill, Robert Hodge, Les Jensen, Paul C. Loane, Don Londal-Smidt, Howard M. Madaus, Maine State Archives, Mike McAfee, Ed McGee, Keith Melton, Col. J. Craig Nannos, Deane Nelson, George C. Neumann, John Ockerbloom, Stephen Osman, Norma O'Brien, Mike O'Donnell, Ron Palm, Brian Pohanka, John Powell, Kenneth Powers, William Roden, Dr. Richard Sauers, Sylvia Sherman, Michelle Simmons, James Spears, James Stannmetalos, Glenn Stevens, Bill Turner, Ken Turner, Mr. & Mrs. Richard Ulbrich, Tim Wilson, Michael Winey, Stephen Wood.

I hope to be forgiven for anyone I have unintentionally neglected to mention.

Don Troiani
Southbury, Connecticut

The Colonial Period
1754–1769

THE DEVELOPMENT OF MILITARY UNIFORMS COIN-cided with the emergence of the European nation-states during the seventeenth century. As a monarch rose to supremacy over his nobles during the so-called Age of Enlightenment, so did his need for a standing army loyal to the Crown and able to reinforce his will. The economic pressures of the Thirty Years War and, in Great Britain, the English Civil War, demonstrated the economic value of mass production of arms, accoutrements, and clothing to equip newly raised corps. The Swedish army of Gustavus Adolphus was noted for its "green," "blue," and "yellow" regiments, so-called because they had been issued clothing made of colored cloth purchased in bulk and issued out in consistent batches by regiment. By the close of the English Civil War, a brick-red cloth —a dye inexpensively derived from the madder root— became predominant in the British Army. As France emerged preeminent in European affairs following the Thirty Years War, many nations began to follow French practices. The jus-taucorps—a long woolen coat originally derived from French peasant dress—had been adopted in the French Army and soon found its way into civilian fashion. By the 1680s, Louis XIV's French troops had achieved remarkable consistency in dress, with blue or red for royal household troops, while natural grayish-white cloth was adopted as a cheaper dress for the many standing regiments in the royal army.

Marked improvement in textile production and dyeing soon allowed other nations to achieve similar uniformity in color of cloth as well as in the cut of military clothing. Whether by intent or coincidence, by the opening of the eighteenth century white seemed to be the predominant color adopted by Catholic nations such as France, Spain, and the Holy Roman Empire (Austria). Blue appeared to be pre-ferred by Protestant states (first achieved from cheap woad dye, later derived from the more expensive indigo), although Britain, Hanover, and Denmark kept their rather small armies in madder-red uniforms. As the century progressed, the loose-fitting justaucorps, or coat, worn by soldier and civilian became more fitted, as did the breeches and waistcoats worn underneath. With this "suit of clothes" would be work stockings and shoes and a low-crowned, broad-brimmed felt hat.

Changes in military technology, as well as in the practical needs of the soldiery, led to further modifications in military clothing. The mass armament of troops with flintlock muskets and the employment of close-order formations led to sewing, or "cocking," up the brim of the hat to the crown to prevent its interference with the musket during drill and combat. Soon, the three-cornered, or "tri-corn," cock became the popular mode, and the brims became both shorter and more rigid, often bound with worsted tape or lace to further strengthen and support the edges. Canvas coverings to protect the stockings, shoes, and knees of the breeches from thorns and mud were developed, which became known as gaiters, or "spatter-dashes." The long tails, or "skirts," of the soldiers' coats were hooked back to aid in marching, thereby exposing their colored linings, which became known as "turnbacks." Similarly, varicolored cuffs, collars, and lapels were added to the coats, termed "facings," which became popular by the midcentury. Buttonholes and coat edges were frequently bound with both cloth tape or lace to reinforce the cloth, often done in the livery pattern of the ruler or a proprietary colonel or commander. Now, not only one's country but the regimental affiliation of an individual could be determined by the uniform clothing issued to him, which became known as "regimentals."

In the Anglo-American colonies of North America, however, uniforms were a rare occurrence prior to the mid-eighteenth century. True, an occasional red-clad British independent company or even regiment did arrive to garrison key frontier posts, suppress local rebellions, or mount operations against the French colonies to the north, but such occurrences were rare. Occasionally, groups of gentlemen would band together and form a nominal troop of horse or foot company—as much social club as of any military utility—and this custom was little practiced outside of the largest cities or towns on the Atlantic seaboard. During the War of Austrian Succession, or "King George's War," New England militia volunteers on the Louisbourg expedition purchased "slops"—cheap, mass-produced clothing—from sutlers to augment their clothing for a long, cold campaign. Frequently of brown or blue, this cheap clothing imposed some degree of uniformity among various companies, although more accidental than by intent. Nevertheless, uniform clothing would come into its own in the colonies during the French and Indian War. Colonial governments, challenged with raising regiments for service against the French and their Native-American allies, resorted to bounties of cash or land, as well as uniforms, as incentives for enlistment. Blue seemed to be the preferred color in Virginia, New Jersey, South Carolina, and Massachusetts, while green uniforms were provided to provincials from Pennsylvania, New York, and the lower counties of Delaware. Wilderness campaigning in North America led to further modifications in military dress and equipment among British, colonial American, French, and even Native-American participants, as the following section will demonstrate.

SOLDIER, VIRGINIA REGIMENT, 1754

Concern over perceived French encroachments in the Ohio country—land claimed by the colony of Virginia—convinced Gov. Robert Dinwiddie that a military force needed to be raised for the protection of the Virginia frontiers and to build a fort at the forks of the Ohio River (present-day Pittsburgh, Pennsylvania). Using the colony's militia laws for authorization, Dinwiddie commissioned officers for two, eventually six, companies of volunteers to be paid from funds grudgingly provided by the General Assembly of Virginia, Britain then being at peace—however tenuous—with France. Recruiting for the Virginia Regiment began in the northern counties of the colony under the direction of a twenty-one-year-old former militia major, now promoted to lieutenant colonel, by the name of George Washington.

Washington reported to Dinwiddie that raising troops for hard service on the western frontiers at 8 pence per day proved difficult, even among "the generality of those who are to be enlisted, . . . loose, Idle Persons that are quite destitute of House, and Home, and I may truly say many of them Cloaths." In March 1754 Washington requested and received permission to clothe his men in a simple uniform of red coats and breeches, to be paid for out of stoppages from their pay. Locally procured, the red uniforms were made of "thin, sleazy cloth without lining," and at least the first two companies also received "flannel waistcoats of an interior sort." Some, if not all, of the red coats were "turn'd up with blue" —an attempt at a more martial appearance. Deserter descriptions verify the issue of red breeches, although leather breeches seem to have been in widespread use as well. Coarse and checked linen shirts, shoes, and stockings were also furnished, as well as blankets for the men that had none.

The Virginia Regiment was furnished with arms and accoutrements drawn from the Williamsburg magazine. The muskets appear to have been of standard British issue, either Tower or contractor-furnished Long Land Pattern with wooden ramrods and barrels engraved "Virginia 1750" to denote colony ownership. Cartridge boxes were worn on narrow straps, and bayonet frogs—for those soldiers fortunate enough to have been issued bayonets—were suspended from those straps. The other soldiers carried belt axes or tomahawks in their place.

This reconstruction portrays the probable appearance of the troops in garrison at Alexandria in April, before marching westward toward the forks of the Ohio. The soldier wears his hat, although a private purchase, cocked in a military style. Prior to their departure, the men were issued cloth "Indian leggings" to protect their legs from the rough underbrush. It would be in such garb, although threadbare and ragged from their rugged service, that Washington's men would appear when they surrendered to the French at Fort Necessity on July 4, 1754, following the first bloodshed of what would rapidly accelerate into worldwide conflict—the Seven Years' War.

COL. J. CRAIG NANNOS

D. Troiani
© 93

British Eighteen-Hole Cartridge Box, Belt, and Frog, 1759–84

The design of this simple set of accoutrements had its origins in the early eighteenth century and continued in usage by the British Army for nearly a hundred years virtually unchanged in form. The cartridge box was a simple, curved block of black-painted popular or beech wood drilled to hold eighteen rounds of musket or carbine cartridges. A royal cypher was embossed on the black leather flap, which was nailed to the back of the wooden block, and two leather belt keepers were similarly attached to the front. The cartridge box was worn on a narrow belt of blackened harness leather that closed with a simple square iron buckle. A sliding frog, made of two pieces of harness leather, crudely sewn together and reinforced with tinned iron rivets, held the bayonet of the soldier's firearm.

New recruits to British regiments were issued a "stand of arms" before joining their regiments. The box with frog and belt were part of this stand, in addition to the musket with its sling, bayonet, and scabbard. This specimen of the cartridge box is stamped with the GRIII cypher in false gold leaf, denoting its production during the reign of King George III (1760–1820). Nearly identical cartridge boxes survive in other collections with the cypher of King George II (1727–60). Simple and cheap to produce, tens of thousands of these sets were made under contract for the Board of Ordnance until replaced by the twenty-four round tin "magazine," adopted in 1784. Although the most common British Army accoutrement of the Georgian period, this example is the only complete cartridge box set that survives today.

SHAWNEE WARRIOR, C. 1750–80

By the mid-1700s, the Shawnee had firmly established themselves north of the Ohio River in what is now southern Ohio. An exceptionally fragmented people, this Algonquian-speaking tribe had been widely scattered during the previous two centuries, with groups known in Illinois, among the Alabama Creek, and a heavy concentration in Pennsylvania. At one time, under the domination of the Iroquois Confederacy, the Shawnee grew in strength and independence as they moved westward into the Ohio country, from which they had earlier been dispersed by the Iroquois before European contact. By the opening of the Seven Years' War, they controlled much of the fur trade of that region, principally deerskins.

Trade brought the Ohio Shawnee into allegiance with the British, but they were forced to side with the French out of self-defense, after the British failed to protect them from attacks by the French and their Indian allies in 1752. They accompanied the French against Washington in 1754 and were instrumental in achieving Braddock's Defeat the following year, which left the Virginia and Pennsylvania frontier settlements open to their frequent attacks. French influence waned in the Ohio Valley following the fall of Fort DuQuesne in 1758, and the Shawnee established an uneasy truce with the English. They even sided with them on occasion, until postwar policies and fear for their land led them to join in the Indian alliance commonly called Pontiac's Conspiracy. They made peace in 1756, which was maintained until 1774, when there was an outbreak of hostilities with Virginia known as Lord Dunmore's War. During the Revolutionary War, and intermittently afterward until the close of the War of 1812, the Shawnee sided with the British, devastating Kentucky and other frontier areas. Likewise, American forces repeatedly destroyed Shawnee settlements.

Skillful and resourceful warriors, the Shawnee excelled in raiding and ambush tactics. During this period, the Shawnee, like most Eastern Woodlands Indians, used a mixture of traditional Indian articles of dress (though often made of trade goods) and European garments, such as shirts, coats, and blanketing, which they wore as "matchcoats," a traditional Indian garment of togalike form. As related by an eyewitness who served against them in 1764:

SCOTT FERRIS

Their dress consists of the skins of some wild beast, or a blanket, a shirt either of linen, or of dressed skins, a breech clout, leggins, reaching half way up the thigh, and fastened to a belt, with mokawsons on their feet. . . . They shave their head, reserving only a small tuft of hair on the top; and slit the outer part of their ears, to which, by weights,

they give a circular form, extending it down to their shoulder.

They adorn themselves with ear and nose rings, bracelets of silver and wampum, and paint their faces with various colours. When they prepare for an engagement they paint themselves black, and fight naked.

Their arms are a fusil, or rifle, a powder horn, a shot pouch, a tomahawk, and a scalping knife hanging to their neck.

When they are in want of fire arms, they supply them by a bow, a spear, or a death hammer, which is a short club made of hard wood.

This Shawnee warrior is thus armed and accoutred, carrying a French-made fusil, ball-headed club, and "scalping knife." His knife sheath is covered with an elaborate pattern woven of flattened, dyed porcupine quills, and his moccasins are decorated with similar quillwork. His trade cloth leggings are edged with brass tinkling cones, tufted with dyed deer hair or horsehair, and his finger-woven garters and pouch strap are trimmed with trade beads. The slits in his elongated earlobes are wrapped with quillwork, and trade silver ornaments decorate his upper body. This finery, coupled with the black and vermilion paint, signify that he is prepared for the war council or ceremonies prior to setting out on a raid. In actual combat, he would appear less showy and more fearsome, and often nearly, if not completely, naked.

Halberd Tomahawk

Among the ample array of weapons available to the American Indian warrior of the eighteenth century, none captures popular imagination as does the war ax, or tomahawk. The battle weapon of choice for close-quarter combat, it begot a host of distinctive variations. Although the pipe and spike tomahawks are probably the best known today, the halberd, or battle-ax, type may have been equally prevalent during the eighteenth century. European artists frequently show this pattern in paintings and engravings, notably the mezzotint portrait of the Mohawk chief King Hendrick published before his death at the Battle of Lake George in 1755 and *The Death of General Wolfe,* by Benjamin West.

The design is essentially a European military halberd, reduced somewhat in size with a much shortened haft. Most specimens had a head forged of one piece of steel and featured a splayed blade at the front, a dagger or spear point at the top, and a long, curved spike at the back, assuring the user a variety of equally gruesome death-dealing options. The spike was particularly adapted for nearly puncturing skulls. Although they were common in their day, few examples have survived the ravages of hard usage and the passage of years. Many have been reworked or discarded as the style fell from favor toward the early nineteenth century.

The presentation specimen shown here bears an inscription on the flat of the blade, "WCT to GWM," in addition to the appropriate decorations of crossed arrows and bows. The height from the base of the forged socket to the tip of the dagger is ten inches. Extremely well crafted, this fine piece may have been given as a token of friendship or respect to parties now unknown. A few similar specimens are extant in institutions and private collections.

Scalping Knife, c. 1779

Found underwater offshore of Fort Haldimand, a British-built fortification constructed on Carleton Island during the Revolutionary War, this is an outstanding example of what was commonly called a "scalping knife" during the eighteenth century. Although the tip of the corroded blade is now missing, the knife is in excellent condition, considering that it was submerged for two hundred years, and retains its original wooden handle or grip. Similar blades have been excavated at numerous forts, trading posts, and Indian villages through eastern North America and figure prominently in period artwork depicting warriors of the Eastern Woodland tribes. Bone- and wood-handled scalping knives are listed among the supplies furnished to the British Indian Department, as well as among the stores of most frontier trading establishments.

French Colonial Cutlass or Saber, 1750–60

On July 8, 1760, following two weeks of sporadic fighting with British warships, the French frigate *Machault* was abandoned and scuttled on the Restigouche River to avoid capture. The frigate was part of a small squadron that sailed from France with needed arms, munitions, and supplies for the relief of Montreal (the capital of French Canada, after the fall of Quebec the previous year), and its loss helped seal Canada's fate in Britain's favor.

Sabers or cutlasses were part of the ship's complement of small arms listed in her original 1758 fitting-out manifest. When the *Machault* was excavated by Parks Canada underwater archaeologists in 1969–71, brass guards and pommel caps from a hilt form known as *pontet simple* were recovered. These were probably from the ship's sabers or cutlasses but could possibly have been part of a supply intended for land troops. The iron blades had long ago rusted away, but the form of a corresponding leather scabbard proved that the blades were of saber form—single-edged weapons for cutting or slashing.

This important saber or cutlass is complete and features an identical hilt to those recovered from the *Machault*, including the wreathed head decoration cast into the counterguard. Specimens of this hilt were also excavated from French forts— Beausejour (captured 1755) and Carillon (Ticonderoga, abandoned 1759)—clearly establishing land usage in Canada during the 1750s, as well. It has a wooden grip covered with leather and is mounted with a 34-inch, curved blade with three fullers, or grooves. The blade's form suggests Spanish or Germanic manufacture, and it is likely that this cutlass was made from available parts specifically for colonial usage. Swords and cutlasses were in high demand as trade goods among the Indian allies of the French, and perhaps this multipurpose example could originally have been intended as such.

Private, Companies Franches de la Marine, 1757–60

WILLIAM RODEN

At the outbreak of the Seven Years' War, troops of the *Companies franches de la Marine* were the only French regulars then in Canada. These troops were under the direction of the Ministry of the Marine, which was responsible for the administration of the overseas French colonies. Despite what their name might suggest, these troops were not sea soldiers, but independent companies of infantry troops raised for service in new France (French Canada) and Louisiana, as well as colonial garrisons in the East and West Indies. Most of the enlisted men were recruited in France, the hope being that the discharged veterans would then choose to settle in the colonies, thereby bolstering the minimal French population. However, many of the officers in the Canadian companies were of French Canadian stock by the 1750s, due to official policies that encouraged this practice. There were thirty companies serving in New France in the 1750s, and an increase to forty was authorized in 1757.

Since the 1680s, the *Companies franches* were traditionally clothed in white uniforms, as were most French regiments in the Royal Army. Men of the *Companies franches* serving in Canada received grayish white coats of coarse, unbleached wool, with royal blue cuffs and linings and trimmed with brass buttons. Their "smallclothes"—sleeved waistcoats and breeches—were also of royal blue cloth. Cocked hats with false gold lace binding and white neckstocks completed this simple but striking uniform. Officers wore similar bleached white and royal blue uniforms of better cut and finer materials, including gilt buttons and trimmings.

The *Compagnie franche* soldier was armed with a musket, its socket bayonet, and a brass-hilted sword with a short, straight blade (usually substituted by a tomahawk in the field). Until the 1740s, the muskets were of various Marine patterns procured at the Tulle arsenal; however, by the 1750s, the ministry increasingly purchased muskets from the arsenal at St. Etienne that were nearly identical to the 1728 army model. Accoutrement belts were of buff leather, and by the mid-1750s, the 9-round cartridge box, or *gargoussier*, worn on the waistbelt was replaced by a shoulder pouch (*giberne*) of thick reddish brown leather that held thirty rounds of cartridges in its wooden block insert. A simple knapsack of hemp canvas or hair-on cowhide, suspended by a leather or webbing strap, contained spare clothing and personal effects on campaign.

Long, heavy, and easily stained, the uniform coat was frequently left in barracks when the troops went about their daily duties, being reserved for dress parade or severe weather. For normal garrison activity or field service during the warm season, the blue sleeved waistcoat, breeches, and forage cap proved more than adequate. French troops in Canada were often issued *mitassex*, or cloth Indian leggings, as well as moccasins, and tumpline or burden straps (which carried the blanket roll that often replaced the knapsack) when going on frontier service. The troops of the *Companies franches* served in nearly every battle fought in North America, proving themselves not only as disciplined infantry, but also as skilled partisans or irregulars in the woods warfare that signalized the French and Indian War.

French Grenadier's Saber or Hanger, 1740–60

Although they were the traditional side arms of the infantry, swords were seemingly of little practical use in the densely forested landscape where French and British soldiers campaigned during the French and Indian War. Typically, swords were left behind or turned in to regimental stores when troops took the field, tomahawks or belt axes often proving more practical substitutes, though this was not always the case. The grenadiers that formed part of the French force during the failed winter 1757 expedition against Fort William Henry carried their swords with them, probably as symbols of their elite status. In garrison or on the open battlefield, such as the Plains of Abraham, such weapons were still carried by most French regulars. Grenadiers were armed with curved-bladed sabers or hangers rather than the straight-bladed swords issued to battalion companies. On the curved blade of this saber, which has an all-brass hilt, is engraved "*Grandier d' infantrie.*"

Artillery Linstock, French, 1753

The linstock was the principal firing device for artillery pieces through much of the eighteenth century. A derivation of "lint-stock," it functioned much as its name implies, serving to hold the loosely twisted cord, or "match," used to touch off, or fire, artillery pieces. Match was made of hempen tow, treated with various components or combustibles to ensure constant, regulated burning. There was both "quick match" and "slow match," the latter also being carried by grenadiers to ignite their grenades. A length of match would be doubled at the center and each equal length wrapped in an opposing spiral fashion up the shaft until the loose ends came to the head of the linstock. There the ends would be wedged or threaded into the tips of two opposing arms or holders. More match could be fed from below as the tips burned down. This linstock has serpent-shaped arms. The tips of the match would be wedged into the mouth and at night, when lit, the linstock would give the impression of a dragon spewing fire. Many lintocks were quite plain and did not mount the spearlike tip as on this example, which made it usable as an arm at close quarters. The form of the iron linstock head, dated "1753," suggests a French origin.

French Model 1728 Musket, c. 1741

This smoothbore musket was the standard infantry arm probably carried by the French Army infantry regiments serving in North America from the 1740s onward. Essentially an improved version of the model 1717, the first standardized French pattern, the 1728 was first updated in 1741, when iron ramrods replaced the earlier wooden ones. It had a 44-inch barrel of .69 caliber, firing a ball of slightly smaller diameter than that fired by its .75-caliber British counterpart. Further changes, principally in the configuration of the barrel bands, were incorporated in a new model, the 1746 musket, which probably also saw limited usage here during the French and Indian War. Well made and reliable, many of these muskets found their way into British and American hands and were used during the Revolutionary War, not only by patriot forces, but also by some Loyalist and British corps.

French Artillery Sword or Hanger, 1750–60

Although they rarely drew them in combat, most European foot soldiers of the mid-1750s still carried swords in addition to their principal arms of musket and bayonet. This sword or hanger is of the form issued to enlisted men of the French artillery during the French and Indian War. Detachments from the Royal Artillery Regiment began arriving in Canada in 1756, supplementing French artillery strength, which had earlier consisted only of the *Cannonier-Bombardiers*—the colonial regular artillery of the Ministry of Marine. This sword has a straight, 26-inch blade, on which is engraved "*Regiment Royale Artillerie*," a leather-wrapped grip, and a brass hilt.

GRENADIER, 40TH FOOT, 1759

Originally formed as Philipp's Regiment in 1717 from eight independent companies serving in Nova Scotia and Newfoundland, this unit served continuously in those two British North American colonies until 1758. By 1752 it had been numbered the 40th Regiment of Foot and was also known as Hopson's Regiment, after its third colonel in chief, Maj. Gen. Peregrine Thomas Hopson. Prior to the outbreak of the Seven Years' War, the regiment was scattered in various forts and outposts along the Nova Scotia frontier. The regiment participated in the taking of Fort Beausejour in June 1755 and other small actions that secured the colony from the French advances during that and the following year.

With the arrival of a new British expeditionary force in June 1757, the 40th's detachments were called in from their outlying posts and returned to Halifax to join together as a complete regiment for almost the first time in its sixty years of service. Erratic supply and hard duty had taken their toll on the 40th's men, who were described as making "a very shabby appearance . . . and did not trouble themselves much about discipline," but after the regiment was relieved, reunited, and reequipped, they "re-assumed the air and spirit of expert regular forces" and served with distinction during the siege and taking of Louisbourg in 1758. The 40th was left behind as part of the garrison at that place the following year, when a British force sailed up the St. Lawrence for Quebec, the capitol of French Canada. Before leaving Louisbourg in June 1759, Maj. Gen. James Wolfe detached the grenadier companies of the 22nd, 40th, and 45th from their parent regiments and formed them into a chosen corps titled the Louisbourg Grenadiers, embarking them with the rest of his expeditionary force.

Grenadiers were the picked men of a regiment, selected for their size, strength, and agility. Their origin began in the seventeenth century, when they were used as assault troops to storm into breaches of strong places, hacking down barriers with their hatchets and tossing grenades into enemy positions. By the mid-eighteenth century, although they were still elite troops relied upon to spearhead an attack or occupy the place of honor or peril in a battle line, they made use of the grenades only on rare occasions.

This grenadier of the 40th Foot is dressed much as he would have appeared on the 1759 Quebec Campaign. The shoulder pouch, once used to carry grenades, now contains a wooden box bored to carry eighteen to twenty-four musket cartridges. A brass match case is attached to the broad, buff leather pouchbelt, another carryover from earlier days, when it served as the receptacle for the burning quick match used to light the fuses of the grenades. A slightly

CHARLES HILL

narrower buff waistbelt carries the grenadier's sword and bayonet in a double frog. Over this, an eighteen-round "belly" box is belted, providing additional ammunition for his Long Land musket.

British grenadiers wore tall, stiffened cloth caps shaped like a bishop's miter, elaborately embroidered with devices, including the royal cipher, surmounted by the crown, with the running horse of the House of Hanover below. Another vestigial badge of honor, the cap was originally adopted to enable the granadier to sling his musket over his shoulder while throwing grenades—both problematical exercises

when wearing the broad-brimmed hat then favored among military men. Both the cap and uniform are brick red (a hue derived from the madder root), faced with buff cloth. As ordered by Royal Warrant in 1752, the grenadier coat has "the usual little ornament on the point of the shoulder" commonly known as "wings." The tape buttonholes and edging of the coat and waistcoat are of white worsted, with a narrow yellow line enclosed by two black lines, a form of livery lace that identified the wearer as a member of that regiment. Tight-fitting gaiters of blackened linen, with stiff leather tops to protect the knees of the red breeches when

Sergeant's Halberd, British, 1745

By the eighteenth century, the halberd, or halbert, was an arm that had evolved from its original use in the late Middle Ages as a poleax into the badge of rank or position, typically of a sergeant of foot troops, but also employed by civil officers and town guards or watchmen. The head of the halberd consisted of a spear or lance point grafted to a battle-ax head (with its characteristic hooked rear blade, originally intended for dishorsing mounted knights). Attached to a 6- to 7-foot wooden half, or shaft, it could also be employed by a sergeant in straightening the ranks of his men and was still occasionally called upon to serve as a weapon in actual combat.

This fine example of a British infantry sergeant's halberd is engraved with the date "1745" and "CPT. EDWD. BLACKET." The date probably indicates the period of production or issue, and the name is not that of the owner, but rather signifies that this arm was part of the issue to the company commanded by a Capt. Edward Blacket of an unidentified regiment. The marking of arms with a captain's name was an archaic carryover from earlier times, when companies were raised and equipped by their captain-commandants. However, with the establishment of the British Army and its regimental system during the late seventeenth century, colonel-commandants and the Crown took over such responsibilities. By the close of the Seven Years' War, most regiments employed a letter or numeral designator when marking arms and equipment, especially since commanders changed with each promotion or commission purchase.

kneeling, prevented stones and dirt from entering the shoes and guarded the stockings below from becoming torn or wet during long marches.

Thus uniformed and accoutred, the Louisbourg Grenadiers took part in the surprise landing below the Plains of Abraham, to the west of Quebec, early on the morning of September 13. Scaling the cliffs in darkness, the entire British army was formed for battle against the French, the Louisbourg Grenadiers occupying the place of honor on the right of the line. By midmorning, the battle was in full progress. Leading the Louisbourg Grenadiers and the 28th Foot in a charge on the French left, General Wolfe fell mortally wounded during his moment of victory. The Louisbourg Grenadiers' moment of glory was costly—fifty-five officers and men killed or wounded, nearly one-quarter of the entire corps. Following the surrender of Quebec, the Louisbourg Grenadiers were dissolved, and the companies returned to their parent regiments. The grenadier company, along with the entire 40th Foot, later served with distinction in the 1760 Montreal Campaign and on the expedition against French and Spanish forces in the Caribbean, from 1761 to 1762.

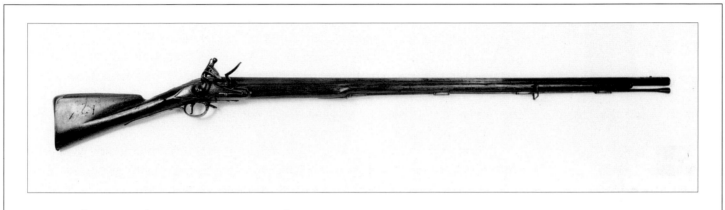

British Musket, Long Land Pattern, 1747–60

Following the ascendancy of George I to the British throne in 1714, there began a series of reforms in the procurement and manufacture of military weapons that would, by the 1720s, result in the establishment of a "King's Pattern" series of muskets. Under the control of the Board of Ordnance, arms makers were furnished approved patterns for the parts (barrels, locks, furniture, and fittings) they were to produce or the arms to be assembled from parts delivered to them, all under the scrutiny of ordnance agents. Completed parts or arms were delivered into the Tower or London or Dublin Castle (the central armories for England and Ireland, respectively) or into the hands of ordnance contractors.

Essentially, three basic musket patterns were recognized: the Long Land, the Short Land, and the Marine, or Militia (a simplified version of the Short Land). The Long and Short Land Patterns differed primarily in length of arm, the former having a 46-inch barrel, the latter a 42-inch. The Long and Short Pattern muskets were the workhorse arms of the British Army through most of the Georgian period, augmented in the 1790s by the simplified India Pattern musket (a wartime stopgap arm) and after the close of the Napoleonic Wars in 1815, gradual replacement by the New Land Pattern arms. Sometime in the late eighteenth century, these muskets became colloquially known as "Brown Bess" muskets, the popular name by which they are commonly called today.

Despite the three basic patterns, a series of minor improvements were introduced to Crown long arms at various intervals during the eighteenth century. In 1742 some newly standardized features, such as a double-bridle lock, were instituted to the Long Land musket. Scholars now classify this as the Pattern of 1742. This example is marked "Farmer" over "1747" on the lock plate indicating the lock's maker and the date of production. It also retains its original iron rammer showing that it was produced or updated sometime after 1750, when these metal rammers began to replace the earlier brass-tipped wooden types. During the French and Indian War, most British troops sent to North America carried muskets still furnished with wooden rammers, although some regiments were able to replace them in the field with iron rammers drawn from ordnance stores.

Officer's Spontoon, 1st Regiment of Foot, c. 1750–70

Also known as the "espontoon" or "half-pike," the spontoon was the badge of rank and polearm carried by commissioned officers of foot companies through the greater part of the eighteenth century. The spontoon was essentially a steel or iron spear point, sometimes with a crossbar below the blade, mounted on a wooden haft that averaged $6\frac{1}{2}$ feet in length and closely resembled the spears used for boar hunting in Europe during that and earlier periods.

During the French and Indian War and again in the Revolutionary War, many British officers left their spontoons behind, preferring to carry light fusils and bayonets on campaign. However, this practice clearly had some adverse effects on the command of troops in the field, leading General Washington in 1778 to order each company-grade Continental infantry officer to "provide himself with a half pike or spear as soon as possible—fire arms, when made use of, withdrawing their attention too much from their men."

The 1st Foot fought in North America from 1757 to 1763, and the first battalion of the regiment served in the Caribbean during the Revolutionary War, surrendering to French forces after the valiant defense of Brimstone Hill Fort at St. Kitts in 1781. The blade of this spontoon is engraved with a British Crown over "ROYAL" and, although undated, is identical to a regimentally marked example belonging to a 25th Foot officer who left his regiment in 1773. It is of a style that could have been employed by an officer of the Royals during either conflict.

THE BATTLE OF BUSHY RUN: THE "SWING ACTION" OF AUGUST 6, 1763

With the close of hostilities with France, peace returned to the trans-Allegheny frontier. Then, suddenly, the Great Lakes tribes launched a series of surprise attacks—apparently coordinated—on British frontier forts and settlements, beginning in early May 1763 with Detroit, which miraculously holds out. But Forts Michilimackinac, Sandusky, St. Joseph, Miamis, Venango, and Le Bouef fall to ruse or siege over the next two months. In western Pennsylvania, Forts Pitt and Ligonier are invested in early June and successfully resist occasional direct attacks, but their supplies are running low. The shattered remants of two Highland corps—the 42nd and the 77th Regiments of Foot —are the only regular troops available to compose an expeditionary force under Col. Henry Bouquet to relieve the

besieged posts. Many of the Scots are ill, recuperating from recurring bouts of malaria and other maladies contracted in the West Indies the previous year. It is not until July 28 that Bouquet and his small army march out of Fort Bedford—the principal staging area for the expedition—and reach Fort Ligonier on August 2.

Bouquet pushes on two days later with his troops and provisions "on the hoof," pack horses bearing flour bags and a small herd of cattle. Besides the Highlanders, his force of some five hundred troops include a small detachment from his own 1st Battalion of the 60th Foot, or "Royal Americans." Observing that "the Highlanders lose themselves in the Woods as soon as they got out of the Road, and can not on that Account be employed as Flankers," Bouquet has recruited a small party of "rangers," or woodsmen, to perform this critical mission. Anticipating an ambush, Bouquet reroutes the march toward the abandoned station at Bushy Run, where he intends to rest his men and animals before attempting a night march across "a very dangerous defile . . . commanded by high and craggy hills."

On August 5, after marching seventeen miles since early morning, his troops are now only one mile from the day's objective and another twenty-six miles to Fort Pitt. But Bouquet's careful precautions are to no avail: the army has been tracked by its invisible foe, and at one o'clock, gunfire and war cries announce the ambush of Bouquet's advance guard. The two light infantry companies of the 42nd Foot move up

Scottish Broadsword, Royal Highland Regiment, Other Ranks Pattern, c. 1755

The traditional edged weapon of the Scottish soldier, the basket-hilted broadsword, was deadly in the hands of a warrior skilled in its use. The heavy, straight blade made it an ideal weapon for hacking and stabbing, while the protection afforded the user by the slotted and pierced iron guard rendered it useful for punching—a form of brass knuckles, as it were. By the mid-eighteenth century, the musket and bayonet had long been established as the principal arms of Highland infantry, although the broadsword was still issued—and used, in close-quarter combat.

This sword is of the form carried by the "other ranks" (enlisted men) of the famed Black Watch (the Royal Highland Regiment) and other Highland corps during the Seven Years' War. Created in 1739 and numbered the 42nd Regiment of Foot in 1751, the Black Watch distinguished itself during its American service from 1757 to 1764, from its disastrous frontal assault on the French lines at Ticonderoga in 1758 to the Battle of Bushy Run in 1763 and subsequent subjugation of the Ohio Indians in 1764. Its blade is marked with a crown over "GR" cipher and "DRURY" on both sides. Drury was an English swordsmith who received most contracts for the production of "Scottish" broadswords during this period. However, it is the marking on the pommel of this sword that makes this a particularly fine and rare example. It was issued to a soldier of the first battalion of the regiment sometime during or before 1758, as evidenced by the engraving "42/A/35," which signifies the thirty-fifth sword issued to the first or Colonel's Company (denoted by the letter "A"). In 1759 the newly raised second battalion was ordered to "have there [sic] Swords Numbr'd, and Lettred, as Soon as possible Beginning with the Letter L. The first Battn having Ended with the Letter, K."

quickly to drive back the Indians beyond the ambush point. As soon as the counterattack halts, however, the warriors are back to the attack, sniping at the regulars from advantageous positions on commanding ground with the firearms and bows and arrows. Bodies painted black, the Indians blend in with their surroundings and move quickly to attack other points along the column and again in front. Each time the regulars fire or charge, the Indians disappear among the trees, only to reappear at some other point along the column. Finally, the pack train in the rear, halted on the top of Edge Hill with its guard, is attacked. Bouquet's entire force now falls back to protect the hillside, where the men extend a circular defense perimeter around the upper slope, with wounded men, cattle, and horses inside.

"The Action then became general, and though we were attacked on every Side, and the Savages exerted themselves with uncommon Resolution, they were constantly repulsed with Loss," writes Bouquet in his evening dispatch to Gen. Jeffrey Amherst, adding that his own losses "in Men including Rangers and Drivers exceeds Sixty killed or wounded." Thirsty cries from the nearby wounded remind Bouquet of his own parched mouth and cracked lips, but the men's canteens are bone dry. The Swiss-born, professional soldier praises his officers and "the cool and steady behaviour of the Troops, who did not fire a Shot without orders, and drove the Enemy from their Posts with fixed bayonets." Realizing that this could possibly be his last letter, Bouquet warns that "Whatever our Fate may be, I thought it necessary to give your Excellency this early Information, that you may at all Events take such measures as you will think proper with the Provinces for their Safety, and the effectual Relief of Fort Pitt." With the vital correspondence now completed, Bouquet focuses his total attention to the task at hand—a daring ploy that will either save his dwindling command or irrevocably sign his men's death warrants. Only the coming dawn will tell.

The diffuse light of predawn creates murky gray forms of the landscapes that had earlier been ink-black. As a dull orange glow appears in the lower eastern skyline, the men perform last-minute adjustments to their weapons and equipment. With the cooler night air already dissipating, some soldiers shed their Highland jackets or coats in anticipation of another hot day, preferring to renew their desperate struggle for survival in their sleeveless, woolen waistcoats or merely their linen shirts. Others strip off waistcoats and pull their jackets back on, recognizing that the white shirts present an attractive target against the dark of the trees. The companies ring the crest of Edge Hill, which is roughly bisected north and south by the road down which Bouquet's troops had marched westward the previous day. North of it, at the apex of the hill, is a makeshift redoubt constructed of flourbags to protect the wounded. This westward portion is the least defensible and therefore considered a position of honor. It is defended by three light infantry companies and 42nd Foot's grenadier company.

As the "Royal Highland Regiment"—an honorary title conferred in 1758—the 42nd's uniforms are faced and lapeled with blue, a color reserved for Royal regiments. The brick-red jackets and waistcoats are edged with distinctive regimental lace, and the buttonholes on the jacket are trimmed with the same, set on in a "Jew's harp" form. Blue Scots bonnets are trimmed with black cockades of silk

Officer's Highland Broadsword, 1740–60

Similar in overall form to the other ranks' broadsword of Highland regiments, this basket-hilted sword is the form favored by officers commanding Scottish troops. The hilt is nearly identical to the sword carried by Lt. (later Capt.) James Grant of the 77th (Montgomery's) Highland Regiment of Foot during his service in North America, from 1758 to 1761. This sword differs chiefly in the form of the blade, having the double edge that characterizes a broadsword rather than the single-edged "backsword" blade found on Grant's. The intricate piercings and fluting on the basket hilt reflect the artistry of the Scottish "hammerman" who designed, forged, and finished it, fitting it to a purchased blade—typical of Scottish sword manufacture.

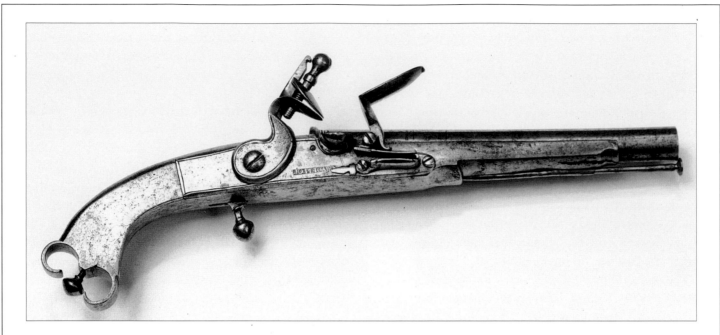

Highland Pistol of The Black Watch, c. 1759

With the introduction of relatively cheap and effective firearms, Scottish warriors quickly developed new techniques of armed conflict that took full advantage of this new technology, as well as their traditional methods of fighting. According to an early nineteenth-century account of the Scottish military, a Highland charge consisted of the following:

> When they had advanced within a few yards of the enemy, they poured in a volley of musketry, which, from the short distance, and their constant practice as marksmen, was generally very effective: then dropping their muskets, they dashed forward sword in hand, reserving their pistols and dirks for close action.... When they closed with the enemy, they received the points of the bayonets on their targets [a small, round shield of leather-covered wood]; thrust them aside, resorted to their pistols and dirks, to complete the impression made by the musket and broadsword.

After firing the pistols, they would fling them at their enemy and charge in with broadswords to complete their work. To prevent the wooden stocks from cracking when thrown, and to add weight to the arm for such usage, Highland pistols were stocked in steel or brass. The trigger or butt of the pistol often featured traditional decorative embellishments, such as an acorn or Scottish thistle, and the more expensive pistols were often elaborately engraved or inlaid with gold or silver.

By the opening of the Seven Years' War, the Royal Highland Regiment (The Black Watch) retained the traditional arms of musket and bayonet, Highland pistol, and broadsword, the targets having been laid aside years earlier. This all-steel Highland pistol is the relatively plain form issued to the Black Watch during that conflict. It is stamped with the cartouche of the maker, "JO. PITCAIRN," a Scottish gunsmith. Similar pistols by English arms manufacturers in Birmingham were also furnished to the regiment at the same time. This example has "RHR 2B" engraved on the top of the barrel, signifying the Royal Highland Regiment, Second Battalion.

In 1759, a second battalion was added to the regiment and sailed to join the first battalion, then serving on the northern frontiers of New York. On April 29, 1759, the second battalion was ordered to engrave its arms in a similar manner to its swords, to which this pistol's markings conform. Following hard campaigning in North America and the Caribbean, the regiment was so reduced in numbers that the men of the second battalion were drafted into the first and the excess officers returned to Great Britain. This pistol was clearly one of those issued to the soldiers of the second battalion before its disbandment in 1763.

ribbon and bearskin tufts, while the men wear "government sett" tartan kilts, or *philabegs*, over blue leggings, tied below the knee with red garters—necessary leg protection in the rough wilderness. Officers wear similar uniforms of better quality, although their scarlet coats are trimmed with "only a narrow edging of gold-lace around the facings, and very often no lace at all . . . to render them less conspicuous to the Indians, who always aimed particularly at the officers." The two light companies of the Royal Highlanders have the same short .65 caliber Highland carbines furnished to the entire 77th Foot, although the rest of the 42nd is armed with heavier Long Land Pattern muskets. All troops are stripped down to essential accoutrements—cartridge boxes, shot bags, and powder horns. Though their comrades in the battalion and grenadier companies still carry basket-hilted broadswords, the light troops carry versatile hatchets in lieu of the traditional Scots' edged weapon.

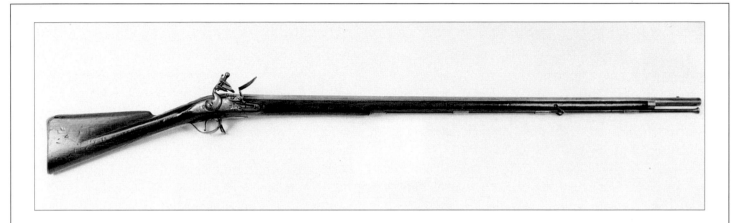

Light Infantry Carbine, c. 1760

At the outbreak of the French and Indian War, Britain had few troops experienced in the partisan or irregular warfare that prevailed in both North American forests and the steppes of Eastern Europe. With the emphasis on increased mobility, improved marksmanship, and partisan tactics came the demand for specialized arms to meet the needs of the new light-armed troops, including Highlanders, light dragoons and horse, light infantry, and ranger units. The carbine, technically a lighter musket carried by horse dragoons, replaced the musket as the weapon of these new corps. Like the fusil (the long arm carried by officers), the carbine was essentially a scaled-down version of a musket and, in British service, had a barrel bore of .65-inch caliber.

In 1756–57 the Royal Artillery Regiment began to receive carbines with 36- to 37-inch barrels and fitted to carry bayonets to replace their heavier arms, as did the new Highland battalions (Montgomery's and Fraser's) then raising for North America. The demand for such light arms exceeded the supply, and in America, during 1759, General Amherst ordered the artillery and spare Highland carbines delivered out to British light infantry and ranger companies. Unfortunately, the slighter stocks and simpler brass mounts of the carbines also proved less sturdy, and the arms were unpopular with many of these units, who turned them in, preferring to draw the reliable but heavier musket or captured French arms.

Back in England, however, the Board of Ordnance contracted for similarly mounted light infantry carbines with 42-inch barrels and furnished with bayonets and wooded (later iron) rammers. Although apparently produced between 1760 and 1762, all known examples of these longer carbines have locks made between 1757 and 1762 and are marked with the maker's name and date of production, in this example, "GRICE" over "1758." Despite their late production, many of these carbines saw service during the war and the subsequent "Pontiac's Conspiracy" in 1763–64. During the Revolutionary War, numerous carbines remained in store in Halifax, Quebec, and Montreal, while many were issued to new Loyalist and militia corps in Canada, as well as to some British regiments in need of firearms to replace the sergeants' halberds on campaign.

Both carbine versions share brass mountings that set them apart from other British arms, including a trigger guard that is flatter and simpler in form than the type found on Land Pattern muskets and the later 1770 sergeant's fusil. Another distinct mounting is the "thumb-piece," or escutcheon plate at the wrist, or "small," of the walnut stock. Parts from these carbines have been excavated at Fort Ligonier, a site occupied by Highland, artillery, and light infantry troops at various times between 1758 and 1764.

Although the Native-American warriors—principally composed of Shawnee, Delaware, Miami, Mingo, Wyandot, and Ottawa—are numerically inferior to the force that they have surrounded, they are masters of forest warfare, and they mask their numbers by lightning-quick deployments and careful use of cover. They, too, are stripped down for combat: naked or nearly naked in breechcloth, "the face and body painted, feathers in their heads, symbols and signals of war, tomahawk and spear in hand," along with a "fusil, or rifle, a powder horn, a shot pouch, a tomahawk, and a scalping knife hanging from their neck[s]." Beautifully wrought quillwork and beadwork adorn some of their accoutrements, moccasins, leggings, and even arms. One or two carrry brass-hilted French or British swords—prized weapons obtained through trade or combat—and others wield spike-headed hatchets or pipe tomahawks for the close work to come. Bluish tattoos can be seen beneath the warpaint annointing the warriors' bodies and heads, done "in such figures as will make him appear most terrible to his enemies."

At dawn, well clear of rifle and musket range, the Indians begin a loud clamor, howling at and taunting the British—a tactic designed to both intimidate an enemy and increase their own valor. Then, the attack on the hill is recommenced. Under cover of a well-directed fire, parties of warriors attempt to break through the defensive line at various points, but are repelled at the point of bayonet. Nevertheless, the British regulars are tiring, and fearsome warriors, "besmeared with black and red paint, and covered with the blood of the slain," become more audacious and press their attack on all sides. Two of the light infantry companies posted to the west file in toward the center of the circle, apparently in retreat. To close these gaps, the defensive ring is pulled in closer—the companies to the right and left extending their own thin lines to fill in the space left by the withdrawing troops. Now certain of success, the Indians increase their fire and ferocity of attack.

Under command of Maj. Allan Campbell of the 42nd, the two companies move quickly across the hill along the path, past the oval-shaped redoubt, and sally out at the eastern perimeter unobserved by opponents bent on pressing their advantage to the west. As the foremost troops reach the eastern base of the hillside, the command is given to halt and face right, forming a two-rank line in open order. With their right flank serving as an anchor and their left covered by a party of rangers, the Scots charge southward in pendulum fashion into the right flank of the Indians. Firing a volley at the warriors, who return their fire, they press home their attack with charged bayonet and push the Indians from their cover. As the line of Highlanders swing farther south along the slope of the hill, the Indians to their front are hit by flanking fire from the seemingly forgotten third light infantry company and grenadiers, who have been waiting in ambush for this maneuver. Springing up, they join in the charge that has succeeded in rolling up the Indians' right flank and dispersing the warriors. Bouquet's gamble has paid off, wresting victory from apparent defeat.

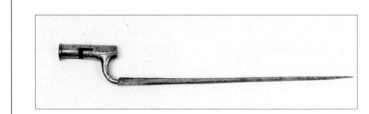

British Carbine Bayonet, 1739–57

By the late 1720s, a distinct form of bayonet for British Land Pattern muskets had emerged, developed from Dutch and German bayonets. It featured a long, triangular-profile blade that was welded at the base of its shank or neck to a socket fitted to the musket barrel, "locking" into place by means of a three-step slot or mortise that passed over a bayonet lug or stud mounted to the top of the musket. Changing but little in design through the eighteenth century, it was the form used when scaled-down bayonets were produced to fit the various carbines and fusils being manufactured.

This carbine bayonet possesses the classic features of the British bayonet, including a raised "guard" at the base of the blade where it meets the shank, as well as a rounded collar or "ring" reinforcement at the base of the socket mount. However, it is the raised attachment shield or collar of the shank's base that identifies this as a particularly early style, as this feature had gradually disappeared from most bayonets fabricated after the 1740s. Though this bayonet may have been made as late as 1756–57 for the artillery and Highland carbine, it is more likely one produced for some earlier form of British carbine or fusil.

The Revolution
1770–1783

THE EXPERIENCE OF BOTH BRITISH AND AMERICAN troops in North America during the French and Indian War contributed significantly to changes in military tactics, weaponry, and military dress by the opening of the Revolutionary War. Earlier wilderness campaigning experience in the forests, waterways, and mountains of the Adirondack and Trans-Allegheny frontiers had made a significant impact on senior British military officers such as Sir Thomas Gage and Sir William Howe, who were now engaged in suppressing the rebellious thirteen colonies along the eastern seaboard. Light infantry companies had been re-established in all British infantry regiments during 1771–72, and camps of instruction were established in England and Ireland to train the companies to work together on the battalion level in the conduct of irregular warfare. The value of light cavalry had been firmly established on the plains of Europe in the earlier conflict, and light dragoon regiments were now a standing feature of the British and Irish military establishments. Though the Board of Ordnance had been reticent about the adoption of rifled military arms, the stellar performance of Virginia, Maryland, and Pennsylvania rifle companies against the British during the first year of the rebellion soon brought about a change in thought, and by 1776, British gunmakers were producing both muzzleloading and breechloading (Ferguson) rifles for use by British and Loyalist corps in America.

Even before the outbreak of hostilities, volunteer companies were formed throughout the colonies, augmenting the handful of uniformed "ancient" corps already extant in the various colonies, such as the Ancient and Honorable Artillery Company of Boston or the Albany Grenadiers. Most of these new corps readily adopted the short coats or coatees characteristic of the light infantry and adopted names such as the Salem Rangers, Charleston Light Infantry, or the Philadelphia Associators (which boasted four uniformed battalions by 1774). The *rage militaire* spilled into the western counties of Virginia, Pennsylvania, and North Carolina, whose companies adopted cheap uniforms consisting of linen hunting shirts and trousers dyed a uniform color or trimmed with a contrasting fringe. Gen. George Washington would recommend these simple and economical hunting shirts and overalls as the stopgap uniform for the entire Continental Army during 1776 (although this was never fully achieved). Military arms, including muskets, bayonets, and swords, were imported from Europe while local gunsmiths began producing American copies of British muskets following Committee of Safety specifications.

Sir William Howe, who had assumed command of the British forces in North America by 1776, adopted a loose-order, two-rank formation for tactical deployment that had first been used in the forests of New York during the French and Indian War. Many officers set aside gorgets, sashes, and epaulettes to avoid the particular notice of American sharpshooters and even removed the metallic lace or embroidery from their coats to further lengthen their chances of survival. Similarly, British regiments began altering clothing and equipment to suit rough frontier conditions before they even landed on American shores. One good example was the Composite Brigade drawn from the three Guards regiments, who marched through the open farmlands of Long Island during the 1776 New York campaign looking very different from how they would have appeared on parade at St. James in London. Their cocked hats had been recut into round hats, their coats had been shortened, and all lace had been removed from their facings. Even accoutrements were modified and lightened. Gaiter-trousers or overalls were readily adopted by both sides as a more practical and comfortable legwear than breeches and tight-fitting "spatterdashes."

As the war progressed, however, Washington and his senior officers were determined to make the Continental Army the equal of any European power, both in point of discipline and appearance. Under the supervision of Prussian-born Inspector General Wilhelm von Steuben, regiments perfected close-order drills, deploying from column into line with parade-ground precision. As supplies from France, the Netherlands, and Spain became more plentiful in the last years of the war and the frequency of combat declined, Continental Army officers vied with each other in keeping their respective regiments in martial splendor. Stoppages from whiskey rations paid for half-gaiters and feather plumes, as well as for black ball and whiting for accoutrements and uniforms. Loyalist corps similarly competed with British regiments to achieve martial perfection, both influenced by the ever-correct appearance and bearing of their German allies.

BATTALION SOLDIER OF THE "VEIN-OPENERS," 1770

Under the protective guns of Royal Navy warships drawn up in battle formation in Boston Harbor, the British 14th and 29th Regiments of Foot were rowed ashore on October 1, 1768. After the often-violent rioting that had occurred in Boston during and following the Stamp Act crisis, Lt. Col. William Dalrymple of the 14th Regiment of Foot had expected physical opposition, rather than the observed mutterings and sullen glances of the watching Bostonians, as the regulars clambered up from the boats and found their places in formation. Under a show of force, he marched the 29th Foot through the town and encamped them on Boston Common, where they quickly began erecting a military tent city on the public green. Drawing a detachment from the troops, he took possession of Faneuil Hall, the unofficial headquarters of the Sons of Liberty, seizing all firearms stored therein. To enforce the collection of importation taxes under the Townshend program, Boston had been placed under military occupation, but this enforced peace would not last.

While the troops settled into their military routine of guard mounts, parade, and drill, emboldened townspeople initiated their own sporadic campaign of opposition, through letters and petitions of complaint, verbal abuse, and finally, random assault with fists, sticks, garbage, and cinders. Off-duty soldiers wisely began to visit shops, alehouses, and "pleasure gardens" in small groups for self-protection, while brawling between civilians and troops became a mounting problem. Despite strict orders on conduct and fear of the lash, the occasional soldier—by no means always innocent—was brought up on charges ranging from theft to fighting to rape. Tension mounted in 1770 as the "jetsam and floatsam" of the town faced off against "lobsterbacks" from similar backgrounds. An off-duty soldier of the 29th, in search of work at a ropewalk, was brutally beaten by a mob, leading to a series of fights that finally resulted in the "fatal fifth of March." On that day, seven soldiers from the 29th under Capt. William Preston fired into a large mob after provocation by insult and outright assault with ice balls, stones, and other objects, killing three and wounding others, two of which later died. Following this "Boston Massacre," the 29th Foot was hereafter known to the townspeople as the "vein-openers."

As the 29th Foot was sailing from Halifax to Boston in 1768, stylistic changes in British military dress that evolved through the 1760s were officially sanctioned by the publication of a new royal warrant regulating the dress of His Majesty George III's land forces. It was only shortly before the Boston Massacre that this overseas regiment received its first issue of uniforms conforming to the 1768 specifications, and following traditional regimental economy, it would take even longer for the older articles of military clothing still in

WILLIAM RODEN

wearable condition to be cycled out of use. Thus the 29th Foot wore, at the time of the Boston Massacre, a curious mixture of both old and new regulation clothing and accoutrements. This reconstruction of a battalion private is based on both the published regulations and eyewitness artwork depicting members of the 29th regiment in Boston, notably the Christian Remick watercolor of Boston Common and the Paul Revere engraving of the Boston Massacre.

Under the 1768 regulations, the new coats of the 29th Foot retained the regiment's traditional facings of yellow, but the color of the "skirt" or tail linings (which earlier matched the coat facings) were uniformly changed to white in all but buff-faced British infantry regiments. This soldier of the 29th Foot, however, wears a pre-1768 warrant regimental coat, with yellow linings and still festooned with an older pattern lace first adopted by the regiment nearly two decades earlier. It was common practice in many British regiments, including the 29th, to retain older coats for routine duties and off-duty wear, thereby preserving the new coats for dress parade and other formal duties. His white woolen waistcoat and breeches are of the new style, replacing the red "smallclothes" of earlier warrants. The regimental hat, its $4^1/2$–inch brim neatly bounded with $1^1/2$-inch worsted tape and trimmed with horsehair cockade button, and loop, is cocked in a military form already outmoded in more fashionable British regiments. His cartridge pouch- and waistbelts are of an earlier issue but have been altered and whitened with pipe clay to conform to the new regulation widths of $2^3/4$ inches and 2 inches, respectively. Linen half gaiters, nearly waterproof from heavy applications of blackball, are buttoned over gray woolen stockings to prevent pebbles and dirt from entering the shoes. The soldier's arms consist of a Long Land Pattern musket and bayonet.

The 29th Foot continued to serve as part of Maj. Gen. Thomas Gage's occupying force in Boston until 1771, when it was sent to St. Augustine and the West Indies, until relieved in 1773 and sent back briefly to England. The regiment later returned to North America in 1776 as part of General Burgoyne's army, destined for Canada and the planned thrust down the Hudson to sever New England—the "hotbed of sedition"—from the rest of the rebel colonies. Only the two flank companies of the regiment, the grenadiers and light infantry, actually accompanied Burgoyne on his ill-fated 1777 campaign and became part of the force surrendered at Saratoga. The rest of the regiment was left behind, destined as garrison troops for the posts along the St. Lawrence. The regiment remained in Canada for the rest of the war, although a strong detachment drawn from the 29th formed part of the expeditionary force that scoured the Lake Champlain corridor in 1780.

British Revolutionary War Buttons

The warrant of 1768 prescribed numbered buttons for the line regiments of the British Army. This proved popular, and many regiments added special devices as well as numbers and other ornaments. Buttons of the enlisted men were generally cast of pewter, with a large iron shank that was pushed through the fabric of the uniform and held with a leather or cloth thong. This allowed the soldier to remove the buttons quickly for cleaning and prevented soiling of the uniform. Officers' buttons were of stamped sheet silver or gilded copper with bone back. These were sewn directly to the uniform. Often they were of different designs than those of the enlisted men of the same regiment.

The excavated enlisted buttons shown here are all made of cast pewter. Top row, left to right: 1) Butler's Rangers, a Loyalist Corps that served on the New York frontier and was notorious for its sometimes brutal behavior against the area inhabitants. 2) The 27th (or Inniskilling) Regiment of Foot. This button bears the turreted castle that was the ancient badge of the regiment. It served in the major campaigns of 1776–77 in New York and Pennsylvania. 3) The 8th (or King's) Regiment of Foot. This regiment served along the Canadian and western frontiers throughout the war. 4) The 10th Regiment of Foot. The flank companies of the 10th Regiment participated in the first engagements of the war at Lexington and Concord Bridge and afterward in

Howe's Philadelphia Campaign, until returning to England for recruiting in late 1778.

Second row, left to right: 5) The 21st Regiment of Foot, or Royal North British Fuzileers. This regiment formed part of the expedition under Gen. John Burgoyne during his invasion of New York State. Most of the regiment surrendered to the Americans at Saratoga in 1777, although some detachments remained in Canada throughout the war. 6) 42nd Regiment of Foot, or Royal Highland Regiment, also known as the Black Watch. The 42nd fought through many of the major engagements in the east and south. 7) The 3rd Regiment of Foot Guards, members of which formed part of the composite Brigade of Guards. Few other British regiments compiled such a record of valor as this provisional wartime unit. 8) The 47th Regiment of Foot. This regiment fought in the early engagements around Boston in 1775 and, with the exception of the flank companies, avoided capture at Saratoga, having been left behind to garrison various posts on Burgoyne's route of march.

British Infantry Hangers, Third Quarter of the Eighteenth Century

Hangers, or short swords, were carried by the enlisted ranks of the British Army until they were abolished for all but sergeants, grenadiers, and musicians, by decree of the Warrant of 1768. In actuality, many units chose to leave their hangers in regimental stores, considering them an encumbrance, and consequently, grenadiers were ordered to cease carrying them in 1784.

The example on the left has a cast brass hilt, composed of a flattened spherical pommel, a boldly ribbed grip, and a dished, heart-shaped counterguard with raised edges. Its unmarked blade is slightly curved with no fullers and may be a period replacement. The importance of this sword lies in the engraved markings on the underside of the counterguard, designating this sword as having been carried by a private of the 59th Regiment of Foot, which served in North America from 1765 to 1775.

Also regimentally marked is the middle example, carried by a grenadier of the 16th Regiment of Foot, which served in the colonies from 1767 to 1782. It also is made of cast brass but has a "dog's head" pommel and a grip imitating a spiral cord binding. The intricate counterguard is composed of two shell guards that are connected to the knucklebow by a series of branches and is engraved "XVI. R^t· Gr. No. 39." The 26^1/$_2$-inch blade is curved and single-edged, with a narrow fuller and false edge, which suggests that this is as a sergeant's sword. Board of Ordnance records mention "dog's head" pommel swords, and this general type is believed to have been the most commonly carried infantry hanger during the American Revolutionary War era.

The semibasket hilted hanger on the right is an example of a higher-quality sergeant's issue sword. Its graceful iron hilt has an olive-shaped pommel, a wire-bound sharkskin grip, and an openwork counterguard incorporating two addorsed "S" scrolls. For extra hand protection, five branches are included in addition to a small lobed quillion, or wrist guard. Since sergeants' swords were to have longer blades, this one measures 27^9/$_{16}$ inches and is marked with an "H" within a running fox, the mark of the Harvey family of Birmingham cutlers.

Grenadier, 33rd Regiment of Foot, 1776

Arriving in the Carolinas in May 1776, the 33rd Regiment of Foot joined the expeditionary force besieging Charleston. Following that failed attempt, it sailed to join Maj. Gen. Sir William Howe's main army then preparing for the New York Campaign. The grenadier and light infantry companies were detached from the regiment and assigned to the provisional battalions of flank companies that had been organized. As part of the 1st Battalion of Grenadiers, the 33rd grenadier company was but lightly engaged until the Battle of Brandywine on September 11, 1777. There, despite heavy casualties received from a heavy fusillade of cannon shot and musketry, including three officers wounded, the grenadiers broke the American battle line and pursued them for two miles before halting. The 1st Battalion of Grenadiers again distinguished themselves during the hard-fought Battle of Monmouth, suffering heavy casualties from enemy fire and heat exhaustion. The 1st Battalion and the 33rd Foot also both fought during the second and successful siege of Charleston in 1780. The grenadier company returned to New York afterward, not sharing in either its parent regiment's impressive fighting record compiled during the southern campaigns or in its captivity following the surrender at Yorktown.

According to 1767 specifications for the varicolored regimental uniform facings, British infantry coats had 3½-inch-wide cuffs, 3-inch-wide lapels, and corresponding fall-down collars—in the 33rd Foot's case, cut from the same red cloth as the coat body. This rather austere uniform was brightened by ½-inch-wide white lace applied to the buttonholes of the lapels, cuffs, collar, and pocket flaps. The distinctive wings of the grenadier and light infantry coats were similarly trimmed with this worsted lace. Each regiment had lace of a different pattern, that of the 33rd having a single red line running through the center.

The five-sided shape of the buttonhole trim employed on the 33rd Foot's uniforms was known, among British military tailors, as a "flowerpot" from its resemblance to a ceramic planter. Other regimental buttonholes then in use in the British Army included the "straight," "Jew's harp," "scallop-headed," and "pointed" forms. Generally, buttons and their corresponding buttonholes were placed equidistant on most regimental coats during this period, although some

British regiments used a "two and two" or "by twos" arrangement, as seen on this 33rd grenadier's coat. A handful of corps, such as the 3rd Regiment of Foot Guards, employed a "by three" arrangement, necessitating a reduction from the ten buttons prescribed by the 1768 warrant to nine buttons on the lapel of each coat, and a similar reduction from four to three buttons on each cuff.

As long as his regiment's uniforms and accoutrements conformed to the general specifications laid out by the Crown, a regimental colonel had a certain amount of freedom in determining such minor regimental distinctions. His taste or preference was governed only by his pocketbook and the approval of his peers—a board of general officers that met each year to review the pattern clothing and equipment submitted by the regimental agents. This board ensured that the quality and form of the goods supplied for a regiment fully met Crown guidelines. This rather subjective system of quality control and inspection continued well into the nineteenth century. During the Revolutionary War, the regimental colonel of the 33rd Foot was Maj. Gen. (later Lt.) Charles Cornwallis, who took great pride in the appearance and welfare of his regiment, even purchasing in 1775, from his own funds, kersey cloaks to protect each man during cold and rainy weather.

Wearing full marching order, consisting of goatskin-covered knapsack (with cloak stowed therein), linen haversack, and tin water flask in addition to his accoutrements, this soldier of the 33rd Foot wears the impressive bearskin cap that proclaims his enrollment in the elite grenadier company. Other devices, such as his coat's shoulder wings and the traditional brass match case—now little more than a decorative embellishment—also announce his status. His waistbelt, fixed with the brass regimental belt plate in front, bears two frogs on the left side—one for his bayonet, and the other for his brass-hilted hanger. After 1768 only sergeants and grenadiers were permitted to carry such short swords in the "marching" English regiments. His white woolen waistcoat and breeches have been pipe-clayed to hide any stains, and he wears the more comfortable half gaiters in lieu of knee-length full gaiters or "spatterdashes," which were frequently reserved for parades and similar full dress duties.

British Bayonet Belt Plates, 1775–83

Frequently referred to as "clasps" in eighteenth-century British regimental accounts and correspondence, belt plates were used to secure the ends of the waistbelts and shoulderbelts used to carry the edged weapons of officers and soldiers. They were first adopted in British regiments shortly before the opening of the Revolutionary War and replaced large buckles used earlier for such purposes.

Nearly all known examples of the plates worn on the belts of the "other ranks," or enlisted men, in British regiments were of brass or copper alloy, while officers' plates were either gold- or silver-plated (sometimes of solid silver). The enlisted plates were either cast or, more frequently, cut from sheet brass, with the regimental number, device, or initials engraved or cast on the face of the plate. They were fastened to the thick leather belting on the underside, usually by means of a hook at one end and two studs at the other.

Clockwise from upper left: plate of the 80th Foot or Royal Edinburgh Volunteers, as denoted by the script

"REV" engraving (the 80th was raised in 1778 and surrendered at Yorktown in 1781, where this plate was found; oval plate of the famous (or infamous) Butler's Rangers, a Loyalist corps raised in 1778 that wreaked havoc on the New York frontier through most of the war; plate of the 64th Regiment of Foot, dug in South Carolina, where the regiment served during 1779–82; and the 33rd Foot plate, excavated near Saratoga, where a fifty-man detachment of the regiment surrendered with Burgoyne's Army in 1777.

Three of the four plates are rectangular and horizontal in form, denoting their original attachment to bayonet waistbelts. As shoulderbelts began to replace waistbelts in popularity in the late 1770s, there was a corresponding change to vertical marking (seen here on the Butler's Rangers plate), at which time the oval form also came into favor. The hole drilled through the face of the 80th Foot plate originally held the hook that was soldered or brazed on its reverse.

British Grenadier Cap, 1768 Warrant

Following the French and Indian War, many British regiments began to request royal sanction to change the form of their grenadier and drummer caps from the traditional cloth miter form to fur caps copied from those worn by Austrian and French grenadiers. The popularity of this form led to its official sanction for all such troops, with the publication of the royal warrant of 1768, which specified: "The caps of the Grenadiers to be of black bear-skin. On the front, the King's crest, of silver plated metal, on a black ground with the motto, 'Nec aspera terrent.' A grenade on the back part, with the number of the regiment on it . . . the height of the cap (without the bear-skin which reaches beyond the top) to be twelve inches."

Drummers were to wear similar caps, but with metal front plates bearing the "King's crest . . . with trophies of Colours and drums" and instead of a grenade (unless a grenadier drummer), the "number of the Regiment on the back part," usually engraved on a small drum device cast of brass or white metal. Fusilier regiments were authorized similar bearskin caps, "but not so high; and not to have the grenade on the back part."

This grenadier cap conforms fully to the above 1768 specifications, although the small metal grenade device, originally sewn over the narrow fur edging at the rear bottom, is now missing. Nearly identical grenadier and drummer caps, still bearing their "97"–engraved grenade and drum devices, are in the collections of the National Museums of Scotland and the National Army Museum in London. Also not visible in this photograph is a large oval of red cloth centered on the back of the cap; this is the vestigial remnant of the earlier miter cap's cloth "bag," or crown. Beneath the exterior front, with its stamped front plate surmounted by bearskin, is a thin, spade-shaped plate of tinned iron, which allows the cap to keep its upright form yet still be of minimal weight. The cap has a leather sweatband and is lined with natural linen.

PRIVATE, BATTALION COMPANY, 15TH REGIMENT OF FOOT, 1777–81

The British 15th Regiment of Foot, then serving in Ireland, was part of the reinforcement sent to Sir William Howe, commander in chief in North America in December 1775. It arrived in time to join in the unsuccessful expedition against Charleston, South Carolina, during May to July 1776 and fight in the battles of Long Island and Fort Washington later that year. During 1777 it took part in the Tryon's raid on Danbury, Connecticut, and fought brilliantly during the Battles of Brandywine and Germantown. In the latter, its lieutenant colonel, John Bird, was killed while leading a counterattack at the head of the regiment.

Following the evacuation of Philadelphia and Battle of Monmouth in June 1778, the 15th sailed with Sir James Grant's expeditionary force to the Caribbean, serving against the French in the hard-fought actions at St. Lucia in 1779. It was part of the force under Admiral Rodney that seized the Dutch island of St. Eustatius (Statia) in 1781 and, with the 13th Foot, became the occupying garrison of that small, rocky island, minus its flank companies, which were sent to St. Kitts. Statia was captured by a French amphibious force under the Marquis Bouilly later that year, the garrison surrendering after only minimal resistance, so completely were they caught by surprise. The light infantry and grenadier companies of the regiments, however, served with great credit among the defenders of Brimstone Hill Fort at St. Kitts during its famous siege the following year.

Before being sent to North America, the regiment was furnished with a "slop" dress to save the full uniform from soilage during its Atlantic voyage and subsequent land-based fatigue duties. Regimental tailors made simple, single-breasted jackets or "roundabouts" and white ticking breeches for the men, who were also issued "cap-hats," a sort of hybrid between a hat and a cap, made by cutting down the previous year's regimental hats. The cap-hats were trimmed with worsted tape and tassels, as well as a brass cap badge bearing the regimental number engraved on an eight-pointed brass star. The jackets were trimmed with simple yellow cuff and collars—the facing color of the regiment—and small regimental buttons. By 1777 the breeches were replaced by the more practical linen gaiter-trousers or overalls favored by British and American troops alike. The 15th seems to have employed at least portions of this practical dress in the sultry Caribbean, as a cap-hat badge was recovered by archaeologists from a 1781 occupation site on Statia.

This private, seen here loading his Long Land Pattern musket from a 29-round pouch, is dressed in the slop uniform of the regiment and stripped down to light combat order, consisting of pouch with belt and an issue waistbelt converted into a shoulderbelt. With the addition of small shoulder wings to his jacket and a change of belting from buff to black, this soldier could easily pass as a member of the light infantry, which wore similar dress on campaign in the American war and later Caribbean service.

Long Land Musket and Shoulderbelt, 15th Regiment of Foot, c. 1777

The older, standing regiments sent out from the British Isles for active service during the Revolutionary War drew new stands of arms from the Tower of London or Dublin Castle before sailing, as their previous muskets had generally been in use since the close of the Seven Years' War and were too worn for active campaigning. The 15th drew a new issue of the Long Land Pattern musket, the standard arm of the British Army during most of the eighteenth century, its "old Set being worn out & rendered unserviceable." An improved pattern furnished with steel rammer, it was of the form commonly produced from the early 1760s onward, until slowly phased out by the introduction of the Short Land Pattern musket at the close of that decade. The 15th's light infantry company drew Short Land muskets, as did all light troops sent to North America. This Long Land, produced at the Tower of London, is regimentally marked on the barrel and with "XV" on the trigger guard.

The 15th Foot also drew new accoutrements from regimental stores before sailing for America in December 1775. The 1768 Royal Warrant regulating the dress and accoutrements of the British Army called for 2-inch-wide buff leather waistbelts bearing a single frog to contain the bayonet scabbard. This rare example of such a waistbelt conforms to the warrant but was carefully converted into a shoulderbelt, probably by a shoemaker or other leather worker in the ranks of the 15th Foot, sometime after its receipt by the regiment. The branches of the frog were separated and then carefully resewn to the belt closer together, thereby achieving a smoother fit against the left hip of the soldier than could be achieved by merely slinging the original waistbelt over the shoulder, a common practice in other corps.

The musket and the bayonet belt came from eighteenth-century homes in Connecticut and are probably "captured" objects from Tryon's April 1777 raid. The regimental belt plate is still attached to the belt. A bayonet from a British artillery carbine is fixed in the remnants of its scabbard, probably added by its new American owner sometime after 1777.

A Grenadier Officer's Fighting Sword 1775–77

Prior to the Revolutionary War, colonels of certain British regiments had established "pattern" swords to be worn by their officers, along with such distinctive devices as gorgets and belt plates. Almost universally, the form was some variant of the smallsword, either silver- or gilt-mounted, depending on the metal established for a particular corps. Various colonels, however, took this standardization to more precise levels, some describing in regimental orders the "pattern to be viewed" or purchased at a particular swordsmith's establishment, while others took it upon themselves to acquire an entire complement of swords for all their officers (usually debiting the cost of each sword against an individual officer's account in the regimental agent's books). The pattern smallswords were generally reserved for regimental parades and similar duties while more functional edged weapons were carried by officers on campaign. This was true especially among company-grade officers, who were most likely to be engaged in actual combat at close quarters. Typically, a short, lightweight blade was preferred, usually with a slight curve, allowing for both "cut and thrust." The two most popular sword forms for wartime service were the short saber and the hunting sword or "cutteau."

Personally acquired and governed by individual taste, these swords ranged in quality and degree of manufacture and ornamentation. This well-made hunting sword was carried during the Revolutionary War by the Hon. William Falconer of the 15th Regiment of Foot. His sword and scabbard are both mounted in silver, which was the regimental metal of the 15th Foot. The hilt has a shell guard with full knuckle bow and the grip is black-dyed, fluted ivory. The reverse of the scabbard's throat bears the engraving "Will$^{m.}$ Falconer Lieu$^{t.}$ Grenadiers."

During the Battle of Brandywine on September 11, 1777, while under a "heavy Fire of Artillery and Musquetry," the grenadiers "advanced fearlessly and very quickly; fired a volley, and then ran furiously at the rebels with fixed bayonets," driving them back two miles "without firing a shot, in spite of the fact the rebel fire was heavy." The 1st Battalion suffered heavily for their valor, with 12 killed and 70 wounded. Commissioned officers were particularly hard hit—7 wounded (including the 15th company's captain) and 3 killed, among them the unfortunate Lieutenant Falconer. This sword, as well as Falconer's other personal effects, were sent to his family in England, and a postmortem memento engraving was placed on the scabbard throat: "The Honble Lieut. William Falconer of the 15th Reg$^{t.}$ at Foot Commanded by Lieut. Colonel Bird was killed in the Action at Brandewine Sept. 11th 1777 in the 19th year of his Age."

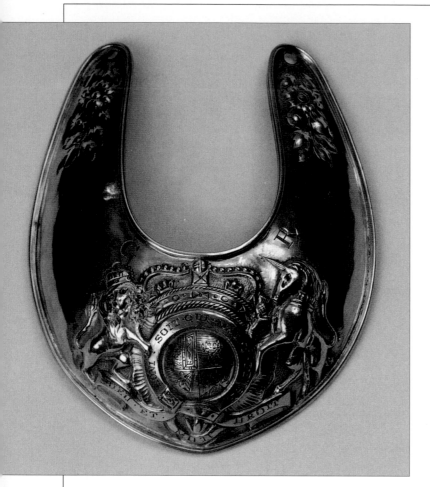

British Officer's Gorget, 1750–70

A vestige of feudal times, the gorget head evolved from the metal breastplate or cuirass, and by the eighteenth century, it served as a badge of rank or office for military officers. The half-moon-shaped British gorget typically bore in its center the royal coat of arms (with militia or volunteer corps, this was sometimes replaced by the arms of a colony or municipality) or the regimental badge of an authorized "ancient" regiment, sometimes flanked by the regimental number or title. The metal or color of the gorget was to match that of the uniform's buttons, silver or gold, usually plated, but sometimes of solid silver. It was made of sheet metal that was then engraved or struck with the device in relief, as on this solid silver specimen.

Featuring the British royal coat of arms in raised relief, this gorget is identical to one depicted in a 1772 portrait of the 15th Foot's colonel and is of a form popular in the 1750s to 1770s. The gorget was suspended from the neck by a ribbon, usually of the facing color of the regiment, that fastened to the gorget by running through the holes at each end, tied off in front with small rosettes of similar ribbon. British officers typically wore their gorgets in the field while choosing (or sometimes being ordered) to leave their sashes behind—another badge of rank that was merely an encumbrance in bushy country.

The gorget also found limited usage among colonial American militia officers and even some Continental Army officers during the early part of the Revolutionary War.

Private, Battalion Company, King's American Regiment, Summer 1777

The King's American Regiment was raised by Edmund Fanning in New York in early 1777. Recruits initially attracted to the regiment included both Loyalist refugees seeking revenge for the wrongs inflicted on them and captured patriot soldiers seeking refuge from possible death aboard the diseased-filled British prison ships anchored in Jamaica Bay. Under strict discipline, the regiment soon became known as one of the best Provincial corps and was one of five such units accepted on the American Establishment of the British Army and redesignated the 4th American Regiment on March 7, 1781. It served during the capture of Forts Montgomery and Clinton in 1777 and distinguished itself in numerous actions in the South before being disbanded in Canada with the cessation of hostilities in 1783.

Responding to a requisition from Sir William Howe, the Treasury Board contracted for the production of 5,000 uniforms for corps then raising or anticipated from the Loyalist population in the colonies. Shipped to North America in September 1776, the uniforms consisted of "Coats Green & Lined with White baize, Waistcoat & Breeches White & White Buttons" and felt "round hats." While awaiting the arrival of this clothing, his regiment still dressed in a mix of civilian clothing and patriot uniforms, Colonel Fanning directed "that their Cloaths be clean . . . Hats brush'd and trim'd up, fastened up on one side, their Hair cut short & all Remnants or badges of the Rebel Service on the Cloaths or any of them Carefully taken off and conceal'd." Two months later, the *New York Gazette* was proud to report that Fanning's and other Provincial regiments were "mostly clothed, and make a very handsome Appearance" in uniforms of "Green, faced with White, and made of the best Materials."

Fanning was a stickler for details and in August 1777 reminded his men in strong terms that "in every Part of dress" they were to maintain "the most exact Uniformity." In preparation for field service that autumn, the men of the King's American Regiment was ordered to affix their cartridge boxes to the straps of their cartridge pouches, the intent being to convert the waist-mounted, supplemental ammunition containers to a more effective shoulder arrangement. They were likewise ordered to sling their narrow waistbelts, with bayonet frogs, over the opposite, or right, shoulder. The regiment was also furnished with linen gaiter-trousers, paid for by "stoppages" from the men's pay and made by the regimental tailors.

PAUL SCHIERL

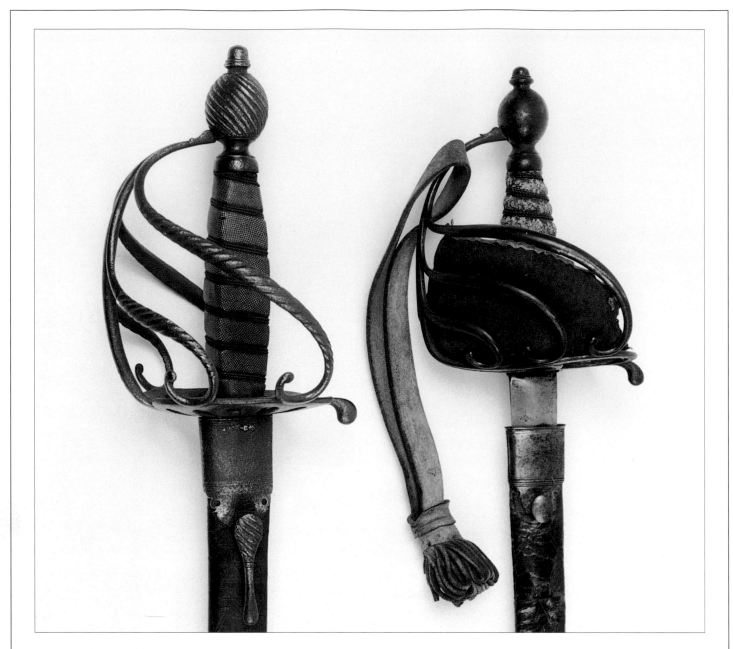

British Officers' Swords, c. 1770–80

While enlisted men in the British Army were issued with plain utilitarian swords, officers were responsible for arming themselves and were somewhat free to choose whatever style weapon they saw fit. The only regulation pertaining to their swords was the Warrant of 1768, which dictated that the color of the hilt's metal match the color of the lace on the coat. Contemporary portraits show that swords of the following types were very much in vogue during the period of the American Revolution.

This basket-hilted saber on the right was intended for use by a mounted officer, evidenced by its large hilt meant to accommodate a gloved hand. It has an openwork, bilobate counterguard and a copper-wire-bound, sharkskin-covered grip. Both its olive-shaped pommel and its four branches are covered with finely executed fluting known as gadrooning. Its straight, single-edged blade has two fullers, one wide and one narrow, with a false edge. Also surviving is the complete original scabbard, mounted with an iron chape and locket, and a hook gadrooned en suite with the hilt. The reverse of the locket is rocker engraved "Bibb Newport Street," a London cutler listed at this address from 1758 to 1775.

Similar to the sword on the right is a fine example of an infantry officer's sword known as a "spadroon," due to its fullered, single-edged straight blade. The iron hilt is composed of an olive-shaped pollem; wire-bound, white-sharkskin-covered grip; and a pierced heart-shaped counterguard supporting three scrolling outboard branches. The *ricasso* of the blade is marked "S&G Harvey," a father and son partnership who worked together till Samuel died in 1778. In addition, the sword is complete with not only its original iron-mounted black leather scabbard, but also its rarely encountered buff leather sword knot and red cloth and leather hilt liner. Officers had at least two sword knots, a fancy one made of bullion for use on parade and a leather one for use in combat.

PRIVATE, BATTALION COMPANY, THE ROYAL NORTH BRITISH FUZILEERS, SPRING–FALL 1777

The 21st Regiment of Foot was first raised in 1678 as the Scots Fuzileers Regiment, although it was redesignated the Royal North British Fuzileers Regiment of Foot in 1712. The Fuzileers (or "Fusiliers," as it began to be spelled during the late eighteenth century) was one of the "ancient" and royal regiments of the British Army and, therefore, was entitled to display its traditional badge or device on colors, drums, caps, gorgets, and certain other regimental appointments. In the case of the 21st, the Scottish thistle had long been accepted as the regiment's distinctive device—an appropriate selection for a Scottish corps. Arriving for the relief of Canada in May 1776 and participating in the southward thrust down the Lake Champlain corridor later that year, the 21st wintered in Canada with the rest of Maj. Gen. John "Gentleman Johnny" Burgoyne's army. It was part of Brig. Gen. Hamilton's 2nd Brigade during the 1777 campaign, fighting at the two battles of Freeman's Farm, before being interned as part of the Convention Army following capitulation at Saratoga on October 17, 1777.

The uniform worn by the 21st Foot followed the 1768 regulations, which specified dark blue facings, the facing color worn by all royal regiments. The regimental buttonholes were applied "singly" or equidistant on the facings and were made of white lace with a single dark blue stripe along the outside edge. The 1777 uniforms shipped for the use of Burgoyne's army had been captured at sea and now clothed many Continental soldiers. Thus, in April 1777, while preparing for the expedition southward, orders were given to Burgoyne's regiments to cut the skirts of their coats down and use the excess fabric to patch their threadbare coats of 1776 issue. To replace the worn, woolen breeches for the warm-weather campaign, gaiter-trousers or overalls were made from linen drilling or striped ticking. Hats were similarly ordered to be cut down into caps or cap-hats, with a vertical front plate and a crest made from cow tails, dyed a particular color for each regiment. With such field alterations, Burgoyne's British regiments all resembled light infantry troops, and clearly this was the intent, as the men were also trained to march and fight in the loose tactical order necessary for forest warfare.

The 21st, as a fusilier regiment, was authorized bearskin caps by the 1768 warrant, but there is little evidence to suggest that the regiment brought such caps with them to North America. If they did, the caps remained in store in Canada

PAUL SCHIERL

when the regiment went on Burgoyne's Expedition of 1777, according to a watercolor by a German eyewitness. For campaign, the 21st also wore felt cap-hats, trimmed with a white crest and featuring a thistle device of cast pewter affixed to the front plate. The fusiliers' coats were altered to closely imitate light infantry jackets by removing the horizontal, or "cross," pocket flaps and reattaching them "long," or vertically. Bayonet waistbelts were slung over the shoulder to alleviate constraint on the abdomen. This soldier of the 21st, who carries a Long Land Pattern musket, with which the battalion companies were still armed, has slung his linen haversack reversed to protect the flap from catching on brush.

British Officer's Fusil 1760–70

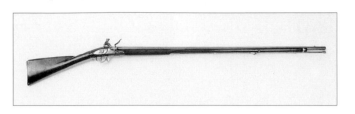

Fusil, fuzil, and fusee are all corruptions of the Italian word *fucile,* meaning flint. In its earlier usage, it referred to all long firearms that incorporated a flintlock ignition system. In context, three "ancient" musket-armed regiments in the British Army, "The Royal Fuzileers," the "Royal Welsh Fuzileers," and the "Royal North British Fuzileers," received their titles in the late seventeenth century. By the mid-eighteenth century, however, the term *fusil* came to mean a light musket carried by an officer, at least in the British lexicon. Although commissioned officers of foot troops were to be armed with spontoons, according to Royal warrant, by the early 1750s some regiments (such as the Royal Artillery) were permitting officers to carry fusils in lieu of the proper polearm. During the French and Indian War, this became an established practice and was sanctioned by the successive commanders-in-chief in North America. The carrying of fusils was officially authorized for officers of fusilier regiments in 1770, as well as for officers commanding grenadier and light infantry companies.

By 1776 the approved used of this arm was extended to other corps, such as Highland and guard officers serving in America, and unofficially, it was probably carried by most foot officers on campaign. Many American officers carried similar arms, although this practice was officially prohibited in the Continental Army after 1778.

Privately purchased, fusils varied greatly in quality and decoration and were variously mounted in brass, iron, or silver, depending on taste and budget of the owner. Some British regimental commanders regulated the pattern or form to be carried by their officers, directing them to procure such from a designated maker. This brass-mounted officer's fusil by Jover has a narrow-bore 42-inch barrel, and the front of the forestock is cut back 4 inches to allow for the mounting of a socket bayonet.

British Twenty-Nine-Hole Cartridge Pouch, 1768–84

Before 1784 there was no established pattern or model for cartridge pouches in the British Army. Procurement of uniforms and accoutrements, such as pouches and bayonet belts, was the responsibility of the proprietary or colonel in chief of a regiment, usually a general officer, who would turn over the actual responsibilities to a regimental agent, usually a merchant or financier, who would then be reimbursed for his troubles by a commission (typically 2 percent above actual purchase costs). The colonel, in turn, would be reimbursed by the Crown at a set allowance for clothing and equipage.

This well-made cartridge pouch is one of perhaps three patterns in widespread use among the infantry regiments of the British Army during the Revolutionary War, yet only five examples are known to survive today. Made of thick, substantial blackened leather, it contained a wooden block (usually beech) drilled to accommodate twenty-nine cartridges. Below the block, there was space for an additional eleven rounds or so, plus musket tools and spare flints, accessed by a pull-down flap cut into the front of the pouch under the large covering flap. The flap of the pouch was heavily polished with "blackball," a substance somewhat like shoe polish, made of beeswax, tallow, and lampblack. When well rubbed in, it made the pouch nearly impervious to water. The width of the buff shoulder belt is $2\,3/4$ inches, as governed by specifications in the 1768 royal warrant, which was not superseded until 1784.

TROOPER, THE QUEEN'S LIGHT DRAGOONS, DISMOUNTED DIVISION, 1777

In anticipation of sending the "Queen's" or 16th Regiment of Light Dragoons to America, it was augmented by the addition of 9 mounted private men per each of 6 troops, plus an additional cornet, sergeant, 2 corporals, and 29 privates per troop to serve dismounted, bringing it to a full wartime authorization of 490, officers included. The dismounted dragoons were intended to act together as a dismounted division or light infantry detachment under the command of a captain and lieutenant. Structured in this manner, the 16th Light Dragoons was also capable of acting as an independent legion, having its own combined-arms complement of horse and foot.

Arriving near New York in late September 1776. the 16th distinguished itself during minor actions in New Jersey, including the capture of Maj. Gen. Charles Lee, the second-ranking officer of the Continental Army. A detachment of the dismounted men were at the battle of Princeton, and the entire regiment served with Howe's army during the 1777 Philadelphia campaign. The 16th fought its final battle on American soil on June 28, 1778, at Monmouth, New Jersey. Shortly afterward, the officers and noncommissioned officers were sent to England to recruit, while the men were drafted into the 17th Light Dragoons.

The regiment's lieutenant colonel, the Hon. William Harcourt, took great pains to properly prepare his men for American service, proudly writing to his father on May 23, 1776, about "the Dismounted part of the Regiment, which I have vanity enough to think are at least as well trained and much better armed and appointed than any Light Infantry in the army." The arms and appointments to which he referred included a short rifle or rifled carbine, a billhook or hatchet in lieu of saber, and—according to a Hessian eyewitness—a pistol, probably worn in a simple holster or boot attached to a waist- or shoulderbelt. The men were issued haversacks and tin canteens, both with leather straps. Cloaks provided for inclement weather were carried rolled on top of the knapsacks. Belting was of whitened buff leather.

Uniforms were of the same style as those furnished to the mounted men, although cut shorter in the skirts like those worn by the light infantry. As appropriate to a royal regiment, the madder red coats had blue facings, with buttons and holes placed "two and two," trimmed with white royal lace with blue and yellow stripes. Epaulette straps of blue cloth, edged with narrow white tape and trimmed with worsted fringe, were fastened to each shoulder. Instead of the boots worn by mounted troopers, the dismounted men were supplied with brown cloth gaiters and shoes. Leather caps of

WILLIAM RODEN

"an entire new construction," were purchased in 1776, trimmed with cloth turbans painted to resemble leopard skin, "three rows of iron chains around the crown," and surmounted with bearskin "roaches," or crests.

British Light Dragoon Pistol, 1760

In addition to the saber or horseman's sword, cavalry and light dragoons were armed with single-shot flintlock pistols. Carried in a pair of leather holsters mounted across the cantle of the saddle, the pistols were inaccurate at all but point-blank range when fired from horseback. As such, they were considered secondary arms to the keen-bladed horseman's sword or saber. They could still prove highly effective, however, in the close and brutal personal combat into which most mounted actions invariably devolved.

With the official creation of light dragoon regiments in 1759, the British Army adopted a lighter pistol with a 9-inch barrel. Well made and popular, it remained the official pattern through the Revolutionary War period and was carried by British light dragoons and Loyalist cavalry, as well as their American opponents, during that conflict. This example is marked on the lock plate with the maker's name and date of manufacture: "Vernon 1760."

CAVALRY TROOPER, THE BRITISH LEGION, 1780–81

The British Legion was a mixed command of Provincial horse and foot raised by Lord William Cathcart in 1778, who commanded with the rank of colonel. When the young lord returned to England in late 1779, his second in command, a daring young English cavalry officer by the name of Banastre Tarleton, was named lieutenant-colonel-commandant of the corps. By 1780 the British Legion consisted of six cavalry troops and four light infantry companies.

The legion, which soon established its reputation as an effective fighting force, was part of the British expeditionary force that encircled Charleston in 1780. Tarleton, leading his own British Legion and other detachments, successfully surprised and defeated the Patriot horse posted at Monck's

Corner on April 14, establishing the Tory corps as a particularly ruthless and savage opponent and earning its commander the epithet of "Blood Ban" and the implacable hatred of the Patriot foe. At the British defeat at Cowpens, revenge would be inflicted on the legion and its commander with the capture of its infantry, most of its cavalry fleeing the field after being but little engaged. Tarleton and a remnant of his legion, now mostly cavalry, continued to fight as part of Cornwallis's army until its surrender following the siege of Yorktown on October 19, 1781.

Lord Cathcart felt that "the Provincial clothing was too gaudy and the accoutrements too slight," and arranged to have the men outfitted according to his own notions of what was most appropriate for a partisan corps. In 1780 the British Legion cavalry was described by a London newspaper as follows:

> *The cavalry that Coll. Tarleton commands is a provincial corps, and makes rather a singular figure; for as service has been consulted more than show, their horses are all manner of colours and sizes. Their uniforms are a light green waistcoat, without skirts, with black cuffs and capes, and nothing more. Their arms consist of a sabre and one pistol. The spare holster contains their bread and cheese. Thus lightly accoutred, and mounted on the swiftest horses the country produces, it is impossible for the enemy to have any notice of their approach till they actually receive the shock of their charge.*

Officers wore jackets edged with narrow gilt lace and trimmed with gilt buttons, and troopers wore a plainer jacket trimmed with pewter buttons. Bearskin-crested helmets, similar to those worn by the 16th Light Dragoons, were adopted, with green turbans or sashes round the crown and plumes made from black ostrich feathers. Breeches of white cloth and whitened buckskin were both worn as legwear, along with snug-fitting black light dragoon boots. Both the horse and cavalry accoutrements were of black, tanned leather, and the saddle-mounted pistol holsters had "caps," or covers, of bearskin. The iron-mounted saber had a "stirrup hilt" and a curved blade—the "hussar" style just coming into vogue among British light dragoons and readily copied by the Americans.

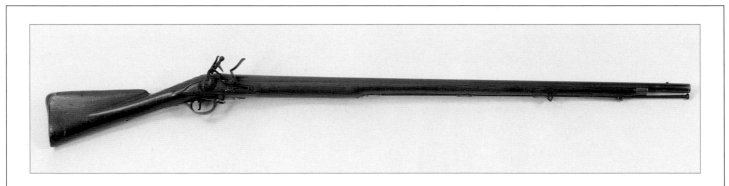

Sergeant's Fusil, Royal North British "Fuzileers," c. 1770

During the French and Indian War, British sergeants frequently left their halberds in store and carried "firelocks" in their place when serving in the field. On March 12, 1770, orders were circulated authorizing ordnance to produce and issue a new "particular Pattern" fusil that had been selected for the use of grenadier sergeants of infantry regiments. This authorization was also extended to light infantry sergeants upon the reestablishment of such companies later that year, the battalion company sergeants retaining their traditional halberds.

This fusil is regimentally marked on the top of the barrel, "ROYL. N[orth] B[ritish] FUZILEERS"; the 21st Regiment of Foot, which arrived in Canada in 1776, served in the 1776 and the 1777 Northern Campaign, and was interned after Saratoga. It is of the pattern authorized for flank company sergeants in 1770, essentially a scaled-down version of the Short Land Pattern musket, with a 39-inch barrel .65-caliber bore. It is unclear whether this example was carried by a flank company sergeant in the 21st, as all battalion sergeants in fusilier regiments were also rearmed with such fusils by the Revolutionary War. Similarly, some British units during the Revolutionary War, such as the Composite Brigade of Guards and the 71st Highlanders, drew fusils in lieu of halberds for all sergeants before sailing for America in 1776. Prior to the New York Campaign later that year, Gen. Sir William Howe ordered all British regiments to turn their halberds into store at Halifax, drawing muskets for their sergeants when fusils were unavailable.

A GRENADIER OF THE BLACK WATCH, WINTER 1779–80

CHARLES HILL

Perhaps the most famous regiment in the British Army, the 42nd, or "Royal Highland Regiment," as it was then officially known, is perhaps best remembered today as "The Black Watch." Having served in America in 1757–61 during the French and Indian War and again during the 1763–64 Indian campaigns, it returned to North Amer-

ica once more in 1776. At the Battle of Long Island, the 42nd Company, along with its battalion, joined in the fierce fighting that raged around British-occupied western New Jersey during spring 1777 and in the Philadelphia Campaign of 1777, where it fought with great distinction at the Battle of Brandywine.

As part of the 1st Battalion of Grenadiers, the 42nd played a key role in the hotly contested Battle of Monmouth on June 28, 1778—the last pitched battle fought in the North between the Continental and British armies. Throughout that long, hot day—fought under a blazing sun with temperatures in the nineties—the British grenadiers (wearing their heavy woolen uniforms and fully-loaded packs) pushed back superior forces of attacking Americans, until coming upon the main American battle line. There, following a see-saw struggle for control of high ground that exposed them to heavy artillery fire, and suffering heavy casualties from both the fighting and heat exhaustion, they finally withdrew under cover of darkness. The 42nd continued to serve with the 1st Battalion of Grenadiers for the remainder of the war; they would only fight together in one final campaign—during the 1780 Siege of Charleston.

The uniform coat of the 42nd Foot was similar to that prescribed in the 1768 warrant for the other infantry regiments in the British Army, with the exception of short skirts to allow for wearing the belted plaid in lieu of breeches. Issued to all men of the regiment were knitted blue Highland bonnets with a diced band of red, white, and green, trimmed with a round cockade of black ribbon, regimental button, and white loop surmounted by black ostrich plumes.

The broadswords were left in store when the regiment sailed for America, in keeping with their lieutenant colonel's 1775 declaration that during the previous war "the Highlanders on several occasions declined using broad-swords in America, that they all prefer bayonets." Before departure, 392 new "Cartridge Boxes, with Straps and Frogs . . . to replace a like number worn out and rendered unserviceable" were issued by the Board of Ordnance, and every soldier was furnished with a Short Land Pattern musket and bayonet. Capt. John Peebles of the grenadier company thought the cheaply produced "accoutrements bad," and in May 1779, "got a Set of tin Cartridge boxes for the Co[mpan]y from N[ew] York." Using the new tin cartridge boxes with the old "belly" boxes, the grenadiers were able to carry the full "50 rounds of Ammunition" per man required on field service during the 1780 Charleston Campaign.

On December 4, 1779, Captain Peebles noted that "the Mens brown tr[o]wzers are almost finished, the Taylors a cursed plague." Made by the company tailors from brown "donation cloth" and trimmed with black horn buttons, these gaiter-trousers would be worn by the 42nd grenadiers on the voyage south and during the campaign until replaced by similar warm-weather trousers made of Russia drill in May 1780. The grenadiers' coats, worn since April 1779 and described as "very ragged" the following April, remained on the men's backs until September 1780, when new ones were issued upon their return to New York.

Highland Accoutrement Badges, 1776–83

The traditional Scottish thistle appears as a motif in the buttons and other distinctive devices of Highland corps from the eighteenth century to this day. The circular device on the left is the "cartridge box ornament" or badge produced for the 71st Regiment of Foot (Fraser's Highlanders), as can be seen from the '71' engraved below this thistle. This example was found near Savannah; others have been excavated near Charleston and New York. Nearly identical, but unnumbered examples were worn by the "Royal Highland Emigrants" (later the 84th Regiment of Foot) and have been found on their campsites in Canada and Georgia. Officers' versions of the badge are known for both regiments, made from thin sheet silver. The cartridge box badge has frequently been misidentified as a "bonnet badge" among collectors.

The heart was another popular form among the Scots, and heart-shaped devices were frequently used to trim the tips of their broadsword belts. This sheet brass example has a thistle engraved on it and is believed to be a tip from a sergeant's swordbelt of the 84th; numerous plain examples, of slightly smaller dimension, are believed to be those issued to the "other ranks" of the same regiment. Both types have been found at Fort Haldimand, occupied by elements of the 1st Battalion, 84th Foot during 1779–83. Another Revolutionary War artifact that has its own lore built around it, the belt tips are commonly said to be "turnback hearts" that once decorated the skirts of officers' coats.

PRIVATE, CAPTAIN McINTOSH'S COMPANY, "FRASER'S HIGHLANDERS," 2ND BATTALION, 71ST REGIMENT OF FOOT, WINTER 1780–81

The 71st Regiment of Foot was authorized in November 1775 to consist of two battalions, "each Battalion to consist of Ten Companies of 4 Sergeants, 4 Corporals, 2 Drummers and 100 Private Men in each Company, with 2 Pipers to each of the Grenadier Companies." Raised and recruited that winter in the Scottish Highlands by the Lt. Gen. Hon. Simon Fraser, the regiment sailed with a fleet bound for America on April 21, 1776. "Fraser's Highlanders" was the first of a number of new Highland corps during the war, there previously having been only one permanent Highland regiment, the 42nd, on the prewar establishment of the British Army. According to one of its lieutenants, the men "were excellent, nothing, indeed, could be superior, for the recruits, having been collected chiefly from the lands of their chief [Fraser], were, with few exceptions, young, able-bodied and full of attachment to their superiors, whom for the most part, they followed from motives of hereditary affection." During the dreary two month voyage, the fleet was scattered by an Atlantic storm, after which three transports, containing some of the companies with their arms and equipage, were captured by American privateers and brought to Boston as prizes.

Most of the regiment, however, safely joined Howe's army on Staten Island in time to fight during the New York Campaign of 1776. Elements of the two battalions fought in the Philadelphia Campaign of 1777, while a smaller contingent remained in New York and participated in the taking of Forts Clinton and Montgomery. In 1778 the regiment was stationed on Staten Island, then sent to Savannah, Georgia, fighting at Briar Creek, Stone Creek, Augusta, and the Siege of Savannah in 1779. The regiment marched overland from Savannah in December 1779 to join Clinton's army for the Siege of Charleston. After the taking of that city, it fought at Camden and other actions in the Carolinas during 1780. The 1st Battalion was captured at the Battle of Cowpens, while the men of the 2nd continued their exemplary fighting record in Lord Cornwallis's army, fighting at Wetzell's Mills, Guilford Courthouse, and Green Spring, until they were interned following the capitulation at Yorktown in October 1781.

As with the 42nd Foot, the 71st was clothed and armed in the Highland fashion, which included short coats or "Highland jackets" of red, faced with white. Buttons were placed in pairs on the facings and the "Lace for the Button holes to be White with a Red Worm." White woolen waistcoats were worn underneath and instead of the breeches worn in English regiments, "belted plaids" of "government sett" tartan were issued, serving as garments by day and blankets at night. Short Land Pattern muskets were issued to all enlisted men, while officers and sergeants carried fusils, and each man also carried a Highland broadsword and steel-mounted side pistol. Unlike the 42nd, the 71st resolutely clung to their Highland plaids and weapons, however impractical, long after the senior regiment had discarded their own for American service. This can be partly explained as a matter of stubborn pride, as Fraser's men were almost entirely Highland-born, while the 42nd had many Lowland Scots in its ranks.

This soldier of Capt. Aenas McIntosh's company in the 2nd Battalion is dressed as he would have appeared during the winter campaign of 1780–81 in North Carolina, based on the 1779–81 company account book and other supporting documentation. His uniform coat is worn and patched, though his white waistcoat is in slightly better condition, redone with new woolen fronts that autumn. He wears tartan gaiter-trousers or "trews" made from his old plaid, although new brown trousers of wool had also been issued to his company. The latter pair, as well as a spare shirt, stockings, and personal items, are carried rolled in his blanket, which is worn slung over the left shoulder in lieu of carrying the red-painted knapsack usually worn for such purpose. Accoutrements have been minimized to the belly-mounted cartridge box, on its narrow waistbelt with bayonet frog. The flap of the box still bears the regimental "cartridge box ornament" of cast brass. On the opposite shoulder from the blanket roll is carried the haversack and tin water flask. His Highland bonnet is trimmed according to battalion practice, with two black ostrich plumes above his horsehair cockade denoting his status as a battalion company private.

Short Land Pattern Musket, 20th Regiment of Foot, 1770–77

On March 15, 1776, the 20th Regiment of Foot, then serving in Ireland, was transferred to the British Establishment and ordered to North America. Before sailing, the regiment drew a new set of arms from stores at Dublin Castle. Apparently, as can be seen in this regimentally marked survivor from the Saratoga Campaign, the 20th Foot received the Short Land Pattern musket, as did many other regiments departing from Ireland. Approved in 1768 as "more convenient" than the heavier Long Land muskets, the 42-inch-barreled Short Land Pattern muskets were first issued to the light infantry companies reestablished in British regiments during 1770 to 1771. However, it was not until the Revolutionary War that their usage became widespread in the British Army, the bulk of Short Lands having remained in store until the outbreak of hostilities.

Short Land muskets were used widely and with great success as the war progressed, although it was not until 1790 that they fully replaced the Long Land, with a final halt in production of the longer barrels. The various Land Pattern muskets are commonly called "Brown Bess" muskets today, a late-eighteenth-century nickname probably inspired by the natural brown walnut stock of such arms, earlier pattern muskets and marine muskets frequently having been painted black or red ocher.

British Cartridge Pouch Badges, 1775–83

This representative sample of British cartridge pouch badges reflects the diversity of forms used by British infantry regiments during the Revolutionary War. These devices or ornaments were both functional and decorative. Cast from heavy brass, they helped weigh down the leather flaps of cartridge pouches when in use, thereby preventing the accidental spillage of cartridges. At the same time, they served to show unit affiliation. They were popular from the late 1750s through the 1780s, but their use was officially prohibited after 1784, except by the three regiments of Foot Guards. Pouch ornaments are among the rarest of all Revolutionary War excavated artifacts.

These four badges were all excavated from Revolutionary War sites and are identified by regiment and context as follows clockwise, from top: 9th Regiment of Foot grenadier company badge, found on the 1777 route of Burgoyne's army along Lake Champlain; 43rd Foot light company badge, recovered from an American 1781–82 winter cantonment on the Hudson Highlands, probably cast off from a pouch captured at Yorktown; 60th Foot grenadier's badge, found in St. Augustine, Florida; and a 3rd Foot ("the Buffs") dragon device, dug on a battlefield in South Carolina. Grenadier companies typically favored a flaming grenade device, as can be seen from the two examples, whereas light infantry badges were made small to suit the lighter pouches carried by these companies. "Ancient" regiments of the British Army were permitted to place their distinctive regimental devices on their accoutrements and caps—in the case of the Buffs, a stylized dragon or griffin motif in use prior to 1742. Badges cast with open work, such as the pictured "GR" and "43" badges, were handsomely backed with red cloth for additional effect.

"LIGHT BOB" PRIVATE, 16TH REGIMENT OF FOOT, 1777–81

The 16th Regiment of Foot had a rather unremarkable military record during the Revolutionary War, though by all accounts it appears to have been a good regiment. Serving in detachments at various southern posts during most of the war, it had few opportunities to distinguish itself, although it fought with great credit during the successful 1779 defense of Savannah and the 1781 siege of Pensacola, where most of the regiment was surrendered, with the rest of the garrison, to the Spanish forces of Gov. Gen. Bernardo de Galvez of Louisiana. The light infantry company, however, had earlier been detached for active field service in a provisional light infantry battalion consisting of itself, the light infantry companies of the 1st and 2nd Battalions, 71st Foot, and that of the Prince of Wales's Volunteers (a Provincial regiment). This "battalion of light infantry signalized themselves on many occasions" but were captured during the fierce fighting at the Battle of Cowpens on January 17, 1781.

First formed during the French and Indian War to deal with the French irregulars and their Indian allies, the provisional light infantry formations of the British Army were disbanded with the coming of peace. The importance of permanent light-armed troops was finally officially recognized during 1770–71, with the establishment of a permanent light infantry company in each of the "Marching Regiments of Foot." In selecting men for such service, officers were advised to take into account that as "the Attack may frequently become personal between Man and man, It is therefore necessary to be particular in selecting Men for this Service not only of Activity and Bodyly Strength but also some Experience and approved Spirit." Light infantrymen were expected to be equally proficient in both loose, skirmish order and in the closed ranks of battalion formations, with special attention given to their skills as marksmen.

Clothing and equipage were selected appropriate to the service expected of these new troops. Coats with short skirts were adopted; these soon became known as "jackets." Waistcoats were of red wool and a short, "squared-front" form. Leather caps and lightweight accoutrements of tanned leather replaced the felt hats and heavy buff belting worn by battalion troops. Tomahawks or hatchets supplemented muskets and bayonets of the new Short Land Pattern, the light infantry companies being the first recipients of these new arms. Although broadly governed by the 1771 guidelines, great variety existed in the form of both equipage and dress between different regiments' light companies.

This soldier of the 16th, called a "light bob" because of his shortened clothing, wears the winged, yellow-faced jacket

and the distinctive red waistcoat of his company. With the exception of the brown, woolen gaiter-trousers issued for winter campaign wear in North America, he is dressed very much in accordance with the prewar specifications for light infantry troops. His cap is closely modeled on that "fixed upon" in 1771 but also includes a short flap, or visor, worn turned up but capable of dropping down to occasionally shield the eyes from light or glare. He wears crossbelts of blackened leather; a powder horn suspended by a cord is attached to that of his cartridge pouch. The horn was to be used for "loose loading" with powder and ball, saving the fixed cartridges of the cartridge box or pouch for fast firing at close range. It was frequently left in store during the Revolutionary War by seasoned light troops, being viewed as an inconvenience, and its issue was rescinded in 1784.

English Officer's Horse Pistol, c. 1770

Despite the profusion of pistols that survive from the Revolutionary War period, only a relatively small number have a history of ownership and usage during the war. Although of private purchase, this officer's brass-mounted horse pistol was obviously inspired by the British Light Dragoon pattern then in use. Made by Hadley of Charing cross, it is marked "Henry Harnage/ Major/62nd Regt./1770" on the wrist escutcheon plate.

Harnage served with his regiment during the northern campaigns of 1776 and 1777 and until the surrender of Burgoyne's army at Saratoga. Paroled to New York City, Harnage was permitted to keep his arms and personal belongings with him. The butt of the pistol was later engraved with the name of his son, Sir George Harnage, baronet and last of the family line, and is dated "Belswardyne 1845." As a mounted field-grade officer, Major Harnage likely carried this pistol, and probably an identical mate, in his saddle holsters.

British Light Infantry Cap, 1776–98

The standard headgear issued to many British troops during the Revolutionary War proved poorly suited to active campaign service. Particularly unpopular was the light infantry cap pattern, a form selected by the board of general officers that had established the dress and accoutrements of the light infantry in 1771. Essentially a skull cap of "jacked" leather (leather stiffened by heated application of a mixture of rosin, beeswax, and turpentine), it had a vertical front plate decorated with the cipher of King George III surmounted by the British crown and a regimental number below. It was trimmed with three rings of light chain around the crown (ostensibly to render the cap saber-proof) and had a leather or ribbon cockade on the right side.

Few of these caps adequately fulfilled the need for which they were first adopted—providing functional and comfortable headgear for these fast-moving, lightly equipped infantrymen. The leather helmets were heavy and hot and were often discarded or left behind, replaced by "cap-hats" made from cut-down hats or by simple "round hats" with narrow brims, but the felt caps and hats were less durable than leather, and continued replacement ultimately made them more expensive. A simplified leather cap capable of collapsing flat was introduced during the Revolutionary War. It was considerably lighter, made of thinner leather, with a soft, easily folded center or crown, as can be seen on this fine original that came from a British collection.

This form of cap seems to have first made a midwar appearance among Loyalist "Provincial" corps, notably the Queen's Rangers. Its commandant, Lt. Col. John Graves Simcoe, purchased similar but visorless "light and commodious" caps for his men in 1780. By 1782 the Royal Artillery had adopted such "forage caps" for fatigue duty, folded and stowed in the knapsack when the regimental hat was worn for full dress. These caps often had a regimental badge affixed to the upright front panel, although this particular example never carried such a device.

JAEGER, 2ND COMPANY, HESSE-CASSEL FIELD JAEGER CORPS, 1776–77

HERMAN BENNINGHOFF

The Field Jaegers were the elite troops of the Hesse-Cassel forces serving with the British Army during the Revolutionary War. Recruited from hunters, gamekeepers, and other marksmen, they were famous for their skills as riflemen and skirmishers, as well as for discipline and bravery under arms in the most trying of circumstances. Mustered into British service during March 1776 in Hesse-Cassel, the jaegers were described as "a stout, active Body of Men, armed with Rifle-Barrel Guns, to the Use of which They are thoroughly inured . . . commanded by skillful, experienced Officers. They cannot fail of being very serviceable." In June 1776 two companies of foot jaegers accompanied the second contingent of Hessian units sent to North America. They were augmented in 1777 with three additional companies of

foot and one mounted company, forming a provisional Field Jaeger Corps of nearly 500 officers and enlisted men.

The jaegers were originally commanded by the stern but beloved Col. Carl von Donop, who was mortally wounded during the October 22, 1777, assault on Fort Mercer, and afterward, by Col. Adolphus von Wurm. The most famous and talented officer of this exceptional corps was Capt. Johann Ewald, commander of the 2nd Company of Field Jaegers, who developed the practice of the *petit guerre* into a science. Usually serving in a company-size or smaller detachments, the jaegers could be found in the van of advancing British columns or covering the rear of those withdrawing. Widely deployed and serving on campaigns that ranged from

New York to the Carolinas, the jaeger corps was able to amass an almost unexcelled battle record during the war.

The Hesse-Cassel Field Jaegers wore uniforms coats of grass green, faced and lined with crimson red. Almost identical to those worn by the Prussian jaegers, on which they were modeled, the coats had six brass buttons arranged in pairs on each half lapel, and their round Prussian-style cuffs had a slit on the underside. Grass green waistcoats (changed to buff in 1782) were worn underneath. Legwear consisted of buff-colored leather or cloth breeches, substituted by ones of linen during hot weather. Foot jaegers wore gray leggings trimmed with brass buttons to protect their lower legs from brush and damp. All companies wore large cocked hats, nearly bicorne in form. The hat was trimmed with a red and green feather, a green cockade with yellow loop and button, and round, white worsted tufts with crimson centers at the hat's corners.

The coarse clothing of the jaegers suffered from the hard and prolonged field service to which it was subjected and wore out long before the annual replacement suits were sent from Hesse-Cassel each year. While inspecting the jaeger advanced posts outside of New Brunswick, New Jersey, on January 9, 1777, Lord Cornwallis was impressed that they "were very cheerful despite their ragged clothing and hard duty," and he informed Ewald that "plentiful provisions would arrive any day and each jaeger would be clothed at his [Cornwallis's] expense."

By January 23 the promised gift was delivered, drawn from 3,000 ready-made suits of regimentals recently arrived from England to clothe Provincial corps then raising. Colonel von Donop was quick to assure his own commander that although the green coats, "facings and turnbacks are indeed understood to be white," they could "easily be changed to red and they will all be made like our uniforms." He also noted that "they are lighter and more comfortable for the conditions of a campaign than our own." The 200 Provincial coats, as well as the white woolen smallclothes that accompanied them, were fully issued to the jaegers in early May, presumably with all the necessary alternations in color and cut accomplished.

The principal arm of a Hessian jaeger was his short rifle, produced at the Pistor Manufactory in Schmalkalden. The rifle had a near 29-inch, swamped, octagonal barrel of .65-caliber bore, a wooden patch box, and brass fittings. His accoutrement belts and cartridge pouch were of brown leather, and the rifle sling was dyed a reddish color. A short, brass-hilted hunting sword was carried by each jaeger, with the exception of those in the mounted company, who differed in dress and equipment only by "wearing Sabres instead of Swords; and having Spurs fix'd to the Heels of their Boots." Their musicians also carried "Trumpets instead of French Horns," which they used for signaling commands to dismounted companies. The waistbelt was occasionally fitted with a cartridge box and supplemental ammunition and, notwithstanding in-garrison orders to the contrary, was frequently worn slung over the shoulder in the field.

Hessian Infantry Officer's Sword, 1752–88

While British officers had a certain degree of latitude in the selection of arms and equipage, the dress, weapons, and accoutrements of Hessian officers were strictly regulated by Frederick II, ruler of Hesse-Cassel. When he was informed in 1776 that his officers—following the lead of their red-coated brethren—had removed the metallic lace from their hats and coats to minimize their becoming targets for American riflemen, he furiously ordered the lace restored and a strict adherence to regulation dress in the future. As such, it is doubtful that a Hessian infantry officer would dare to carry any blade other than the type pictured here, a design borrowed from the Prussian Army. Although classified as a small sword by its form, the heavy cast-brass hilt and substantial double-edged blade rendered it an effective fighting weapon. A near-identical sword, with its Hessian engraving still visible on the blade, is in the collection of the Morristown National Historical Park.

FUSILIER COMPANY PRIVATE, FUSILIER REGIMENT VON LOSSBERG, 1776

The Fusilier Regiment von Lossberg was part of the 1st Division of Hessian troops sent to North America from Hesse-Cassel after Frederick II signed a treaty on January 15, 1776, with the British government to supply troops to serve in the subjugation of the rebel colonies. Fighting with distinction at Long Island, Fort Washington, and White Plains, the regiment enjoyed a fine reputation until it, along with the rest of the Hessian garrison at Trenton, was captured in a surprise attack on Christmas morning, 1776. The regiment was eventually reraised in 1778 from survivors, escaped prisoners, and new recruits and served at New York until 1780, when it was sent to Quebec, where it remained till the close of the war.

Frederick II was heavily influenced by the military system of nearby Prussia, as were many other rulers. As a result, the uniforms, equipage, and organization of Hessian regiments closely resembled those of corresponding Prussian corps. The Fusilier Regiment von Lossberg wore a short, blue coat of Prussian cut, with orange facings and red linings. The half lapels had six buttons set in pairs, a standard feature on all Hessian coats that were also borrowed from Prussia. The collarless coats were heavy and made of coarse materials that by the winter of 1776 had already begun to wear thin from the active campaigning. Neckstocks of stiff, black leather were worn by the regiment. "Smallclothes"—waistcoat and breeches—were of white cloth, and the lower legs were encased in snug-fitting gaiters of black cloth.

Caps of miter shape, with stamped brass fittings over a stiffened cloth crown, were worn by all Hessian fusilier companies. Grenadier companies wore similar, but higher caps. The front plates featured the arms or device of the Hessian ruler, a rampant, crowned lion over the letters "FL," signifying Frederick II, the Landgrave. One such fusilier cap, kept as a Trenton souvenir by a Massachusetts soldier, is now in the Smithsonian Institution, and brass fragments of others have been excavated in New York and Philadelphia. The troops were armed with a musket and bayonet of the "Potsdam" pattern and a brass-hilted hanger. Cartridges were carried in a large cartridge pouch, its flap embellished with stamped brass devices and slung by a broad, whitened buff leather belt. The waistbelt was of the same construction, and the musket sling was of red-dyed leather.

SCOTT FERRIS

Brunswick Dragoon Sword, 1760–83

The Dragoon Regiment *Prinz Ludwig* formed part of the Bunswick contingent sent to America in 1776. It marched south with Burgoyne's army in 1777, most unfortunately still on foot, as few horses had been found to mount these horsemen. More than 150 of these dragoons made up part of a detachment that was sent to gather horses and supplies but was attacked and overrun near Bennington; the remainder of the regiment served until the surrender at Saratoga. Among the arms captured by the Americans were the heavy, dragoon broadswords that were still carried by the *Prinz Ludwig* dragoons. One hundred forty-nine of these swords were shipped south for the use of the 2nd Continental Light Dragoons, and their receipt in February 1778 was acknowledged by Maj. Benjamin Tallmadge, who wrote, "They are very strong & heavy having steel Scabbards."

Few of these Brunswick swords are known today. Four documented examples are in museum collections, and the fifth, pictured here, is now in the Troiani collection. It has a heavy, double-edged blade and basket hilt with a domed pommel of brass. Cast into the sword's guard is the "C" under crown cipher of Charles, Duke of Brunswick. It was originally carried in a leather-covered, wooden scabbard reinforced with steel that was buckled to a broad, buff leather waistbelt.

German Musket, 1750–80

The muskets carried by German troops during the Revolutionary War are poorly documented, and few examples of such firearms are extant. Despite the surrender of significant numbers of German troops with their arms, only a few hundred were listed in postwar American inventories. However, in the collection of the Massachusetts State Archives is a musket captured at Bennington and presented by Gen. John Stark to the state as a memento of his victory over the Brunswickers. Although unmarked, this trophy weapon is nearly identical to the Prussian model 1740 musket, manufactured at Potsdam. Musket parts have been excavated from the Brunswick camp at Saratoga that identically match this musket, leaving little doubt that at least some of that principality's muskets were of the Prussian pattern.

This example, also unmarked, is nearly identical to the Stark musket and other unmarked muskets of purported Hessian provenance. The heavily faceted brass mountings, large lock plate with rear point, and high comb and pronounced relief carving around the lock plate, breech, and lower ramrod pipe on the walnut stock are characteristic of German military arms of this period and are found on muskets produced not only at Potsdam, but also at other arms manufactories such as Herzberg, Schmalkalden, and Suhl. The barrel is 41 inches long and the bore is .72-caliber, allowing the use of standard British musket cartridges as issued from ordnance stores. Parts from these muskets were also incorporated into American-made muskets produced under the direction of the Continental Board of War, and a number of these muskets survive.

GENERAL GEORGE WASHINGTON, COMMANDER IN CHIEF, CONTINENTAL ARMY, FALL 1777

MR. & MRS. RICHARD ULBRICH

George Washington was forty-three years old when the Second Continental Congress unanimously elected him general and commander in chief of "the Continental forces raised or to be raised for the defense of American liberty" on June 15, 1775. He accepted with the reservation that he did not believe himself "equal to the command I am honored with," confiding to a fellow Virginia delegate that from this appointment "I date my fall and the ruin of my reputation." Eight days later he set out to take command of the motley force of New England citizen-soldiers then besieging British-held Boston.

Although Washington was convinced of his "own incapacity and want of experience," there was much to recommend the wealthy planter to such a command. He had served with distinction as commander of Virginia's Provincial forces during the French and Indian War and was the only native-born American to hold a brigade command of British-American forces during the war. He was also one of the few experienced senior military leaders still in his prime. A member of the Virginia landed gentry, Washington was well connected both socially and politically. Appointing the Virginian to overall command of the combined colonial forces could only further the American cause by allaying the "southern" colonies' fears and suspicions of New England dominance in political and military matters. Finally, Washington was one of the most imposing figures of his age, both in physique and demeanor.

Considered "the best horseman of his age and the most graceful figure that could be seen on horseback," Washington was no less distinguished on foot. Standing nearly 6 feet, 2 inches, he towered over most of his contemporaries. Wide of shoulder but narrow of chest, with broad hips, large bones, and well-developed muscles, Washington conveyed the impression of great strength and vast reserves of energy. His "well shaped" head revealed strong features: reddish hair, a "large and straight" nose, steel blue eyes, firm chin, and ruddy complexion. Men and women were impressed by his "pleasing and benevolent though . . . commanding countenance" that seemed to support the observation that not "a king in Europe but would look like a valet to chambre by his side."

Washington had attended Congress in May 1775 wearing the uniform that he had selected for the independent companies of Fairfax and Prince William Counties, which he commanded. This plain yet elegant dress, consisting of a blue coat "turned up with buff, with plain yellow buttons, buff waistcoat and breeches and white stockings," continued to be worn by Washington when he took command of the Continental forces. Blue and buff were the colors of the Whig Party, the opposition party to the Tory administration in England, hence their original selection by Washington. Washington's aides and general officers began to adopt this mode of dress, and it soon became the unofficial uniform of the Continental Army's general staff, until formally adopted in 1779.

The lack of uniform clothing in the Continental Army and the need to recognize and distinguish various officers' grades led Washington to implement an expedient system of rank devices in 1775 that would not involve the purchase of expensive epaulettes and other trimmings. He, as commander in chief, would be distinguished "by a light blue Ribband, wore across his breast, between Coat and Waistcoat." Other generals would wear pink ribbands in a similar fashion, while aides-de-camp were identified by ones of green. Field-grade officers were to wear red (or pink) cockades in their hats; captains and lieutenants wore cockades of yellow (or buff) and green, respectively. Sergeants would be recognized "by an Epaulette, or stripe of red Cloth, sewed upon the right shoulder: the Corporals by one of green." This simple but effective system continued in force until replaced by another in 1780.

The brown-uniformed regiment marching past Washington and his aide-de-camp in this painting already shows the wear and tear of hard campaigning. Many of the men wear fringed linen hunting shirts (once proposed by Washington to be the official uniform of the army, for their cheap cost and versatility), and most sport sprigs of evergreen in their hats, signifying their unity in the Patriot cause. The troopers of the 1st City Troop, or Philadelphia Light Horse (shown here in the background), frequently served as Washington's escort and are shown in brown regimentals with white facings, unanimously adopted by this volunteer unit's membership in 1774. They are wearing leather dragoon helmets with vertical front plates, light blue turbans, and bucktail crests, which had replaced the silver-bound, round hats worn by the troop early in the war.

American Silver-Hilted Small Sword, 1760–74

A popular civilian style of the period, the small sword was both arm and badge of rank for a man of gentility. The hilts were light, with simple knuckle bow and counterguard, and the blades were narrow and straight, suitable to the thrust-and-parry technique learned from fencing masters or manuals. As a result, the small sword was readily adopted by the eighteenth-century military as a form befitting gentleman officers. Its common availability also led to widespread use as an officer's edged weapon among American troops during the French and Indian and Revolutionary Wars. American swords were made by adding locally crafted hilts to imported European blades, like this triangular blade of German origin. The silver-mounted hilt is by William Swan of Worcester, Massachusetts, who died in 1774.

LEXINGTON "MINUTE COMPANY," MASSACHUSETTS MILITIA, 1775

In 1774 the Massachusetts Provincial Congress adopted a plan that would ensure the loyalty of its colony militia and render it more effective to oppose the Crown's troops, if necessary. The Whig, or Patriot, officers in the colony's three militia regiments resigned their commissions, and most of the Tory, or Loyalist, officers were intimidated to do the same, thereby allowing for the reorganization of the militia into seven regiments, led by officers of strong patriotic principles. The officers of each town company were to enlist a third of its men ready to act "at a minute's notice." Thus reorganized, the militia "alarm" companies and the new corps of "minutemen," were furnished with officers of their own choosing. The latter, composed of the young and active, was further organized into regiments. The minutemen companies had only a brief, six-month existence, but their role in the Battles of Lexington and Concord on April 19, 1775, has immortalized them in the annals of the Revolutionary War.

In 1775 each Massachusetts militia soldier was required to carry "a good firearm with a steel or iron ramrod . . . a bayonet fitted to his gun, a scabbard and belt therefor, and a cutting sword, or a tomahawk or hatchet, a pouch containing a cartridge box that would hold fifteen rounds of cartridges at least, a hundred of buck shot, a jack knife and tow for wadding, six flints, one pound of powder, forty leaden balls fitten to his gun, a knapsack and blanket, a canteen or wooden bottle sufficient to hold one quart."

This minuteman is equipped in such a manner, and he carries the same Long Land Pattern musket that he used during the French and Indian War. His civilian clothing consists of a single-breasted frock coat of London brown broadcloth and light blue, woolen waistcoat and breeches. The laced half boots, or "hi-lows," are a form that found great favor with farmers and outdoorsmen, merging the protective attributes of gaiters with the comfort of a laced shoe. A tricornered, civilian "cocked hat" and neckerchief round out his rather unmilitary ensemble.

American Cartridge Pouch or Box, 1775–83

During the Revolutionary War and later, Americans frequently referred to all cartridge containers worn by soldiers as "boxes," as differentiated from the British system, which distinguished the more substantial shoulder "pouches" from the belly-mounted "boxes" discussed earlier.

This cartridge box was carried by a Connecticut militiaman during the 1776 New York Campaign, and the front of its wooden block bears the following inscription: "Benjamin Fogg is my Name and with my hand I wrote the same. Bought at portland [Connecticut] price one dollar." It still contains two original paper-wrapped musket cartridges in the nineteen-hole block, which is enclosed within the early bag-style pouch of black leather. The shoulder sling is of linen upholstery webbing, with the ends inserted and sewn into place at the back seam of the pouch flap. This form of pouch was also commonly issued to Connecticut Continental troops, although by 1779 it had fallen out of favor in preference of improved models and was already being referred to as of the "old construction."

A "JERSEY BLUE" OF 1776

"Jersey Blues" was a nickname first given to New Jersey fighting men during the French and Indian War, when the colony had clothed its Provincial regiment in blue uniforms with red facings. Two decades later, in late 1775, the nickname resurfaced when the first two New Jersey regiments raised for Continental service adopted similar uniforms. Later this appellation was globally applied to all New Jersey regulars, whatever the uniform worn. Blue, a color long associated with the Whig or opposition party to the Tory government in England, was a logical color for the Patriot forces raising in America, and soon wartime demands exceeded available supplies. As a result, many regiments received coats of less popular colors, such as green, gray, and "drab"—an aptly named dye of greenish brown cast, ranging in shade from light to dark.

For the 3rd New Jersey (authorized on January 10, 1776), a uniform consisting of coats and belted waistcoats of light drab (almost a tan shade) and buckskin breeches was decided upon as it was organized and equipped during February to May 1776. The short coat had dark blue facings consisting of narrow lapels and cape, and pointed cuffs with "slashed sleeves," that buttoned on the underseam. Coat and waistcoat buttons were pewter, cast with "New Jersey" in raised script letters. The men's cocked hats were neatly bound with white tape, and half gaiters were purchased to complete their legwear. Accoutrements made by New Jersey saddlers were furnished with buff leather crossbelts of the new fashion, and muskets were drawn from colony stores, supplemented by market purchases. This soldier, shown here advancing while loading, carries a "NEW JERSEY"-marked, Wilson-contract musket of the type purchased by the colony during and following the French and Indian War.

Despite its rather dull-colored uniform, the 3rd New Jersey Regiment was, in the words of one of its officers, "esteemed and allowed . . . to be the completest and best Regiment" when formally mustered into Continental service at New York City on May 1, 1776. The eight-company regiment sailed up the Hudson as part of Gen. John Sullivan's brigade, intending to join the Northern Army in Canada. However, the 3rd was instead detached and marched to the Mohawk Valley, to intimidate Loyalists from attempting to organize any armed resistance and maintain, at the least, the neutrality of the Oneida Iroquois. A substantial portion of the regiment was stationed at Fort Stanwix, rechristened Fort Schuyler, where it played a major role in the rebuilding of the crumbling fortification. In October the 3rd New Jersey was ordered to Fort Ticonderoga, where it remained in garrison until the end of February, then marching homeward to Morristown, New Jersey, where it was discharged on March 20, 1777.

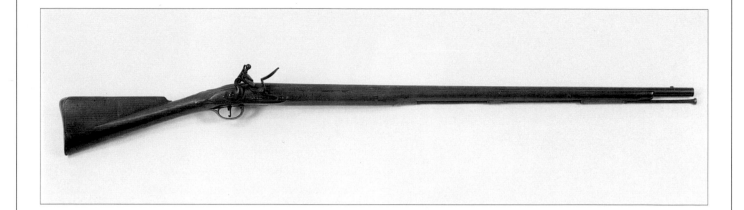

"Wilson" Military Fusil 1750–60

Fusils, or "fuzees," are essentially lightweight versions of the smoothbore muskets typically carried by officers. Military-type fusils generally had the same furniture as their heavier counterparts, but were scaled down in size. Barrels were lighter and smaller, both in caliber (usually .65 to .68) and length (36 to 42 inches). Marked "WILSON" on the lock plate, this 42-inch-barreled fusil was made by the firm of Richard Wilson and closely resembles the Long Land Pattern musket that inspired it. Wilson was a contractor to the British Ordnance, the East India Company, and the Hudson's Bay Company, as well as to various British volunteer or militia corps.

This weapon's furniture and workmanship are much simpler than that usually found on an officer's privately purchased fusil, suggesting a similar contract procurement or common issue. Commercially produced military arms were purchased by British colonial governments in North America, including New Jersey, Virginia, Massachusetts, South Carolina, and New York City during the French and Indian War period, and a small number of Wilson muskets marked "NEW JERSEY" or "CITY OF NEW YORK" still survive.

American Wooden Canteen, 1776

An essential item of a soldier's personal equipment in the field, the canteen was officially considered part of the "camp equipage" of a regiment, along with haversacks, camp kettles, and tents. As such, it was (in theory, at least) to be turned in to stores when the regiment went into winter quarters and reissued at the coming of the next campaign season. Whereas British soldiers usually received tin flasks or water bottles, the predominant form of water carrier used in the Continental Army was the wooden canteen or cask.

This unpainted canteen is of a form known to collectors as a "cheesebox" canteen, because of its resemblance to a wooden cheesebox. Typically made of white cedar, it was formed by wrapping a one-piece wooden band around two circular wooden faces and pegging or nailing the band into place. A hole was drilled for the mouthpiece, plugged with carved wood or cork, and a carrying strap or cord was attached by means of wire loops driven into the banded side. This cooperage style has a strong tradition in western New England and eastern New York.

Carved into one face of this canteen is the following inscription: "JOSEPH AMES x THE 10 x Day 1776 AD." One "J. Ames" served in the 2nd Continental Artillery Regiment, raised principally in New York, and "Pitckills" probably refers to the town of Peekskill, New York, a major Continental Army supply and recruiting center on the Hudson River.

PRIVATE, 4TH NEW YORK REGIMENT, 1778–79

WILLIAM RODEN

The 4th New York Regiment was authorized in November 1776 and organized during the early part of 1777. Commanded by Col. Henry Beekman Livingston until his resignation on January 13, 1779, the regiment continued in service under Lt. Col. Frederick Weisenfels until its disbandment with the reduction of the New York Line in January 1781. Assigned to the Northern Department and attached to the New Hampshire Brigade in August 1777, it fought bravely and well during the Battles of Freeman's Farm. Reassigned with the brigade to the Main Army in October, it again proved its mettle during the Battle of Monmouth—the last pitched battle in which the regiment would fight.

On September 3, 1778, the firm of Otis & Andrews, which served as Continental Army clothiers in Boston, complained to the Board of War that Maj. Gen. John Sullivan had requested them to provide Colonel Livingston's regiment with "400 suits of white regimentals turned up and lined with scarlet" with a corresponding number of "caps with black hair," pairs of brass knee and shoe buckles, black worsted knee garters, white stockings, and black or scarlet stocks with clasps, most of which they considered not in keeping with normal Continental Army requisitions. Livingston and his officers had already provided themselves with such distinctive uniforms, however, and political pressure was brought to bear on the regiment's behalf.

By late 1778 the 4th New York appears to have received white uniforms with red or scarlet facings, trimmed with brass buttons. Leather caps were unavailable, but caps were made from felt hats and trimmed with hair crests per Livingston's specifications. Overalls were issued in lieu of buckskin breeches and knee garters, and it seems more likely that black, rather than scarlet or red, leather neckstocks were received, black-dyed leather being commonly used for both that item and accoutrement belts. The entire 4th New York drew newly imported French model 1766 muskets in June 1777, part of the shipment earmarked for the New Hampshire regiments.

A "BLACK IRISHMAN" OF THE 2ND PENNSYLVANIA REGIMENT, WINTER 1778–79

The 2nd Pennsylvania Regiment was constituted in early 1777 from the remnants of the 2nd Pennsylvania Battalion of 1776. Later that year, the 13th Pennsylvania Regiment was incorporated into it, and command of the regiment was given to Col. Walter Stewart. As part of Brig. Gen. Anthony Wayne's 1st Brigade of the Pennsylvania Division, the 2nd suffered through the winter at Valley Forge and stood up to the British grenadiers in the hard-fought Battle of Monmouth in June 28, 1778. Late that year, the 2nd, along with the rest of the Pennsylvania Division, took up winter quarters near Middlebrook, New Jersey, constructing log hut cantonments along the rocky hillsides during the short, cold days of December. While the troops felled trees and cleared the land at their encampment area in the tattered remnants of last year's clothing, the long-promised new uniforms were finally delivered out.

The Pennsylvanians drew royal blue coats with scarlet facings, along with white woolen waistcoats and breeches and gray yarn stockings. These ready-made uniforms were drawn from a stock of more than 30,000 suits received from France earlier that year. They had been procured by the American commissioners in Paris, Silas Deane and Benjamin Franklin, who contracted for uniforms equal in quality of materials and workmanship to those made for the Royal Army of France. Cut in the three standard sizes used for French uniforms, the clothing was made to specifications and patterns developed by the commissioners. Rather than copying the French military fashion of half lapels, the coats were made with full lapels capable of fully covering the torso when buttoned over—a critical feature given the cold American winters. Cuffs were slashed in the French manner, buttoning at the underseam of the sleeve. The bodies of the coats were lined with twilled, white serge and finished with plain-faced, pewter buttons.

New hats had not been included in the shipment. The Pennsylvanians' old hats were in terrible condition and of varied styles, leading Wayne to order that all hats "which do not Admit of been Cockd" in the proper military fashion be converted into caps of a standard form, achieving at least some degree of uniformity in the headgear of his troops. This was accomplished by cutting off all "but About half An Inch" of the brim around most of the crown. The remaining flap was cocked up, and the cap was "bound Round with White Tape Linnen."

COL. J. CRAIG NANNOS

After receiving his new French-made clothing, Pvt. Andrew McCarty of the 2nd Pennsylvania, who had enlisted for two years' service that spring, "was taken sick" and "obtained permission to return to his family with whom he continued in a bad state of health for about eighteen months." While home, his enlistment expired "about six months previous to his being restored to his health," and thus "he had not on that account obtain[ed] a discharge." So McCarty would claim in a pension application filed in 1818, although an earlier historical document puts a different twist to the story. Shortly after McCarty went on furlough, the following advertisement was placed in the February 27, 1779, issue of the *Pennsylvania Packet:*

Stolen out of the subscriber's stable last night, by a certain Andrew Carty, a bay horse. . . . The said Carty is about five feet seven or eight inches high, black hair, pitted with the small pox; had on a blue regimental coat lined with white, a ruffle shirt, red flannel leggings, and a sort of cap dressed up with fur. He belongs to General Wayne's division, had been upon furlough, and was on his return to camp. Whoever takes up said horse and thief shall have the above reward . . . paid by the subscriber in West-Caln township, Chester county. JAMES STANLEY Feb. 24

History does not record whether Mr. Stanley ever recovered his horse, but Carty or McCarty ended his days in western Virginia, in what is now Jefferson County, West Virginia. Our reconstruction of Private McCarty depicts him shortly before the furlough, wearing the new uniform and the "sort of cap" made to Wayne's specifications. The Irishman is armed with a captured Hessian musket and bayonet, and his accoutrements include a cartridge box "of the new Construction," one of thousands first issued to the Pennsylvania and Maryland Division at Middlebrook that winter.

American Bayonet Shoulder Carriage, 1775–83

This bayonet carriage is a fine early example of the shoulderbelt style that evolved during the Revolutionary War period. The rather oversize frog section securing the bayonet scabbard is reminiscent of the form found in the earlier waistbelt arrangement. The scabbard contains its original American-made bayonet and is well constructed of brown harness leather, as is the crossbelt. Slung over the right shoulder, the socket of the bayonet rested closely against the soldier's left side, just above the hipbone, so as not to interfere with the musket when performing the manual of arms or when on the march. The oval, "double D" brass buckle that secures the belt would be centered at the wearer's breast, allowing him to adjust the length of the belt with ease. Buckles of this form have been excavated at campsites of the Continental Army, as have forged iron scabbard tips or finials nearly identical to that found on this scabbard.

Continental Army Buttons

Following the examples of the British and French Armies, the newly formed Continental Army specified marked buttons for its regiments in late 1775. Many state units adopted their own buttons, while others used the generic "USA" pattern. Unlike British buttons, most of the American buttons were of one-piece cast pewter with an integral loop shank. Large quantities of military buttons were imported from France along with other war materials.

From left to right, top row. 1) 1st Pennsylvania Battalion of 1776. The center of this button bears the raised device "1B.P" surrounded by the words "Continental Army." Three battalions of Pennsylvania troops served as garrison of Fort Ticonderoga during this period. 2) Button of the Rhode Island Regiment, 1781–83. Composed of white and black troops, this regiment maintained a well-deserved reputation for valorous conduct on the battlefield. 3) Button of the 10th Continental Regiment,

c. 1775–76, found near Lake Champlain. The regiment was formed of men from Connecticut. A small detachment served with Arnold's fleet at Valcour Island.

From left to right, bottom row. 4) Enlisted man's button of the Continental Artillery. Made of stamped false-gilt sheet copper over a Haitian boxwood backing, these elegant buttons were first imported from France about 1780–81. They replaced a cruder cast brass American manufactured version, also decorated with a cannon and flag device. 5) The "USA" pattern button. Adopted in early 1777, this button was widely used in all theaters of the war and by many Continental units. There are many variations of this design. 6) Officer's button of the 8th Massachusetts Regiment, 1781–83. Made of silver-plated brass over a wooden backing, these very elegant buttons bear the number of the regiment over a skull-and-crossbones motif.

PRIVATE, CAPTAIN GEORGE LEWIS'S TROOP, 3RD REGIMENT OF CONTINENTAL LIGHT DRAGOONS, 1777–78

NATIONAL PARK SERVICE

Although he received authorization to raise a regiment of light dragoons on January 9, 1777, newly promoted Col. George Baylor had proceeded with only limited success by spring of that year. Recruits and horses were relatively easy to obtain in his native state of Virginia and nearby Maryland, but horse equipage, weapons, and clothing were scarce commodities, stocks in Virginia having nearly been depleted in equipping the 1st Continental Light Dragoons in 1776–77. By spring 1777 only one fully supplied troop was able to march north to join the Main Army —Capt. George Lewis's. General Washington ordered Baylor to send up detachments from the regiment as soon as they could be horsed, with or without arms or uniforms, so great was the need for cavalry. Lewis, a relation of Washington's, was attached with his troop to Washington's headquarters guard, serving primarily as couriers and escorts. Soon Lewis's troop became referred to as "Washington's Bodyguard" or the "Lady Washington Horse."

Lewis's troop continued on this detached service until late 1778, when it rejoined the regiment. Baylor and 104 men from his regiment were surprised in their billets near Tappan, New York, by British light troops under Maj. Gen. Charles "No Flint" Grey on September 19. Fewer than half escaped death or capture, and of the latter, Baylor included, most had been repeatedly bayoneted. The regiment was reraised from its survivors and new recruits but never reached full strength. A squadron of horse under Lt. Col. William Washington, consisting of men from this regiment and the 1st and 4th Light Dragoons, served with great credit during the southern campaign of 1780–81, notably at the Battles of Cowpens, Guilford Courthouse, and Eutaw Springs.

Baylor selected for his command a distinctive uniform of white coats with blue facings that continued in place for most of the regiment's existence. During 1777–78, it was cut in the French dragoon fashion, featuring interrupted half lapels, slashed cuffs, and small collars of light or medium blue cloth. Pewter buttons of the regiment, bearing the letters "LD" in an intertwined script cipher, have been excavated at the site of Baylor's Massacre. The sergeant's coat had shoulder straps edged with silver lace. The officer's uniform was similar but was made of finer materials and furnished with a silver strap epaulette with bullion fringe on the right shoulder.

A helmet cap worn by a member of Lewis's troops during 1777–78 still survives. It is made of jacked black leather with a white horsehair crest and the "several rows of small chains" prescribed for such caps—similar to the headgear shown in contemporary depictions of Baylor's Light Dragoons. Black feathers were provided to trim the caps of the officers in Lewis's troops during 1778.

This reconstruction shows a well-equipped private of Lewis's troop during his headquarters service. Under his coat he wears a white, belted waistcoat. His legwear consists of buckskin breeches and boots. He is fully armed with saber, holstered pistols, and carbine. Accoutrement straps are of black leather, including the "belt for the carbine with a running swivel," by which that arm is suspended, its nose secured a carbine "boot" strapped to the saddle. Few if any of the other troops in the 3rd were as well armed and equipped; carbines were scarce from the start and after 1779 were no longer carried by the regiment.

French Model 1763/1776 Pistol, Second Manufacture, 1770–79

The most common pistol imported to the United States during the war seems to have been the second production of the French model 1763/1776. This production incorporated the modifications of 1769, which included a shorter barrel and simpler furniture. More than 23,000 pairs were fabricated between 1773 and 1779, the year production ceased. All French pistols made during the *ancien regime* had brass mountings; those with iron fittings are from the later French Revolutionary period, iron being a cheaper, stopgap substitute.

Thousands of these brass-banded 1763/1776 pistols were purchased by Continental and state agents in France, for the use as both cavalry arms and naval boarding weapons. Horse pistols were always in short supply among the Continental light dragoons; a trooper was lucky if he had a pistol of any pattern in good, firing order, and the receipt of a fine weapon like the model 1763/1776 must have been a very welcome addition to his armament. These pistols were fabricated at St. Etienne, Maubeuge, and Charleville. This particular pistol was made at Charleville.

LIGHT INFANTRY PRIVATE AND LIGHT DRAGOON OFFICER, LEE'S PARTISAN LEGION, 1779–81

In April 1778 Capt. Henry Lee was authorized to create an "independent corps" of two troops to be expanded from his original 5th Troops of the 1st Continental Light Dragoons. Lee, an aggressive young cavalry officer from one of Virginia's foremost families, had demonstrated his mastery of the *petit guerre* while on outpost duty near Philadelphia, skirmishing with the enemy and forwarding intelligence, cattle, and other necessary supplies to the army wintering at Valley Forge. He had obtained his command partly through merit and partly through political connections, and it well suited his obvious military talents. The following month an additional troop was added, and Lee was in overall command with the rank of major. He wasted no time in obtaining coats of buff, faced with green, for his new command, which was described as "completely uniformed and extremely well mounted."

In June 1779 Capt. Allen McLane's light infantry company, officially part of Patton's Additional Regiment but long operating in an independent capacity similar to that of Lee's was attached to Lee's "Partisan Corps." It was formally annexed as its 4th Troop on July 13, 1779. McLane's original command was augmented with the dismounted dragoons from the other troops, and this overstrength "light infantry" command soon became known as the "Partisan Rangers." It was McLane who had performed the reconnaissance that enabled the capture of Stony Point by "Mad Anthony" Wayne that month and, in August, the taking of Paulus Hook by Lee. McLane and his Rangers also distinguished themselves in the assault.

McLane's men were poorly clad in comparison to the smartly rigged light dragoons when they first joined Lee's corps, but in September 1779 they procured "Uniform light linnen Jackets dyed a Purple & all there Ovrehalls the same." Completing this rather whimsical costume were leather caps with green turbans (of silk for the officers), surmounted by a bearskin roach—the same as worn by Lee's mounted dragoons.

During July and August 1779, ninety-six muskets, along with cartridge boxes, bayonets, and black crossbelts, were drawn by McLane for his men. A year later, forty-seven "light Infantry pieces" were listed as having been cleaned for McLane at the Continental Armory in Philadelphia. While

SCOTT FERRIS / WILLIAM RODEN

this accounting entry may merely refer to the muskets of his light infantry company, it may also indicate that at least some of his Partisan Rangers were furnished with light infantry carbines or fusils. Whether muskets or carbines, the arms were probably of British make, and the private depicted is armed with a Short Land Pattern musket and bayonet.

On February 14, 1780, Lee's command was designated the "Partisan Legion" and reorganized to consist of three mounted and three dismounted troops in anticipation of sending them to the Carolinas, where cavalry and light corps were most needed. During spring and summer, the legion received little assistance from the Continental Board of War as they began to refit for the march southward. Finally, overalls were obtained for the Partisan light infantry and leather breeches for the light dragoons of the legion, who were then "bare of clothing." The command eventually marched southward following their official transfer to the Southern Department on October 31, 1780. Although the source of supply is not clear, the entire legion received "short green coats, with other distinctions exactly resembling some of the enemy's light corps" prior to their departure. A Loyalist eyewitness in the South described the uniforms as "jackets," and as Lee's Legion was frequently mistaken for the Queen's Rangers or the British Legion, the green jackets must have been of the simple "roundabout" form as worn by those two Loyalist corps.

"Light-Horse Harry" Lee and his men wore this practical uniform while performing many notable exploits during the numerous engagements of the 1781 campaign, including the taking of Forts Motte and Granby, the Battle of Guilford Courthouse, Orangeburgh, and the Siege of '96. This dragoon officer of the famous command is shown in such attire, privately purchased but closely matching that issued to his men, although of finer quality and tailoring. A gold bullion epaulette, a gift of the Marquis de Lafayette to each officer in the legion, and gilt buttons and trimmings proclaim his status as an officer, as do his well-fitted "jockey" boots. His sword, normally slung on a black shoulderbelt, is of the Potter style. The enlisted dragoons were similarly armed, with the addition of short carbine suspended from a shoulder "swivel belt," and all mounted men carried pistols in their saddle holsters.

SCOTT FERRIS / WILLIAM RODEN

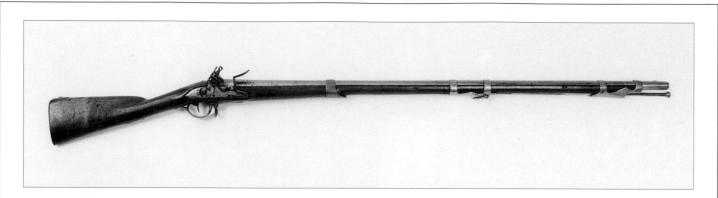

French Model 1770 Dragoon Musket, c. 1774

With the exception of distinctive barrel bands and brass mountings, notably the upper and lower barrel bands, trigger guard, and side plate, the model 1770 dragoon musket has a similar overall configuration to the French infantry muskets of 1770 to 1774. Only about 5,000 were produced between 1772 and 1778 before it was superseded by the model 1777 dragoon

musket. Originally intended for the French dragoons, who functioned as a cross between mounted infantry and light horse, surplus model 1770 dragoon muskets may have also been used by American troops. At the surrender of Charleston in 1780, the British noted "French cavalry fusils" among the captured arms.

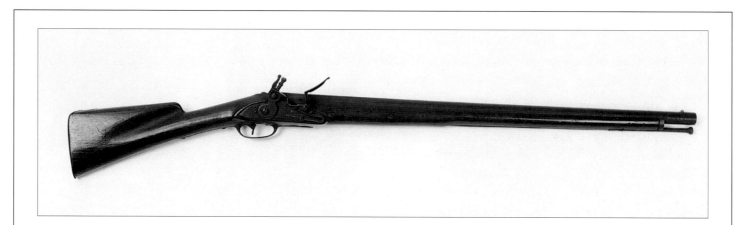

Dutch-American Cavalry Carbine, 1776–83

Perhaps a unique survivor of the Revolutionary War, this light horse or cavalry carbine was cheaply "cobbled" together from various musket parts and resembles no other known example. The lock plate is marked "J. VALET" Over "A. LIEGE," and the 28 1/2-inch barrel has "ROUGET FOUBIER" marked on it, as well as a "US" surcharge. Liege, now in eastern Belgium, was the center of arms production in what was then the Austrian Netherlands in the eighteenth century. Though the car-

bine may have been assembled in the Netherlands, it could possibly have been created by an American gunsmith working from imported parts. Great numbers of lock plates and other parts were shipped from the Netherlands and France during the Revolutionary War. This carbine has a sling bar on the reverse side opposite the lock plate, which was used to clip the weapon to the leather shoulder sling of a cavalryman.

VIRGINIA MILITIAMAN, 1780–81

The Old Dominion, having been little troubled by enemy incursions since 1776, became the target of two separate British expeditions that devastated the state, first in 1779 and again in 1780–81. For the next two years, Virginia would repeatedly call up its militia for active service, not only for the protection of its state borders, but also for service in the war-wracked Carolinas. The performance of the Virginia militia was less than stellar during 1780, both in the Battle of Camden and in the defense of their native soil. But well-led and bolstered by the presence of many discharged Continentals in their ranks, they redeemed their flagging reputation during the Battles of Cowpens and Guilford Courthouse, as well as in the Yorktown Campaign.

Virginia militiamen were expected to provide themselves with "a good Rifle, if to be had, or otherwise, with a common Firelock, Bayonet and Cartouch Box, and also with a Tomahawk." This former Continental is armed with a Short Land Pattern musket and wears the blue-faced green regimental coat drawn from the state public store just prior to his discharge. A pair of natural linen breeches, blue stockings, and a flopped hat complete his attire, along with a "spotted" handkerchief of silk knotted around his neck. Shoes are a common civilian form, closed by ties of linen tape, rather than with metal buckles. A seasoned soldier, he has stowed extra clothing and personal items in his blanket roll, and three days' rations are contained in his haversack.

The Battle of Cowpens, January 17, 1781

The men of Gen. Daniel Morgan's "Flying Army" blow on their hands and stamp their feet to keep warm against the cold of a Carolina winter morning. A battle is in the offing, pitting the nearly 1,700 patriot troops, mostly militia, against Lt. Col. Banastre Tarleton's command of 1,200 British and Tory regulars. It is Wednesday morning, January 17, 1781, at a place in northwestern South Carolina known to locals as "the Cowpens."

Morgan has positioned his troops wisely, taking full advantage of their abilities and weaponry as well as the existing terrain. The first line and second lines are composed of militia and volunteers from the Carolinas, Georgia, and Virginia. The riflemen in the front are to act as sharpshooters, skirmishing with the British from long distance. Morgan entreats the militia of the second line to fire two volleys into the British at close range, then retire to safety behind the third line. The third and final line of battle consists of the corps of Light Infantry, "picked men" drawn from the remnants of the Maryland and Delaware Line, augmented by two Virginia companies and one small North Carolina company. These 380 men are under the command of Lt. Col. John Eager Howard of Maryland and are posted on the rising ground at the northern end of Cowpens. To their left are 125 Virginia riflemen, many of whom are discharged Continental Army veterans, and a small detachment of North Carolina regulars guard their right flank. In reserve to their rear is Lt. Col. William Washington's cavalry: 80 troopers from the 1st and 3rd Continental Light Dragoons, reinforced by some volunteers and state horse units. The regulars are masters of their trade, hardened from constant deprivation and severe hardships, and Morgan depends on them to deliver a victory or at least, to prevent a complete rout.

From a distance, Howard's light infantry looks impressive, most dressed in the blue-faced red uniform prescribed in 1779 for Continentals of the Mid-Atlantic states. Although reclothed in October through the efforts of their state, the Maryland regulars' uniforms already show wear from an active winter campaign. Their new, short regimental coats of blue-faced red are already wearing at the shoulders from the constant rubbing of crossbelts and slings. Once white, woolen waistcoats are darkened with grime, and pewter buttons are missing here and there. Drummers and fifers wear coats of reversed colors: the red coats provide quick recognition of the field music, whose drumbeats and tunes relay critical commands amidst the din and smoke of battle. Seemingly forgotten by their states, the Delaware and Virginia troops wear even more ragged blue and red coats—the remnants of

much earlier issues—supplemented with new clothing loaned from Maryland stores, principally overalls, shirts, and shoes.

The men's overalls are torn and stained from constant marching along muddy traces and through rain-chocked streams, while shoes are in an even more miserable state, with few spares and no opportunity to repair those in use. Hats, always in short supply, are mostly remnants of the previous year's issue, the black wool felt now a rusty brown. Some of the cocked hats have been cut down into practical narrow-brimmed, round hats to make them last longer. The men's muskets are in good repair, however, and primarily of French make. Their bayonets are keen-bladed, and each man's substantial "New Model" cartridge box holds forty "buck and ball" cartridges—the standard combat load of the Continental Army.

As the dawn light begins to filter in from the east on this cold, crisp day, "Bloody Ban" Tarleton files his troops to the right from the Green River Road across the southern terminus of the intended battleground, although he cannot see Morgan's dispositions clearly in the murky shadows of early morning. The open woods are ideal terrain for the swift form of warfare waged by his mixed force of horse and foot. He knows from his local Loyalist scouts and guides that Morgan's line of retreat to the north is cut off by the rain-swollen Broad River. The aggressive, twenty-six-year-old British commander orders his men to drop their knapsacks, canteens, and haversacks, leaving them unencumbered of all but the necessary arms and accoutrements for the impending action. Here and there a few veterans, remembering parched mouths and pilfered packs from previous battles, retain their canteens and hurriedly stuff a few valuables and foodstuffs into their pockets "just in case."

His right wing consists of four crack companies of light infantry. Loyalist infantry from Tarleton's own British Legion compose the center—active, resolute regulars with a reputation for brutality almost as great as their commander's. The proud 7th Regiment of Foot, known as the "Royal" or "British Fuzileers," takes up the left. Two three-pounder battalion guns and their Royal Artillery crews move forward with the line with one cannon placed between the two divisions of the 7th and the other in the interval between the fusiliers and the legion infantry. Each flank of the line is further covered by a troop of horse, ready to gallop in for the kill once the Americans are broken. The 1st Battalion, 71st Regiment of Highland Foot are posted in reserve, along with Tarleton's remaining cavalry.

Of the 200 Royal Fusiliers under Maj. Timothy New-marsh, probably fewer than half had been with the regiment when it first came to North America in 1773. More than 250 fusiliers became prisoners of war with the surrenders of St. John and Chambly in 1775, although some were later exchanged and are now back in the ranks. Others died in battle or from wounds, while others succumbed to the dis-eases endemic to an eighteenth-century army. Although well-drilled under the watchful eyes of veteran commissioned and noncommissioned officers, the wartime recruits that augment these ranks do not have the steadiness normally expected in

such an "ancient" and famous regiment. Also left behind from the Canadian campaign are the tall but impractical bearskin caps worn by fusiliers in the British Army, replaced with cocked hats bound and looped with white worsted tape. Officers and sergeants carry their traditional fusils as befitting a fusilier regiment, while the men carry Short Land muskets. Blue facings to the brick-red fusilier coats and royal livery lace festooning drummers' clothing still clearly identify the 7th Foot as one of the "King's own" regiments. From a dis-tance the fusiliers can easily be mistaken for any one of a number of Royal regiments, now that their bearskins are replaced with the standard infantry hat. Up close, however, one cannot mistake the script "RF" motif placed on both their brass waistbelts and cartridge box badges.

Tarleton opens the battle at sunrise "by the Discharge of two pieces of Cannon and three Huzzas" from his men. They march forward in the loose, open-file, two-rank formation that the British Army has employed to advantage for the past six years of the American rebellion, allowing the battle line to move forward quickly through the pine and oak trees with a minimum loss of order. The fusiliers soon begin suffering casualties, notably among their officers, whose scarlet uniforms and gilt trim set them off as special targets for the riflemen of the American first line.

Some of the fusilier recruits, excited, confused, and enraged over their losses, open fire although no command has been given. The officers restore order, but Tarleton, impetuous and impatient for battle, moves the line forward before Major Newmarsh completes posting his officers. Soon the sharpshooter fire withers away, and they dodge away "from One tree to another" to escape the bayonets and fire of the British troops as they get within closing range. The second American line is now attacked and more fusiliers lay writhing in the grass after they receive its general discharge. The fusiliers now return a volley, shoulder arms, and charge bayonets. Cheering madly as they advance, the British push the militia from the field. Only now do they clearly see the closely massed ranks of Howard's Continentals on the ground to their front, who have commenced firing on the British.

Tarleton orders a general halt and carefully redresses his battle line, which has become disordered by the charge. The fusiliers dress to the right of the three-pounder on the Green River Road, which brings them opposite the left flank of the Continental light infantry. He now advances the Highlanders into line to the left of the fusiliers. Tarleton's line—still in open order—now greatly overlaps the American flanks, an advantage that he hopes to exploit.

As the fusiliers and Highlanders prepare for a final thrust to break the right wing of the American third line, the fifty red-coated dragoons posted on the British right flank are given the opportunity for which they have been waiting. Tarleton orders them to charge the opposing left flank of the American line, around which the militia from the retreating second line are retreating to apparent safety. The troopers are a detachment from a proud British unit, the 17th Regiment of Light Dragoons. Their red coats, with paired buttonholes on white facings, set them clearly apart from the green-jacketed cavalry of the British Legion. More distinctive still

are their stiff leather helmets with brass trimmings and red horsehair crests. The helmets' metal frontplates bear a white metal skull over crossbones on a black background, trimmed round with brown-fleeced goatskin. This sinister device represents the regiment's motto, "Death or Glory," a motto the troopers intend to uphold.

Charging in compact formation around—and through—the skirt of the volunteers posted on the left flank, they come almost instantly on the reforming militia in the rear, where they "began to cut down the militia very fast" with their hacking, dragoon blades. Morgan and some officers rally the volunteers and militia, who reload and hit the dragoons with well-directed rifle fire, "emptying many a British saddle." Already disorganized by the success of their charge, the "Death or Glory boys" are now charged in turn by Washington's 125 American cavalrymen that have been held in reserve. Supported by un-uniformed volunteers and militia horse units in their rear, white-coated 3rd Light Dragoons and other veterans from the 1st Light Dragoons smash into the redcoats. Outnumbered nearly three to one, the redcoats "pretty much scattered" after "leaving in the course of ten minutes eighteen of their brave 17th dragoons dead on the spot." The success of Tarleton's strategy is now completely dependent on the infantry of his left wing.

The fusiliers and Highlanders advance briskly against Howard's Continentals. The 7th, now closer, halt and return their own volley fire. As the acrid, black powder smoke disperses in the wind, the fusiliers and Highlanders see the rebel regulars withdrawing by platoons. Cheering and huzzahing wildly, they charge bayonets with their already fired weapons and rush on, their loose order now deteriorating completely. Suddenly, the seeming Continental retreat is no more, and once again, a wall of blue and red—bristling with bayonets—confronts the British soldiers. First one, then another, platoon volley crashes into the fusiliers and Highlanders. Under such a withering fire, confusion soon reigns and few officers and noncoms are left standing to exert any control over the dazed fusiliers and Highlanders. Howard, sensing his opportunity, orders his men to charge bayonets. The American counterattack completely shatters any and all resistance. Panic is now at near-epidemic proportion among all the British and Loyalist infantry. Though small pockets of men still try to defend themselves or escape, most throw down their arms in desperation or club muskets to signify surrender to the Continentals, whose mad, scrambling charge has completely disordered their own ranks.

RICHARD CONTE

Sensing a complete and decisive victory, the Continentals, from the mounted Colonel Howard down, vie with each other to capture trophies of honor. Seen here, Howard slashes at a silk-epauletted fusilier corporal, who resolutely stands his ground in defense of the regimental colors. But the effort is futile—the regimental standard is already in the hands of one Marylander, while the ensign carrying off the Royal standard is captured by point of sword. His sergeant (distinguished by scarlet coat with plain white lace, blue and scarlet worsted sash, and a lion-headed sword hilt) witnesses all with a back-ward glance before continuing his own race for self-preservation. A drummer, brilliant in his bearskin "music" cap and coat bedecked with lace and fringe, is too panicked to even think of throwing off his drum to aid in his retreat. At first the colors are taken, then in turn, the two cannon, and the last resistance melts among the British and Loyalist infantry, who reverse muskets or raise hands in surrender—all witnessed by Morgan and his staff from their point of advantage on the hill behind. The battle ends in a stunning American victory.

American Horsemen's Sabers, 1775–83

The principal arm of the light cavalry during the Revolutionary War was the horseman's saber. Although the national origin and form of such edged weapons varied greatly among the Patriot mounted troops, the preferred style was clearly that favored by British light dragoon regiments. This form of saber was distinguished by its slotted guard, stirrup- or D-shaped hilt, and long, heavy blade with a slight curve. Many of these American sabers used foreign-made blades, typically Spanish or German; these blades had three fullers or grooves running down the blade, while American blades were usually plain or single-fullered. One American swordsmith, James Potter of New York City, became so adept at copying British horseman's saber that the form itself became known as a "Potter sword."

These four swords all share the standard characteristics of British broadswords but reflect the wide diversity of workmanship and styling found in the American copies. The uppermost sword has a turned wooden grip with a brass hilt, single-fullered blade, and the oblong, ball-headed pommel that characterizes this arm. The second is a classic example of the cavalry weapon manufactured for enlisted men by James Potter, with a leather- and wire-wrapped grip and plain iron mountings. The third example is also iron mounted with a leather-covered wooden grip, although much cruder in its lines than the Potter. The bottom sword was carried by Capt. Samuel Mills of the 2nd Light Dragoons during the war; its bone grip and circular iron pommel make it a rather unique variant. Maj. Benjamin Tallmadge of this regiment carried a Potter-made broadsword, similar to the second sword but of finer quality.

Imported "Virginia" Grenadier and Artillery Swords, 1778–83

In late spring 1778, Jacques LeMaire returned to his native France after a year in Virginia, newly-commissioned as a captain in the Virginia State forces and carrying with him letters of introduction signed by Gov. Patrick Henry. LeMaire also brought with him lists of much-needed ordnance and war materials for Virginia's Continental and state regular forces as well as the militia, in whose capacity he was to act as military agent. LeMaire was from a prominent French family and Henry recognized that his political social connections would open doors more readily than the more formal diplomatic channels then being pursued by William Lee, the state agent already in France. Lee was the younger brother of Arthur Lee, one of the three commissioners to Europe appointed by the Continental Congress to secure treaties of alliance and acquire military goods on behalf of the United States.

William Lee had departed Paris for Vienna in search of ordnance when LeMaire arrived and Arthur Lee instructed the young Frenchman to travel to Strasbourg "to engage the sabres, etc. for the light horse." By June 1778 he was already in negotiation with the sword and tool manufacturers for edged weapons, shovels, axes, and other military tools. Forwarding William Lee quotations for such materials, Lee wrote back on June 27 advising him that "time will not allow for our waiting till the Sabres are made" and that "we must find them ready made to be transported immediately." Before Lee's letter reached LeMaire, "he had made contract on the 4th [of July] . . . at a higher price than the manufacturer's first price." These swords were custom-manufactured for Virginia at Klingenthal, located southwest of Strasbourg in France's Alsace region, where the French government had established its sword manufacturing center in the early 18th century.

Two of the three pattern swords were intended for Virginia foot troops and had brass hilts that conformed closely to the French model 1767 hanger or briquet. The hilts were two-piece castings, consisting of a ribbed grip with large capstan-pommel and a stirrup-shaped guard. The first pattern had "Grenadeer of Virginia" inscribed below a panoply of arms on its blade just above the hilt, with "Victory or Death" similarly marked on the reverse. The second type of sword had "Artillery of Virginia" marked on it, with flat, slightly curved blades—26 1/2 inches long for the former and 23 3/4 inches for the latter. The artillery hanger's blade was slightly wider, while the grenadier saber had a rather unique, wider upper blade section with false edge, running approximately eight inches to the tip. A third pattern sword for dragoons was also manufactured, with different form hilt and straight blade.

The estimated 1,500–2,000 swords were completed in early 1779 and eventually shipped to Virginia, arriving in August. Initially stored at Cumberland Court House, they were dispersed by direct issue to regular and militia troops, as well as shipment to other military depots. During April 1781, Gov. Thomas Jefferson ordered militia cavalry troops be formed to augment the limited existing horse, and "Grenadier swords" were authorized for issue in lieu of cavalry sabers, ensuring "that the want of that Article need not keep them from the field." State regular corps, including Dabney's Legion and Clark's Illinois Regiment, were also furnished with grenadier sabers and artillery hangers, which were variously referred to as "Sergeants swords" and "cutlasses." Post-war issue of the weapons continued from Point of Fork Arsenal during the 1790s until its closure, when the remaining 900 swords were shipped to Richmond. During the first decade of the nineteenth century, many of the grenadier sabers were cleaned, refurbished, and engraved with Virginia militia regimental markings at the Virginia Manufactory of Arms before issue to militia artillery companies.

Company Officer, Continental Line Infantry Regiment, Mid-Atlantic States, 1780–83

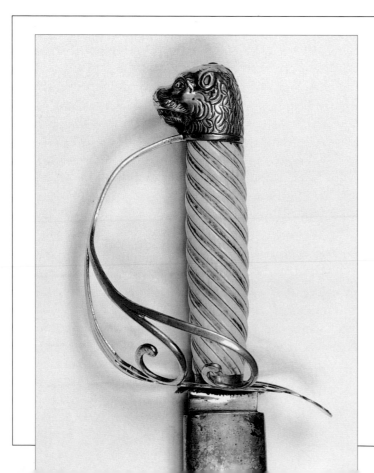

O n October 2, 1779, the Continental Congress established blue as the ground for all Continental Army uniforms. White facings were prescribed for regiments from New England states, buff-colored facings for those of New Jersey and New York, and red for those from the Mid-Atlantic states. Blue coats faced with blue were to be worn by the southern states, with buttonholes bound with white tape. Linings and buttons for all infantry regiments were to be white. Blue coats faced and lined with scarlet and trimmed with narrow yellow tape and buttons were reserved for the artillery corps. White facings, buttons, and linings were to be used by the light dragoons. All woolen smallclothes were to be uniformly white. To varying degrees and with some exceptions, compliance with this regulation was generally achieved during the remainder of the war through the extraordinary efforts of various commanders and the Continental and state clothiers.

Perhaps the most successful at achieving relative uniformity were the regiments of the Mid-Atlantic states, which had already been uniformed in blue and red since the arrival of imported French-made clothing during fall 1778. Pennsylvania, Maryland, Virginia, and Delaware all strove to purchase or import (within their abilities and means) fine broadcloth and trimmings to clothe their officers in similar, but better-quality uniforms than those procured for their enlisted men. For example, Lt. William Lamar of the 1st Maryland Regiment drew the following to make a regimental coat in 1781: $1\frac{3}{4}$ yards of blue cloth, $\frac{1}{4}$ yard scarlet cloth, and $1\frac{3}{4}$ yards with shalloon, plus linen for sleeve and pocket linings, buttons, twist, and other trimmings.

This company officer is dressed in such a blue and scarlet uniform, with white shalloon lining and silvered buttons. His breeches and waistcoats are white, woolen for winter and linen or "janes" for summer. Although the cloth was state supplied, the uniform coat and smallclothes were made up at the officer's expense, frequently done by paying a regimental tailor from the ranks. A single silver epaulette on the left shoulder denotes his rank as a lieutenant, and his spontoon and short saber similarly symbolize his officer's sta-

NATIONAL PARK SERVICE

A Work of Art in Silver

A merican silver-mounted horsemen's sabers of the Revolution are extremely rare. Most cavalry officers preferred a sturdier arm, with hand protection of iron or brass, rather than of soft silver. This lion-headed specimen with spiraled white ivory grips, exhibits the finest workmanship and design. Originally found in Providence, Rhode Island, it bears a similarity to the work of New York silversmith, William Gilbert (active 1767–1818). The imported Spanish blade has triple fullers and was a type in wide use throughout the colonies during much of the eighteenth century.

Swords with pommel caps of animal heads were highly popular and although lions were the most favored, dogs and eagles were also in use. American-made swords of this era are often somewhat more rustic in design and craftsmanship than that of their British cousins. This magnificent lion's head, however, is certainly worthy of any good London maker.

tus. He is fortunate in possessing both weapons, as many junior-grade Continental officers were armed solely with the polearm, creating the "unmilitary appearance" commented upon in some inspection returns of the army. His cocked hat is of beaver, rather than the coarse wool felt as worn by his men. It is trimmed with the black and white cockade first

authorized on July 19, 1780, to be "Emblimatack of the expected Union" of the Continental and French armies. Instead of shoes, he wears the laced half boots favored by European sportsmen and woodsmen, a form commonly known in the eighteenth century as "hi-lows" or "start-ups."

American Swordbelt 1775–83

R are indeed are eighteenth-century military sword-belts of American origin; scarcer still are artifacts of this nature with Revolutionary War provenance. This buff leather shoulderbelt was probably made prior to or during the war, and was apparently altered or modified in that conflict. There are empty rows at awled stitch-holes at the rear branch of the frog, indicating repair from heavy use or perhaps conversion from an earlier waistbelt form to the shoulder arrangement. At the same time, the original horizontal slot cut in the front channel of the frog was sewn closed. Originally intended to retain the clasp or button of the scabbard, it shows no evidence of having ever been so used; instead, there is a similar slot cut on the belt just above the frog's mouth that clearly shows hard usage. The belt is $2^3/8$ inches wide, but has been tapered near the top to accommodate the brass ornament that was clearly added during the swordbelt's eighteenth-century refurbishment. Metallic ornamental tips of various patterns are frequently encountered in paintings of both Continental Army offi-cers and cavalrymen.

This tip ornament is particularly interesting because an identical one has been excavated at a Continental Army cantonment site in the Hudson Valley. The exca-vated example, however, still retains its original brass clasps or tongues on the back, which were used to cling the device on to a leather belt. The brass tip of this par-ticular swordbelt is attached by small iron pins driven through the face and peeled over the buff belting on the reverse, a period repair to replace the fragile original attachments. Perhaps most exciting is the actual design of the ornament, the center of which forms a triangular shape made of an arrow supporting thirteen rings. It is

derived from one of the most famous patriotic motifs of the Revolution—a circle of thirteen interlocking rings symbolizing the unification of the thirteen colonies.

NORTH CAROLINA MILITIAMAN, 1780–81

The North Carolina Line ceased to exist with the fall of Charleston in May 1780, its three understrength Continental regiments having been part of that besieged city's defending force. The state, now open to enemy invasion, mobilized its militia and created a state legion composed of cavalry and foot, principally made up of drafts from the militia. The North Carolina militia, like that of Virginia, had a mixed record of service. Posted in the center of the American battle line at Camden, most of the North Carolinians ran without firing a shot after witnessing the Virginia militia to their left flee in a similar manner. However, they fought well as irregulars in numerous small actions and during the Battles of Cowpens and Guilford Courthouse.

North Carolina was perhaps the poorest of the thirteen original states, but it did its best to provide for the needs of its own militia and the Continental forces of Gate's "Grand Army" and, later, Greene's Southern Army, during the Carolina Campaigns of 1780–81. The militia called into service for the 1780 campaign were to be riflemen, clothed in "cloth coloured" hunting shirts with blue capes and overalls of the same materials. Though this attempt at uniformity was not fully achieved, the almost universal use of linen hunting shirts by Carolina militia is well documented. As early as 1777 the Marquis de Lafayette noted that "hunting shirts, loose jackets of gray [natural] linen, [were] very common in Carolina."

This Carolinian has replaced his rifle (thrown away at the Battle of Camden) with a Long Land musket, although he still employs his rifle pouch and powder horn to carry the ammunition for his smoothbore "firelock." He wears a fringed hunting shirt of natural linen and trousers of cotton "oznabrigs," a coarse material commonly produced by North Carolina weavers during this period. His battered and rustic "flopped" hat protects his head from the sun's brutal rays, while he slakes his thirst with water swigged from an oak "keg" canteen.

American-Made Revolutionary Period Sabers

American-made swords of the Revolutionary period were often modeled on contemporary British swords in general form but were unique and distinctly American in character. Since it was easier and cheaper to use an imported blade, many Americans hilts are mounted on them.

The sword on the left is a horseman's sword, established by its lengthy, three-fullered European blade. A single ferrule protects the bottom of its wooden grip. Its hilt is mounted with a smooth lion's head pommel, which anchors the end of the pierced D-shaped brass countergurad. While this sword was intended for use by an enlisted man, some officers did carry similar weapons of munition quality.

The most striking feature of the center example, clearly a foot officer's weapon, is its oversize brass lion's head pommel, which is finely detailed and quite fierce looking. It has a pierced D-shaped knucklebow that flows into a long, downcurving wrist guard and lobed quillion. It has a plain wooden grip that is deeply incised with a single spiraling groove, fitted with a strip of cooper tape and a ferrule at the bottom. Its curved, hanger-style blade has a single fuller and is protected by its original tooled leather and brass mounted scabbard. This sword was meant to be suspended from a waistbelt by either a fine chain or leather straps, evidenced by the small ring attached to the scabbard's mouthpiece. A number of swords almost identical to this one have been found in Massachusetts, and an example of a similar one carried by Gen. Israel Putnam is known.

The right-hand weapon is very similar to the example on the left. Its lion's head pommel is much larger but still relatively simple in detail. The plain wooden grip is bound with a ferrule at either end, and its pierced counterguard is secured in the lion's mouth. Being a horseman's sword, its curved, trifullered blade measures $32\frac{1}{2}$ inches in length.

LIEUTENANT JAMES GILES, 2ND REGIMENT OF CONTINENTAL ARTILLERY, FALL–WINTER 1780

PAUL SCHIERL

The 2nd Continental Artillery, also known as "Lamb's Artillery" after its commander, Col. John Lamb, was created on January 1, 1777. Raised primarily in New York but incorporating companies or men from Connecticut, Rhode Island, and New Hampshire, it served through the entire war. Like the three other Continental artillery regiments, it rarely served in its entirety; instead, companies or sections were often detached to serve with the various infantry brigades, manning the light battalion guns—usually 4- and 6-pounders—that accompanied such formations. Other companies of the regiment manned the artillery at fixed fortifications, such as the works at West Point and Constitution Island, as well as Fort Stanwix on the New York frontier. Most of the regiment marched to Virginia with the combined Continental and French armies in 1781, serving much of the heavy siege cannon in the American batteries.

From its formation until 1780, the regiment was clothed in the red-faced, black uniforms selected for the Continental Artillery by its commander, Brig. Gen. Henry Knox. However, in accordance with the 1779 Continental Army uniform regulations, the 2nd Artillery received new coats of blue with scarlet facings and linings in March 1780. Seven months later, Colonel Lamb prescribed the dress to be worn by officers of the regiment, consisting of deep blue coats faced with scarlet cuffs, lapels, and cape, all 2 1/2 inches wide. The cuffs were slit on the underside and closed with hooks and eyes. There were ten large, plain gilt buttons on each lapel—the "Button holes bound with Vellum—the Buttons on the Lappels, Cuffs & Pocket flaps to be Pair'd." A strap, or contra-epaulette, also bound with gold vellum lace, was placed on the shoulder opposite the fringed epaulette. Waistcoat and breeches were white, with small yellow buttons. The cocked hat was "Large with a Gold Button and loop, and Cock'd up with Gold Loopings."

During the late summer of 1780 Capt. George Flemming and his company of the 2nd Artillery were attached to the 2nd Brigade of the Light Infantry Division, commanded by the Marquis de Lafayette. In a September 23 letter to Colonel Lamb, Fleming wrote that the "Marquis has gave fresh instance of his munificence by presenting each Officer in his Division with a neat gold gilt small Sword" and "has got a French Merchant to supply us with superfine blue Cloth & Trimmings for a regimental Coat, Waistcoat &

Breeches, for four Guineas each." Four days later, Lt. James Giles of Fleming's company signed for 1 1/2 yards of blue cloth, 1 3/8 yards of white cloth, and lining and trimmings for a uniform suit.

This reconstruction of Giles is based on two postwar portraits of the officer. He wears the 2nd Artillery uniform made from the purchased French cloth, and his cocked hat sports the "black & red Feather" of the light infantry, also presented by the marquis to all officers of his division. His sword, scabbard, and sword knot are taken from the originals received in 1780 from Lafayette, which descended through the Giles family and still survive today.

American-Made Revolutionary War Period Officers' Swords

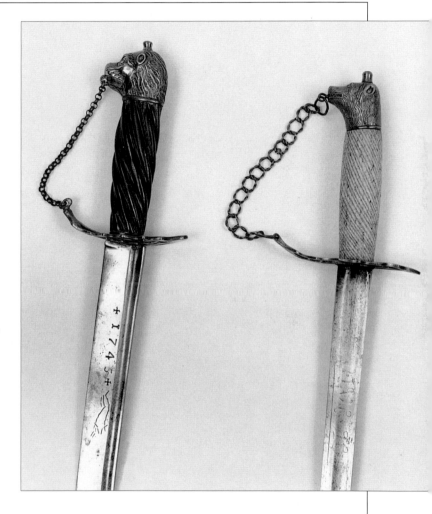

L ike their counterparts in the British Army, American officers, either militia or regular, had to equip and arm themselves. As a result, swords of all sorts, from crude to magnificent and from imported to homemade, were evident in the American officer corps during the War of Independence. The following two examples, with completely American-made hilts and imported blades are good examples of early American folk art. This type of sword is classified as a "cuttoe," which is a military version of the civilian hunting sword.

The example on the left is an imitation of many contemporary British swords, with a finely molded and chased brass, lion's head pommel. Its grip is a piece of green-stained writhen ivory, a popular choice on sword hilts during this era. The pommel is connected to the pierced brass counterguard by a tiny linked brass chain in place of a more practical knucklebow. The blade is slightly curved, with a narrow fuller and a false edge is punch dated "1745," and is engraved with a "running wolf." While this latter mark is often associated with the blade manufactory in Solingen, Germany, it was widely imitated throughout Europe as a mark of quality.

The cuttoe on the right is of similar form but has a simpler brass animal head pommel, with features that are both leonine and canine. It has a white ivory grip that is carved with spiraling, tightly spaced, incised lines and has no ferrules. A large linked chain of twisted brass wire connects the mouth of the pommel to the pierced brass counterguard. The blade is single-edged and exhibits the remains of a French or Spanish inscription. Gen. Ethan Allen is known to have carried a similar weapon, still in existence today.

Sergeant of Light Infantry, New York or New Jersey Line, Spring–Fall 1782

WILLIAM RODEN

In December 1780 a British supply fleet bound for the West Indies, carrying clothing for five regiments then serving in the islands, was captured by a combined Spanish-French fleet under Admiral Cordova. According to American minister John Jay, the military clothing was "presented by the Courts of France and Spain to Congress" and shipped to Boston from Cadiz in April 1781. By summer it was in the hands of Continental Army clothiers, although there was still some confusion as to its ultimate disposition— a matter not fully decided until December. Earlier in the war, captured British uniforms with only minor modifications had been issued out to clothe ragged troops, which led to mistaken identification, sometimes with disastrous results. Finally, in October, Washington was informed that the military tailors were "taking out the Lining" in preparation for dyeing the coat bodies brown, a color more suitable for Continental Army use. After the brown color had set, the facings and linings were sewn back onto the coats.

During the winter of 1781–82, the brown coats were finally issued to the New Jersey, New York, and New Hampshire brigades (which included the 10th Massachusetts Regiment) as "the only way of preserving a compleat uniformity in the three Brigades." Although other troops had "refused taking the British Coats on accout of their Colour & others . . . raised a Report that they Were rotted in dyeing," the uniforms proved to be "of very good quality & . . . received not the least injury in colouring." Some attempt was made to issue the brown-dyed coats according to the facing colors affixed; from British regimental buttons excavated from New Jersey and New York brigade cantonment sites, it is known that green-faced coats were drawn by most of those troops, including the uniforms originally destined for the British 55th Regiment of Foot.

Despite being clothed in the unpopular coats, the Jersey and York regiments exceeded all others in their "Elegant Appearance," according to Col. Walter Stewart, inspector of the Northern Army. The men in these regiments were "furnished with half Gaiters black Stocks with false Collars and ornamental Feathers, partly at the Expence of the Officers and partly by Stoppages of the Whiskey which their Men were entitled to receive." These martial trappings were very much in evidence when Rochambeau reviewed the Continental Army on September 22, 1782. The light infantry (probably of the York and Jersey Line) was "dressed in brown coats with green reverse and cuffs and white linen pantaloons tucked into black gaiters reaching to the calf."

This American sergeant is dressed in such a manner, wearing a light infantry sergeant's jacket of the 55th Foot. The green facings of the 55th have been reattached, with the buttons still placed as originally arranged in pairs. The white buttonholes and wing trim are of white worsted, as worn on sergeants' coats in British infantry regiments. His light infantry cap is of the form established by long usage in the Continental "Corps of Light Infantry," created by cutting down a felt cap and trimming it with a hair crest and front plate. It is further embellished with lace binding and tassels of silver, along with the characteristic red-over-black plume of the light infantry—all gifts of the Marquis de Lafayette to the noncommissioned officers of his Light Infantry Division in August 1780. His rank as a sergeant is further distinguished by two white worsted epaulettes worn over his wings. Another mark of the marquis's pride in his light infantry is the short saber, with scabbard and belt, presented to each sergeant in the corps. It is French-made of the newest military fashion and features an intertwined "USA" engraved on the branch of its guard. A similar "USA" cipher is cast into the brass belt plate of the waistbelt.

Continental Army Waistbelt Plate, 1780–83

When the French expeditionary force under Rochambeau sailed for North America, it brought the swords, accoutrements, and military trimmings that the Marquis de Lafayette had purchased in France as gifts for the officers and noncommissioned officers of his new command. This command, as he had hoped, turned out to be the Light Infantry Division of the Continental Army. In September the promised gifts arrived. Each noncommissioned officer received, in addition to trimmings for his cap, a short saber complete with scabbard and belt. The French-made saber had a branch on which an interlocked "USA" was engraved, signifying the United States of America. It was carried on a buff leather waistbelt that had a cast brass buckle or belt plate, bearing a similar motif.

The plates are of an open oval form, in which is set a cartouch or rondel bearing the "USA" surrounded by a raised rim. Cast in one piece, with two bars set on the back for fastening to belting, it is a form typical of French accoutrement plates of the 1780s and 1790s. Three complete examples have been excavated from post-1780 Continental Army sites in the Hudson Valley, some of which were occupied by Lafayette's light troops. In 1782, another shipment of arms, cloth, and other war stores arrived from France. Procured by Col. John Laurens, one of Washington's former aides, it was consigned to the Board of War. Included in this shipment were additional swords for noncommissioned officers, as well as accoutrement belts and "brass belt buckles." If these swords and buckles were indeed the same "USA" forms originally procured by Lafayette, it is possible that other Continental noncoms outside of the light infantry may have been furnished with such items in the closing days of the war.

GRENADIER CORPORAL, ROYAL DEUX-PONT REGIMENT, C. 1780–83

ILLUSTRATION BY NICOLAS HOFFMANN, TROIANI COLLECTION

The regiment of Royal Deux-Pont was raised on the establishment of German troops in French pay from April 1757 by Christian, duke of Deux-Pont, in his German estates. By August Royal Deux-Pont was with Marshal Soubise's army, which was crushed by Frederick the Great and his Prussians at Rossbach, the regiment's first battle. It retreated in good order, however, and took its revenge the following year in a brilliant charge at Saundershausen, which the French won. Its fine record as a brave and steady unit was reinforced in subsequent campaigns of the Seven Years' War. Thus, in 1763, while many regiments were being disbanded with the end of the war, the regiment of Royal Deux-Pont was kept on the establishment and garrisoned various towns in France until 1780. By that time, France had been at war against Great Britain since 1778, siding with the revolutionary Americans who wished to achieve their independence.

Up to then, France's military efforts had been largely directed toward the West Indies, much to the frustration of the Americans, who pressed for more substantial help. But help was on the way, as a French expeditionary corps was assembling in Brittany to board a fleet in Brest. It consisted of four line infantry regiments, a strong detachment from the corps of artillery, hussars, and infantry companies from the duke of Lauzun's legion of colonial troops. The force was commanded by General Rochambeau, and Royal Deux-Pont was one of four regiments selected to embark at Brest in April 1780 and sail for the United States. They arrived at Newport, Rhode Island, in July 1780. This force considerably impressed the Americans as it marched south in 1781, slowly isolating Lord Cornwallis in Yorktown by September. They were joined by 3,000 more troops that had come up from the West Indies in Admiral de Grasse's fleet, making the besieging Franco-American army some 16,000 strong.

Royal Deux-Pont gained considerable distinction during the assault made on the British fortifications on October 14, when, led by its colonel-commandant, the Count de Forbach, the regiment successfully stormed the British position. The 7,000 British and mercenary Hessian troops finally surrendered on October 19. A slightly wounded de Forbach was chosen to bring the news of the fall of Yorktown to the French Court, carrying with him several of the colors surrendered by the British.

Thereafter, French military operations in the United States almost stopped. On December 23, 1782, most of the French expeditionary corps, including Royal Deux-Pont, left from Boston bound for the West Indies and thence to France.

While most regiments in the French army at that time had white coats, the foreign mercenary regiments had different colors. The Swiss and Irish units, for instance, had red coats. The regimental uniform of Royal Deux-Pont consisted of a dark sky blue coat, the color worn by the German regiments in French pay. Since February 1779 Royal Deux-Pont was distinguished by yellow cuffs and lapels, a dark sky blue collar, white metal buttons that were silvered for officers, and piping of the yellow facing color. The coat had long tails and white turnbacks ornamented with lilies, grenades, or bugle horns in the facing color, depending on whether the wearer was a fusilier, grenadier, or chasseur. The three pointed pocket flaps of regiments with white metal buttons were vertical,

and all were piped in the facing color. Each lapel had seven small buttons, and there were three large ones below the right lapel. The cuffs had two small buttons on the cuff and two above. The grenadiers' shoulder straps were dark sky blue with red piping. In some regiments, however, the grenadiers continued to wear red-fringed epaulettes.

All regiments were supposed to wear hats, but bearskin caps, officially abolished in favor of hats since May 1776, were still worn in some regiments, including Royal Deux-Pont, as shown here. A brass plate stamped with a flaming grenade badge can be seen in front, and a white plume rises from the

Cartridge Box Plate, Foix Regiment, French Army at Savannah, Georgia, 1779

The Foix Regiment of French line infantry, part of which had been sent to the West Indies in 1776, was one of the units that participated in the unsuccessful attempt, by French Admiral d'Estaing, to capture Savannah in the fall of 1779. There had been a number of successful French attacks against British islands in the West Indies, but nothing very elaborate had been done to help the Americans. To capture Savannah seemed like a worthwhile enterprise, however, as it would deprive the British of an important southern port while opening up a new front.

Accordingly, French troops from various West Indian islands were gathered for the expedition during the summer of 1779 and were landed outside Savannah in early September. From September 13 to October 18, American troops joined 2,800 French troops as they tried to capture the town. The British and Loyalist troops gave fierce resistance. D'Estaing, whose force was not strong enough or properly equipped for a full-scale siege, finally gave up, and the French went back to the West Indies. Thereafter, the detachment from the Foix Regiment went to garrison Grenada, an island it had helped conquer from

the British in July 1779.

From 1776 to 1779 the uniform of the Foix Regiment, a unit raised in 1684, was white with green cuffs and lapels, yellow collar, and brass buttons. It also would have been worn later, however, especially by the detachment in America, as the French Army reclothed only a third of the men in each regiment every year. The oval brass cartridge box plate model illustrated was introduced by the royal regulation of April 25, 1767. The design was standard, with the crowned royal arms over assembled flats and below, a scroll bearing the regiment's name. The royal regulation of May 31, 1776, specifically abolished the use of badges on cartridge box flaps, but as with many other items in what proved to be one of the most unpopular regulations in the history of the French Army, unit commanders just went on using the badges until new equipment, which now came without badges, was issued.

rear left of the cap. It is interesting to note that after a twelve-year fight with a swarm of dissident unit commanders, the War Department bureaucrats finally gave up, and the grenadier's beloved and traditional bearskin cap was officially reinstated in 1788. Another feature was the mustache, the traditional distinction of grenadiers in the French Army, an army that was otherwise generally clean shaven at that time.

The waistcoat was white and of a conventional cut, with sleeves, a small standing collar, pocket flaps, and small regimental buttons. The collar and cuffs of the waistcoat were of the yellow facing color. The breeches were white, and each man had several pairs of gaiters: one of white linen, one of blackened linen, and one of black woolen cloth.

The two bars of white lace sewn just above the cuffs indicate the rank of corporal. Sergeants had a silver lace above the cuffs, piped in the facing color. Sergeants major had two silver laces piped in the facing color, one set at the top of the cuffs and the other just above it.

The elite companies in French Army battalions, the grenadiers and the chasseurs, carried the model 1767 brass-hilted hangers. It was carried by its own white shoulderbelt, on which there was also a frog for the bayonet. These crossbelts were also worn by the corporals and sergeants of the fusilier companies, as they also had hangers. The privates of the fusilier companies did not carry hangers and so did not have this shoulderbelt: instead, a bayonet frog was stitched in the lower part of the cartridge box belt.

It is often believed that the model 1777 French Army musket was carried by French troops during the American Revolution. In actuality, however, very few of these muskets had been made and issued, so the army that came to America was armed with previous models, especially the light version of the model 1763, which had been produced in vast quantities. Indeed, the French model 1777 appears to have been unknown in the United States until the late 1790s.

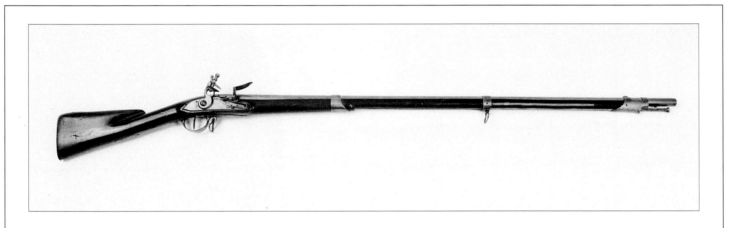

French "Charleville" Musket, Model 1766

With the exception of the British Land Pattern muskets, French muskets were the most commonly carried arm of the Revolutionary War. Indeed, by the close of the war, most soldiers in the Continental Army were armed with one of a number of French models imported to America, the most common being the model 1766. By 1775 it was already considered an outdated pattern by the French Army, which had largely reequipped itself with muskets of newer pattern (particularly the model 1774 and, to a lesser degree as the war progressed, the model 1777). Nevertheless, thousands of surplus model 1766 muskets were purchased and shipped for the use of the Continental and state forces, most notably in 1777, when more than 3,000 reached New England in time to be carried into action at the Battles of Hubbardton and Freeman's Farm by New Hampshire and Massachusetts troops.

The model 1766 differs only slightly from its predecessor, the model 1763, primarily in its elongated lock plate, redesigned barrel bands, and lightened stock and barrel, reducing overall weight by nearly 2 pounds in the later model. These improvements led to its frequently being listed as the "light model 1763 Charleville" on Revolutionary War invoices. The majority of French arms shipped to the United States were from the Charleville manufactory, resulting in the generic application of the term "Charleville" by Americans to all French military muskets. The model 1766 has a 44 5/8-inch-long barrel of .69-caliber bore that is band- versus pin-fastened, making it easier to remove and clean than its British counterpart. This factor, plus its light weight (approximately 8 1/2 pounds), made it a popular arm with American soldiers, and it became the pattern for the first postwar American muskets, the model 1795 Springfield and the 1794 U.S. contract muskets.

The New Republic and Westward Expansion 1790–1850

FOLLOWING THE REVOLUTIONARY WAR, THE NEW United States maintained a fledgling standing army that was dispersed at various frontier posts and a handful of critical seacoast fortifications to guard the principal American port-cities. On the frontier, the army served primarily in a constabulary role, regulating the Indian trade and enforcing American expansionist policies in its newfound western lands. At various times, the U.S. Army would be temporarily expanded in size and receive similar minor improvements in its clothing, arms, and equipage, principally when conflict threatened (as during the Indian campaigns in the Northwest Territory during 1790–95 and again in 1798–99, during the conflict with France). Although the Napoleonic Wars had transformed both the face of Europe and the appearance of its respective armies and equipage, they had but little impact on the tactical doctrine, weapons, or uniforms of the U.S. Army until threat of war with Great Britain loomed imminent, in the wake of the Chesapeake-Leopard Incident in 1807. Once more, the armed forces of the republic were increased and some attention was paid to its modernization, but as the war scare passed, so did the opportunity for full implementation of such proposed changes.

Until almost the outbreak of the War of 1812, the U.S. Army looked little different from its ancestor, the Continental Army. It wore blue uniforms with red facings and white smallclothes, as first standardized in late 1782. Muskets were of French make or American copies of the French Model 1766; accoutrements and equipage included much surplus material from the Revolutionary War. It would not be until 1810 that the army would finally discard the cutaway-style coat, worn since the Revolution with only minor changes in cut and trimmings, and adopt the single-breasted, closed-front uniform already worn by most European troops for more than a decade. By the close of the War of 1812, an all-blue uniform dress was established for the entire U.S. Army, with only minor distinctions in trimmings among the various branches. Again, with only minimal changes in trimmings and some modernization in cut (along with some corresponding changes in headgear, arms, and accoutrements), it would remain in place until 1832, when a uniform closely patterned on the style then worn in the British Army would be formally adopted. Blue would be retained as the traditional ground color, although facing colors would be restored for the first time since 1813. Under the watchful eyes of such Anglophiles as Alexander Macomb (commanding general) and John Wood (inspector general), the United States would continue to be influenced most strongly by British military fashion and practices through the Mexican War, one exception being the infantry exercise, which since 1812 had been based on the French reglement of 1791. As we shall see in the subsequent section, the decidedly French taste of Winfield Scott, Mexican War hero and new commanding general, as well as combat experience in that late conflict (and the Crimean War), would do much to bring about major changes in the army's equipage and doctrine prior to the Civil War.

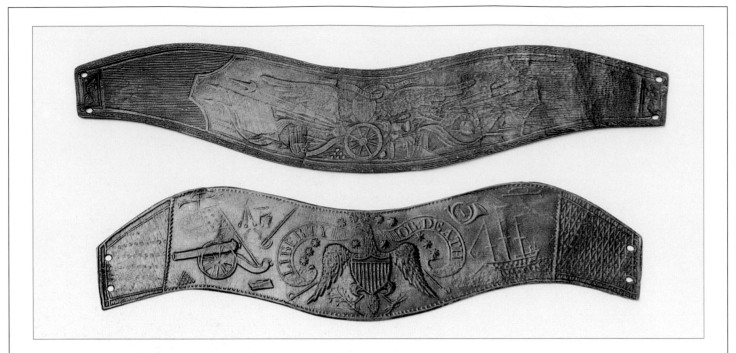

Two Early Neck Stocks

Perhaps no other piece of military apparel was as uncomfortable, chafing, and functionally useless as the neck stock. But in the fashion of another time, appearance often ruled over common sense, and things that seemed foolish also could have a legitimate purpose. A good, stiff leather stock about a soldier's neck forced him to keep his chin up and look straight ahead. In the days of linear warfare, such things were a necessity.

As rifled arms came to dominate the battlefield and military formations became looser, uniforms became more practical and comfortable. During the War of 1812, neck stocks were nearly always prescribed as part of the uniform by both regular troops and the militia on campaign and off. The neck stock did not die an easy death in the U.S. military. Many thousands were issued at the beginning of the Civil War and were promptly discarded by the soldiers as useless.

Top: Artilleryman's neck stock of glazed black leather, with the device of an eagle surmounting a cannon and surrounded by trophies of arms. This specimen probably dates c. 1810–15.

Bottom: The central device of an early Federal-style eagle on this stock is similar to the buttons worn by the U.S. regular army from about 1787 to 1800. A ribband in the eagle's mouth bears the proud proclamation "Liberty or Death"; other devices of a sailing ship, American flag, and sundry military trophies complete the ornamentation. A bugle horn in the corner with a number 1 inside may represent the designation of the regiment that wore this attractive neckwear. Soldiers of Arthur St. Clair's 1st American Regiment of Anthony Wayne's 1st Sub-Legion may have defiantly faced their Native American adversaries with these powerful sentiments encircling their throats.

Marine Corps Uniform Cap Plate, Pattern of 1804

Since 1868, the eagle-globe-and-anchor device has been the enduring emblem of the Marine Corps. It was preceded by several different types. The earliest plate was adopted in 1804, when the Marine Corps switched from brimmed hats to the "stovepipe" shako, a felt cap copied from the British. Evidence for the 1804 plate is sketchy and the precise dates of its use are uncertain. The design was first referred to in correspondence in the 1804 Marine Corps Quartermaster Department as simply a brass eagle on a square plate. By the War of 1812, the description had expanded and was noted as being made of brass, as octagonal in shape, and to be embossed with an eagle, foul anchor, drums, flags, and cannon. This particular plate was found in Florida at a location used by Marines during the 1812–15 period and is consistent with its contemporary description.

THE HEROES OF TIPPECANOE, 1811

I think I never saw a finer Regiment of men than the 4th," remembered one eyewitness, who observed that "they seemed to move like a perfect machine their drill being so perfect." The 4th U.S. Infantry Regiment was part of the massive "additional" regular force authorized on April 12, 1808, in response to mounting threat of war with Great Britain. The legislation called for the creation of five new regiments of infantry and one each of riflemen, light artillery, and light dragoons to augment the one artillery and two infantry regiments that then composed the fledgling U.S. Army. The new regiments had few officers with prior military experience. One exception was John Parke Boyd, the enigmatic Massachusetts-born commandant of the 4th, who had earlier fought in India as a mercenary.

Boyd and his officers, all New Englanders, were able to take advantage of the economic depression strangling that region due to the Embargo Act of 1807 and soon recruited "a choice set of hardy Sailors" from the unemployed mariners then crowding the seacoast towns. The 4th was dispersed in company-size detachments at forts and batteries guarding the New England coast. Ironically, a primary duty of these ex-sailors was in enforcing the very embargo that had pushed them into military service.

Boyd strove to instill a military bearing and esprit de corps among his men. A regimental band was formed by a subscription of the officers, and Boyd instituted alterations to the regulation uniform that would clearly distinguish the 4th from other troops in service. One example was his order to convert the old-style issue hats into caps of the newest military fashion, the additional costs to be drawn from the soldiers' meager pay. Boyd justified this expense under the presumption "that there can be no soldier in the 4th. Regt. Who Does not feel a Pride in his corps" by this stylish change. What the men thought of this measure has not been recorded. Another modification was in wearing the cartridge box on a waistbelt in lieu of the crossbelt arrangement then used by the rest of the army.

In early 1811 Boyd received orders to gather the regiment from its various harbor posts and proceed westward—the first time the entire 4th would serve together since it was raised. On July 17 Secretary of War William Eustis informed Gov. William Henry Harrison of the Indiana Territory that he had ordered the 4th, augmented by a company from the Rifle Regiment, to descend the Ohio River and place itself under the governor's orders at Vincennes. Before their departure, the riflemen were rearmed with the same smoothbore model 1795 muskets carried by the 4th, due to flaws in the rifles made for them at the Harpers Ferry Arsenal. Although inaccurate beyond 50 yards, the muskets, unlike rifles, were

PARKS OF CANADA

easily loaded, fired a lethal mixed charge of one musket ball and three buckshot, and were equipped with bayonets for close fighting.

It was these features, plus the discipline and training of the regulars, that tipped the scale of victory in favor of Harrison's force in the close-fought Battle of Tippecanoe on November 7, 1811. Following their successful defense and counterattack during that costly action, a seasoned militia officer and Indian fighter claimed that "of all the men he ever saw fight those Yankees were the best . . . [and] had it not been for them they would all been destroyed." Boyd himself described the early-morning attack on the camp, were the "Regulars sleeping on their Arms, formed in half a minute, as on a dress parade . . . supported every front . . . and were ever victorious. They gained the battle, & not for them . . . a defeat would have been inevitable." The 4th would continue to serve with distinction in the early days of the War of 1812, notably at the battle of Maguago, until becoming prisoners of war following the capitulation of Detroit on August 16, 1812.

This private wears the new single-breasted 1810 infantry coat that replaced the "cutaway" style that the army had worn since the Revolutionary War. Closed by hooks and eyes, it was trimmed with imitation buttonholes made of white cord. His woolen winter overalls have been modified by cutting off the gaitered bottoms at the ankle and are worn instead inserted into linen summer gaiters waterproofed with blackball, a polish made of beeswax, tallow, and lampblack. This practice, although not sanctioned, was common among soldiers of the 4th during the Tippecanoe Campaign. The 4th never received new uniforms in 1812, and their coats were described as "rag[g]ed" during that summer's service.

Swords for the U.S. Light Dragoons

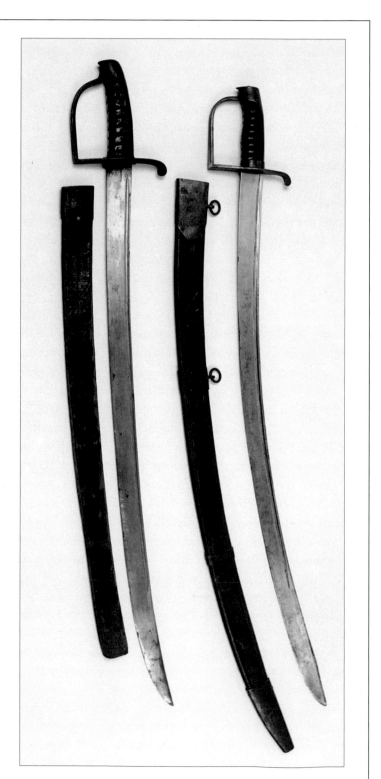

After the Revolution, the need for arms diminished in the eyes of the new Federal government until a potential war with France in 1798 and the raising of a 10,000-man Provisional Army pointed out the danger of relying on foreign sources for weapon production. Not only did stocks of leftover edged weapons prove inadequate, but many were in neglected or damaged state. The firm of Nathan Starr of Middletown, Connecticut, received a contract for 2,000 horseman's swords to be issued to the newly forming cavalry of the Provisional Army. The traditional European stirrup-hilted hussar pattern was adopted, with a plain, iron-mounted leather scabbard (right). The 33-inch curved blades are stamped "N Starr&Co." and "US/1799."

The firm of William Rose & Sons also had a history of supplying swords and blades to the U.S. government as far back as the Revolution; therefore, they were likely candidates to contract for the swords to be issued to the newly raised 1st U.S. Dragoons in 1808. The pattern selected for the 1807 contract was based on a combination of the French hussar sword of 1752 and the British pattern of 1788 Light Cavalry sword (left). Completely mounted in iron, it featured a substantial frame-type scabbard with black leather panels, at a cost of slightly over $5 each. Of the 2,000 swords delivered to the Federal government, 592 were issued to the Light Dragoons. The Rose firm again contracted in 1812 for German pattern hussar swords, along with the Nathan Starr firm, and these improved patterns probably supplanted most of the earlier Rose contract weapons already in use.

As new swords were again needed in 1808, it is likely that many of this contract were issued to militia or volunteer light horse troops in the interim. Although few of these swords have survived to the present, the sturdiness of their manufacture is a testament to the quality of early American industry.

Cap Letters, U.S. Light Dragoons 1808–12

In the wake of the Chesapeake-Leopard Affair, Congress authorized in 1808 an expansion of the standing army of the United States, including the reestablishment of the "Regiment of Light Dragoons." A new uniform was selected for the regiment, including "leather caps or helmets, with blue, tipt with white . . . feathers . . . not to exceed ten inches in length." A prototype cap was developed, which was to be trimmed with a bearskin turban and mounted with a horsehair crest. The pattern cap was accepted by the secretary of war in May 1808, with minor modifications in the form of its perpendicular front plate and crest, while the turban was changed from leopardskin to bearskin. Contracts were let for the production of these caps and Messrs. George Green & Son was awarded a contract to provide 800 sets of brass letters "USLD" for the caps. The cast letters, 1¹/₂ inches high, were to have "good pliable brass tongues to bend and clinch, sufficient to keep them neatly & firmly in place," by which they were to be mounted to the front plates of the caps, the 'US' superimposed over the 'LD' in arrangement.

Frequent complaints were made concerning the method of attachment: the tongues were apparently not strong enough to securely fasten the letters through the leather. Numerous archaeological specimens found on cantonment sites of the U.S. Light Dragoons would seem to support this contention from 1808 to 1812. With the outbreak of the War of 1812, the Light Dragoons were redesignated the 1st Regiment of Light Dragoons and a second regiment was formed. On July 8, 1812, the commander of the 2nd Light Dragoons requested permission to change the metal of his cap trimmings "as white metal letters and Mounting can be had . . . at the same price as brass." The secretary of war approved his request. It is not known if any of these letters were actually produced in white metal, as an October 16 contract described helmets with "plates in front as per pattern," suggesting that another device may have been developed in their stead. The 1st Light Dragoons continued to wear the old-form caps; as an eyewitness at Greenbush Cantonment recalled, on "the front of the caps were 4 raised letters, USLD, which were a puzzle to the boys, but a wag finally translated them into Uncle Sam's Likely Devils."

American Officer's Cocked Hat, c. 1805

By the beginning of the nineteenth century, military cocked hats had evolved from the tricornered shape of the mid-eighteenth century to a bicorne form. The cocked hat would culminate in the *chapeau de bras*—a flat, collapsible form used by officers in the U.S. Army as early as 1808, although not officially described until 1812. This early-nineteenth-century American bicorne is very similar in form and dimensions to the cocked hat prescribed for the Regiment of Artillerists in 1804. In materials and trimmings it is very clearly that of an officer's, probably artillery or staff, as it is trimmed with "yellow" (gilt) eagle looping and button. The cockade is of silk, as is the covering of the hat. Silk hats were a new form just coming into vogue, a form that by the late-nineteenth century would ultimately replace the more expensive beaver felt hats of the genteel. They were made by stretching a napped, silk plush or oiled silk over a body frame made from cheap wool felt or stiffened muslin. "You may also buy some pasteboard and make a cocked hat," wrote a British officer to his brother, which would be covered with "oil-silk" and trimmed with "some broad ribbon for a cockade, and some broad stuff for binding."

PRIVATE, 15TH U.S. INFANTRY REGIMENT, 1812–13

O rganized in 1812 and commanded by Col. Zebu-
lon Montgomery Pike (already famous for his
western explorations in 1806–7), the 15th Infantry
was one of eleven new regiments authorized by Congress in
anticipation of war with Great Britain. With the exception of
Pike and a few of his commissioned and noncommissioned
officers, the regiment was composed of men principally
recruited in the state of New Jersey. Despite the regiment's
inexperience, it soon developed a reputation for precise military bearing under the firm hand of its commander, a strict
disciplinarian and consummate professional.

During the winter of 1812–13, as the regiment trained at
Greenbush Cantonment near Albany, New York, Pike introduced a new system of military drill to replace the conventional two-rank formation then practiced in American and
British armies. Drawing inspiration from a contemporary

English work that recommended reintroduction of a then-
archaic polearm, Pike instituted a three-rank formation, the
first two ranks armed with muskets and the third carrying
twelve foot-long pikes (bayonet-tipped muskets would have
proved too short to be of any effect in such employment by
the third rank). Thus formed and equipped, a battalion could
bring nearly all of its men into direct contact with the enemy
in a bayonet charge, with correspondingly greater shock
power. Pike also equipped his pikemen with muskets for volley firing a greater distance, but with shortened barrels to
reduce weight and for ease in slinging while the pike was
employed. He also acquired 200 swords for these troops for
use in close quarters, as the short muskets were not furnished
with bayonets.

It was in this unique tactical formation that the 15th
Infantry distinguished itself during the amphibious expedi-

tion against York, Upper Canada (present-day Toronto, Ontario), in April 1813. Pike, promoted to brigadier general the previous month, had overall field command, and during the April 27 assault on Fort York, he personally led the principal American column composed of his own 15th and troops from the 16th and 21st U.S. The fall of the fort appeared imminent. As Pike and his men rested briefly during a pause in the action, however, the main powder magazine of the fort exploded. Eyewitnesses recollected the horror of the scene—the tremendous blast tossing broken bodies, shattered muskets and pikes, and rocks into the air. Pike was mortally wounded—crushed by a huge stone—and many of his men were killed or wounded. Despite this tragedy, the fort was taken and York fell—a resounding American victory and a fitting memorial to the gallant Pike.

This pikeman of the 15th Infantry is dressed in the distinctive uniform first received by the regiment in late 1812 and worn during the York campaign. Before the War of 1812, most cloth for the U.S. Army's uniforms was imported from Europe, and the British naval blockade, coupled with wartime speculation, led to shortages and soaring prices. As a result, it was impossible to furnish sufficient quantities of the officially prescribed blue, faced scarlet, infantry uniforms to all of the newly raised regiments. Instead, many regiments drew stopgap uniforms made in a variety of alternative color combinations, such as drab and green or brown and scarlet, although still cut in the accepted pattern. "Mixed" gray uniforms were issued to the 15th, with black cloth tape sent to trim the buttonholes on the breast, collar, and cuffs in lieu of the normal white binding.

The woolen overalls, or "winter pantaloons," are also of gray cloth, and the pikeman wears a cylindrical felt cap trimmed with a regimental plate of tinned iron, leather cockade and pewter eagle, feather plume, and cotton "band & tassels." His sword is one from the Rose 1812 contract for noncommissioned officer's swords, slung on a model 1808 bayonet belt. This belt and the corresponding cartridge box crossbelt are made of blackened harness leather, a wartime substitute for buff leather. His canteen and "Lherbette patent" knapsack are both painted with light blue paint, regularly called for in army contracts.

American Militia Officer's Chapeau de Bras and Wings, c. 1800–20

The *chapeau de bras* was the name Americans gave to a very popular style of hat having something of a half-moon shape, worn by gentlemen from the late eighteenth to early nineteenth century. The name came from the French words for hat, *chapeau*, and arm, *bras*, referring to the practice of carrying the hat under the arm when not being worn on the head. The hat was especially popular with officers of American state militias and volunteers. Even after the War of 1812 and the general adoption of caps, units such as the Salem Artillery in Massachusetts continued to wear the *chapeau de bras*.

The hat shown is an especially fine example that may have been made in France and exported to American military outfitters for sale to the more discriminating militia officers in the Eastern Seaboard cities. Its black felt brim is edged with black silk tape. It has a gold lace cockade loop with a gold eagle button and an elaborate black silk cockade at the center of which may have been a small gilt eagle.

Wings were worn at the shoulders in the same manner as epaulets, generally designating light troops. Wings were also worn by light dragoons in the regular army and by some militia cavalry troops, notably in New York State. They became quite popular in state militia volunteer units of all types for several decades to come. The officer's wings illustrated above are of black velvet with gold embroidery and fringes.

British "Belgic" or "Waterloo" Infantry Officer's Cap, 1812–16

The first cap worn by the British infantry—a cylindrical hat that was nicknamed the "stovepipe" or "bucket cap"—was introduced in 1800. Like all such headgear, it was supposed to provide some protection against a sword blow to the head and also give the wearer an impression of imposing height. British line infantry officers, however, continued to wear bicorne hats until 1812. On December 24, 1811, infantry officers were ordered to wear the cap instead of the bicorne.

On March 18, 1812, a new cap was introduced for all ranks that was intended to last two years before reissue. Said to be of superior quality, it came with a cover of prepared linen to be worn in wet weather. It was later nicknamed the "Belgic cap" or "Waterloo shako," as it became associated with the famous campaign that saw the defeat of Napoleon by the Duke of Wellington at Waterloo, Belgium.

News took time to travel, so the corresponding order was not issued for British troops in Canada until August 3. Some officers of the 104th Regiment, however, had already landed at St. John, New Brunswick, in July wearing the new cap. By September 1812 new "Military Officers Regulation beaver caps trimmed with rich gold chains, Bullion tassels, Gilt plate and Feather" were already for sale in Montreal. By October the officers of the 103rd Foot were reported wearing it, and other regiments followed suit. It can be safely assumed that by 1814 all British line infantry regiments in American had received the new cap.

The design of the British model 1812 cap apparently was influenced by the cap or shako first adopted in the Portuguese line infantry during 1806. The Portuguese shako consisted of a black felt peaked cap with a tall front, bearing a brass plate and ornamented with a feather and cords. The British 1812 cap was generally identical. It had white worsted cords for the men, with a

white-over-red worsted tuff for the battalion companies, all white for the grenadier company, and green for the light infantry company, worn on the left side over the black leather cockade. The brass shako plate had a crown above the "GR" cipher in script. The space below the cipher might be left plain, but often had the regimental number stamped in.

The example shown once belonged to a British officer and is of high quality. For officers, the generic "GR" plate was gilded and might be plain as shown or have silvered numerals, badges, or both. This cap has its original gold and crimson cords and tassels that were regulation wear for all officers' shakos. It would also have had a fine hackle feather on the left side.

ENSIGN AND PRIVATE WITH REGIMENTAL STANDARD, 25TH U.S. INFANTRY, FALL 1813–SPRING 1814

Created by the Congressional Act of June 26, 1812, providing that the "Infantry of the Army shall consist of 25 Regiments," the 25th U.S. Infantry Regiment was recruited and formed during the summer and fall of 1812. It was composed of men primarily from the states of Connecticut, New York, and New Hampshire under the command of Col. Edmund Pendleton Gaines. The regiment trained at Burlington Cantonment during the winter of 1812–13 and formed part of the Sackett's Harbor garrison in Spring 1813. Ordered to the Niagara frontier in May, it received its baptism of fire during the nighttime Battle of Stoney Creek on June 6, 1813. In the surprise of the

American camp, "Repeated charges of the British regulars were repulsed by its fire, and this regiment maintained its ground and was first and last in the action," saving the American force from an abject defeat. Glory did not come lightly. According to Maj. Joseph L. Smith, who commanded the regiment in the action: "42 brave fellows of our regiment fell, either killed, wounded, in their ranks."

The detachment of the 25th left behind at Sackett's Harbor was part of approximately 400 regulars who "sustained the heat of the action" in the unsuccessful British assault on that critical installation. The 25th served with credit in the Battles of Chateauguay and Chrysler's Farm during the American's lackluster fall offensive on the St. Lawrence. The spring of 1814, it was assigned to Brig. Gen. Winfield Scott's 1st Brigade of the Left Division. Honed to razor-sharp fighting condition in camp on the Niagara frontier, it would march to immortal fame under him during the Battles of Chippewa and Lundy's Lane that summer. Upon the reduction of the army with the 1815 peace, the 25th was merged into the 6th Infantry, and its short but glorious wartime history came to a close.

Capt. Henry Leavenworth, then in temporary command of the regimental cantonment outside of Burlington, wrote to Commissary General Callender Irving on February 16, 1813:

The 25th Reg. U.S. Infy. are in great need of Clothing; particularly pantaloons; Hats, Hat plates; Cockades Eagles and Cords. . . .

The Reg. has not yet been furnished with a Standard. . . .

The Regt. has heretofore been furnished with dark brown coats & pantaloons. If those of that colour and of a good quality could be procured they would be preferred.

Leavenworth was referring to the stopgap uniforms of brown faced-red made up for the 25th Infantry and delivered out during fall-winter 1812. These uniforms were cut in the new pattern fixed for the infantry in 1812, but due to shortages of the regulation blue cloth, were made in brown, gray, and drab for many of the newly raised regiments. It is surprising that Leavenworth requested a repeat issue of the unpopular, odd-colored clothing in 1813; during the winter of 1812, other regiments' commanders had refused to accept the brown uniforms shipped to them despite the fact that their men were still wearing the summer jackets and overalls of linen, hoping that their holding out would result in a new issuance of blue uniforms.

By December 1812, however, domestic and imported blue cloth was available in sufficient quantities to clothe the entire army. Writing to the secretary of war, the commissary general proposed a simplified version of the infantry uniform that would nearly halve the amount of time required in

U.S. Light Artillery Officer's Cap Device, 1808–12

With the creation of the U.S. Light Artillery Regiment in 1808 came the demand for proper uniforms and equipage adequate for a fast-moving horse artillery corps. A short-skirted version of the foot artillery uniform was fixed upon, but the felt cocked hat was replaced with a leather cap, "with a circular piece on the front . . . similar to those of the other caps, and a narrow strip of bearskin to appear as a fringe, on the upper Edge of the Front." The stiff leather front plate of the enlisted cap had brass "Roman letters for the Light Artillery"—"US" over "LA"—mounted on it in the same manner as the "USLD" letters for the dragoon caps. What the light artillery officers wore on their caps was completely open to speculation, until the discovery of the artifact pictured here, excavated at Greenbush Cantonment, a major military training post of the U.S. Army during 1812–15. Made of brass and possibly once gilded, it is neatly engraved with the words "LIGHT ARTILLERY."

Its arched shape closely matches that described for the upper edge of the 1808 light artillery cap's front plate. Probably mounted about one inch below the top of the front plate, it replaced the cast letters, which were noted as being "clumsy and not attached sufficiently close to the leather," and therefore susceptible to falling off. As officers were responsible for purchasing their own uniforms and headgear, personal whim sometimes competed with prescribed regimental form. Until another example of this unique device is located, it remains uncertain if this pattern was one prescribed for all officers of the regiment or if it was perhaps an individual affectation.

making the fully trimmed coatee. With the new regulation approved in January 1813 and immediately put into effect, Irvine notified Captain Lawrence on February 23 that his regiment would receive the newly established "Blue Coats with red Cuffs & Collars & White tips [turnbacks] according to the regulations of the War Dept. for the present year." He also noted that the "Standard & Battalion colours of the 25th Regiment Inf shall be forwarded;" the colors, however, were not shipped from Philadelphia until May 15.

The new coats were still cut in the same fashion as the 1812 uniforms, but all tape edging and buttonhole trim was abolished, with the exception of that normally placed on the collars and shoulderstraps. With these coatees were shipped cotton drilling overalls for summer and woolen overalls for winter. The 25th also received, along with other infantry regiments serving on the Niagara frontier, the new leather infantry caps first authorized in January, trimmed with cotton or worsted "pompons" rather than the white feather plumes worn on the earlier felt caps. Pewter cap plates also were furnished, slightly oversized in proportion to the new caps, as they had originally been designed for the cylindrical felt caps.

By May, the use of red or scarlet facings was abolished in the army and new regulations were published establishing an all-blue uniform in the combat branches. All regimental officers, both company and field grade, were to wear a plain blue coat "devoid of lace," turned up with blue on its long skirts. "Blind" buttonholes of silk twist or cord were placed on collar, cuffs, pocket flaps, and across the breast to correspond with the silver uniform buttons. Infantry subaltern field grade officers wore a single silver-bullion epaulet on the left shoulder, captains one on the right, and field-grade officers two epaulets. Dark blue or white cloth pantaloons were worn by officers in winter, while ones of linen or nankeen were popular in summer. Waistbelts of 2-inch-wide whitened buff leather held silver- or steel-mounted swords or sabers—the only weapons officially prescribed for dismounted commissioned officers.

This lieutenant of the 25th Infantry appears in his new 1813 uniform—made in the East by his personal tailor from measurements on file and shipped out to the regiment. His tightly fitted winter pantaloons are tucked into Hessian or hussar boots, and he sports a privately purchased officer's

Eagle-Pommel Artillery Officer's Sword

This handsome, ivory-handled, eagle-pommel artillery officer's sword was made by the New York firm of Lemuel Wells & Co., in New York City, about 1800 to 1807. The well-chiseled bird of prey surmounts a decorative gilded hilt garnished with sprays of leaves and a cannon with rammers.

Typically, most American sword makers imported finished blades from Birmingham (England), Klingenthal (France), and Solingen (Germany), which were the leading European manufacturers of edged weapons. Dealers such as Wells purchased undecorated European blades, etched on their own names and various floral or patriotic motifs, and hilted them to suit the tastes of their clientele. In some cases, the entire weapon might be manufactured overseas, leaving the dealer only to add his own name and address.

U.S. Army regulations in 1812 called for "gilt sabres" for light artillery officers, and no doubt many officers of the foot artillery also used them. It is important to remember that orders and regulations were rarely precise about exact patterns to be used. Generally, that decision was left to the taste of the individual officer, so long as the selection fell roughly within the spirit of what was ordered.

version of the 1813 leather cap, trimmed with silver band and tassels, 1814 eagle plate, and cockade. The regimental standard of blue silk painted with a bald eagle—the national emblem—features the regimental title in gilt on the red scroll below. The private wears the plain blue and red coatee first issued to the regiment in 1813 and worn until replaced with an altogether different uniform in spring 1814. His summer overalls of cotton drilling are tucked into blackened linen gaiters. The black-belted model 1808 accoutrements are from a wartime contract and his musket is of the 1795 model.

War of 1812 State of New York Knapsack and Canteen

Typical of the patterns and construction techniques used at the time of the War of 1812, this painted linen canvas knapsack is significant because it retains white lettering that identifies it as having been issued to the 131st Regiment, state of New York. The "AH" is probably the initials of the original owner. It differs, however, from the other eighteen documented examples of knapsacks (of two different patterns) procured by the state during the War of 1812, which have only a painted set of script letters "SNY" on the outer flap, with no further clue as to the unit.

A few other differences can be noted, as well. This example has a dark blue painted flap, whereas the others have black painted flaps. All of the others also have leather strappings, while this one has heavy canvas straps by which to carry it. Most of the other examples have a bag body with a standard opening at the top, while access to this bag is through the sides, which are closed with small brass buttons. The differences suggest that this knapsack may have been made specifically for the 131st Regiment by an unknown manufacturer.

The canteen matches other known examples of the typical canteen of the War of 1812 period. They were used by both the regular army and the state of New York, differing only in the addition of the letters "SNY" to the light blue painted canteen body. The construction of this canteen consists of a number of staves secured to two sides by two iron bands. The diameter is about 7 inches, and thickness about 3 inches. One stave is raised to help secure the stopper, and wide iron strap retainers are also kept in place by the bands. All of these features are typical of cooperage of the period.

The U.S. Army canteens were made by coopers located in and around Philadelphia; most of the state of New York examples, including this one, have the name of "Arents" branded into one side. Where the Arents manufactory was located remains unknown, although New York City is likely. If the state followed regular-army practice, the canteen was suspended by a $5/8$-inch-wide leather strap that had no provision for adjustment of its length.

PRIVATE, SCOTT'S BRIGADE (9TH, 11TH, AND 25TH U.S. INFANTRY), SPRING–SUMMER 1814

Scott's Brigade of Infantry is perhaps the most famous corps in the early military annals of the United States. Officially, it was the 1st Brigade of Maj. Gen. Jacob Brown's "Left Division" of the American "Army of the North." The Left Division's infantry included veteran regiments, and during the spring of 1814 the responsibility for their training was given to the youngest brigadier general in the army, twenty-eight-year-old Winfield Scott, who swore that if "of such materials, I do not make the best army now in service . . . I will agree to be dismissed from the service." Instituting vast improvements in administration and camp discipline at their camp along the Niagara frontier, Scott focused most of his attention on bringing order and consistency to the drill employed both on the parade and battlefield. At this time, there was no standardization of infantry drill in the U.S. Army, various "official" versions being employed from von Stuben's *Blue Book* to Duane's manual, and some regiments even adopted the British exercise. The 6-foot, 2-inch Virginian soon directed that the "French regulations or the system of discipline laid down by Smyth which are the same will govern the infantry."

The 1st Brigade, in June 1814 consisting of the amalgamated 9th, 11th, and 25th U.S. Infantry Regiments, lived up to Scott's earlier boast and could perform even the most complex maneuvers like a well-oiled machine. Later that summer, it would advance with paradelike precision under heavy enemy fire during the Battles of Chippewa and Lundy's Lane, and from there to the pages of epic history. In those actions, Scott's Brigade not only stood up to the veteran British regiments, including some who had served under Wellington in the Peninsula, but bested them on the open field.

Although composed of "excellent material," Scott's men were poorly clothed and equipped. The state of the 11th Infantry during its April 1814 inspection closely mirrored the condition of their fellow regiments in the brigade:

The arms of the 11th Regt were in good firing order and many of them highly polished. The accoutrements generally fit for service but considerably worn . . . the Guns generally without Gun Slings—with regard to clothing it can hardly be necessary to observe . . . that the situation of the men must be truly deplorable from the want of it many of them without Shoes & hats & some of them with scarcely the vestage of a coat. . . .

Upon complaining to Callender Irvine, the commissary general of purchase, Scott learned that the clothing intended for his men had been diverted by Gen. James Wilkinson. Irvine replied on May 13 that despite his best efforts, the clothing "arrangements are constantly broken in upon" by such counterorders, and he promised to "send clothing from this place [Philadelphia] in the amount and kind corresponding with the accompanying statement." Included in his invoice were the following: 1,500 Gun slings, 2,000 "Leather Caps," 2,000 "Grey Woll Jackets with sleeves," 4,000 linen overalls, 4,000 shirts, 2,000 pairs of gaiters, and 2,000 fatigue frocks. On June 23 the "Clothing so long expected" reached Scott, who informed his men that "Woolen rounabouts with sleeves are to be receiv'd (in lieu of Coats) for summer wear." He ordered all troops who had also received new uniform coats to "leave the same to be carefully boxed" and stored. Scott further decreed that on campaign, each knapsack was to contain only one shirt, one pair each of shoes and socks, one fatigue frock and trousers, and a blanket, noting that "a Brush and one pocket handkerchief may be added but nothing else, these rules shall not be deviated from in the slightest particular without the consent of the General commanding the Brigade."

With the exception of the model 1813 leather infantry caps, which were tall and unwieldy, the clothing received was ideally suited for warm-weather campaigning. The plain, unlined, dark gray kersey jackets were warm enough for cool evenings on the Canadian border, yet ventilated perspiration well in the heat of the sun, and their color also masked dirt and wear more effectively than the indigo blue of the uniform coat. Intended as an undress uniform for all troops in the northern theaters of the war, the new gray jacket was an unfamiliar garment to the British regulars. When Scott's Brigade marched in column toward the British line at Chippewa, their subdued gray dress led the opposing commander to suppose them militia, purportedly exclaiming, upon realizing his mistake, "Those are regulars, by God!"

The linen overalls were made of tough "Russia sheeting," a hempen material known for its durability. With them were worn new-pattern gaiters made of black cloth and extending to the knee. In full dress, the gaiters were supposed to be worn buttoned over the overalls or "pantaloons" of the men, but on campaign the veterans preferred the overalls worn loosely over the gaiters. New slings of blackened leather now graced the men's model 1795 muskets, and their model 1808 accoutrements were slung by similar black, or sometimes whitened buff, crossbelts. The 1813 caps were of an improved pattern from those issued the previous year and were furnished with white cotton "band & tassels" and pompon, a small leather cockade with a pewter eagle, and the new stamped-pewter "eagle" plate adopted for the infantry in January 1814.

Rose 1812 Noncommissioned Officer Sword

Noncommissioned officers are essential for the running of military units. One twentieth-century army general remarked of NCOs, "officers command the units while the noncommissioned officers command the men." Traditionally, the ranks of NCOs were filled by soldiers promoted from within the company, and the army went to some lengths to recognize them with special marks of distinction. One of these marks was the sword. Plain and robust, NCO swords were utilitarian as well as symbolic and usually can be distinguished from their officer counterparts by their simpler lines and heavier construction. The Rose 1812 NCO sword is one of the earliest of its type for which reliable documentation exists of regular army use.

The hilt is brass with a stirrup-shaped guard, a disk quillion, and an urn-shaped pommel that incorporates a collar to house the capstan rivet. Measuring an overall length of 30 inches, the blade is straight with a single fuller and is $1\frac{1}{8}$ inches wide. On this example, the grip is cherry wood, though examples exist with spiral-carved ebony grips. Both William and Joseph Rose received contracts in 1812 to provide the army with NCO swords, and the difference in grips is likely a variation in manufacture between the two brothers.

U.S. Light Dragoon Cap, 1812–14

When the commanders of the two newly raised 1st and 2nd Light Dragoons were solicited for their ideas on proper dress for mounted troops, their responses led to the adoption of the new pattern "Hussar Jacket" of blue, trimmed with white and blue cord. The model 1808 dragoon cap with its "USLD" lettering was continued as the pattern headgear and by July 8, 1812, Col. James Burn was able to inform the secretary of war that the "caps that are making for the 2d Regt of the U S Light Dragoons are nearly finished." Burns went on to request permission to use white metal letters and mountings on the caps of his regiment, "being uniform with the plate and Buckles of the sabre Belts"—noting that they "can be had in Philada. at the same price as brass." Permission was granted, but it appears that Burn used this authorization to acquire trimmings of an entire new form, as an October 16 contract for additional caps called for ones "with plates in front per pattern."

By March 1813 there were 1,238 "new Pattern" caps on hand, as opposed to 37 of the "old plan with brass mounting," suggesting that Burn may have influenced a change not only in the mountings, but the entire cap form by late 1812. The December 1812 regulations for the light dragoon uniform vaguely describe a "Helmet: according to pattern, blue feather with white top." This new cap was another American adaptation of European military wear, resembling the crested helmets worn by both French and British dragoons. It was described in December 1813 as having a "Skull 6 inches in depth the helmet in front to be 3 inches higher than the top of the Scull forming the half Semi to the back part."

The comb was edged with white metal reinforcement strips, with additional bands running down the crown. Made of thin, tinned sheet iron, the strips had more decorative than protective qualities, as did the cap's leather chinstraps, covered with scales made of the same metal. A flowing white horsehair crest was set into the

comb, stepped aback about $\frac{1}{2}$ inch to allow space for the feather, which by 1814 had been replaced with a similarly colored, worsted pompon. By June 1814 fears that there would be "great difficulty in procuring white hair" without excessive costs led to approval of "black hair instead of the white." The dragoon caps that survive today, however, are from the two 1814 contracts (such as this fine example) and they all have white horsehair crests. Thus, the supply-and-demand crisis must not have been as critical as first imagined. That same year the two understrength regiments were merged and later dissolved in 1815. Most of the caps from the 1814 contracts were delivered into stores and never issued, which accounts for their mint condition today.

Flank Company Coatee, Connecticut Militia, c. 1812

At the October 1811 session the General Assembly of Connecticut issued an amendment to the State Militia Act that prescribed "one uniform dress for the infantry," which was to be made "of woollen cloth of a substantial and durable fabric, the color and fashion of which . . . shall be prescribed by the Captain General." On February 17, 1812, the uniform for the infantry was fixed as follows:

> *The non-commissioned officers and privates of the infantry regiments, are to wear short blue coats, lined with white, faced, collared, and cuffed with red; the collar of the coat to be a stiff stand up collar:—the front corner of the coat or forebody, to be turned up with red . . . the whole uniform, trimmed with white buttons, those on the coat to be of a middling size. . . .*

For adherence to this provision, the militiaman would receive a certificate exempting him from the poll tax—certainly an incentive that rendered Connecticut's uniformed militia one of the best clothed in the United States. The order was further modified on December 31, 1812, to exempt "the grenadier, light-infantry and independent companies [as they] have furnished themselves with uniforms, the most of which combine peculiar usefulness with elegance. . . ." This short coat or coatee conforms very closely to the infantry uniform described above. It is provided with shoulder wings piped with red, suggesting that this uniform may have belonged to a member of one of the flank or independent companies. The domestically produced blue and red cloth is rather coarse, but well made. The cut of the uniform, with a pronounced "armscye" or armhole, is a style popular during 1805–17. The use of lapels on infantry coats was abolished by Connecticut in 1813, however, suggesting a terminus date of 1812 for this coat. The Connecticut uniformed militia did see some limited action during the War of 1812, defending their home state from British amphibious incursions such as the Stonington Raid.

Cap Plate, 2nd U.S. Artillery Regiment, 1812–14

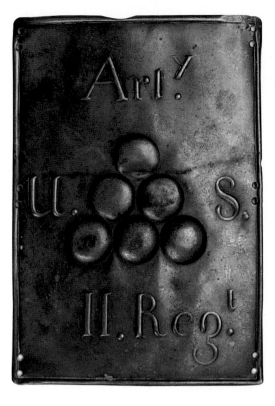

Two new foot artillery regiments, the 2nd and 3rd were authorized in January 1812 to augment the 1st or "Old Artillery." The 2nd Artillery's first commander was Col. George Izard, who had earlier resigned his commission as a captain in the 1st Artillery in 1803 during the purge of Federalist officers from the army under President Jefferson's administration. Izard proceeded to France to further his study of military science, returning to America prior to the outbreak of war with Britain. Izard paid great attention to the uniforms and dress of his new corps and was dissatisfied with the rather archaic appearance of the prescribed artillery uniform. The blue artillery coats had red facings and linings, festooned with more than 18 yards of yellow worsted buttonhole and edging tape, and were cut with cutaway skirts that extended to the knee pan in back. The regulation headgear was a cocked hat that was nearly 11 inches high and 18 inches broad, bound with yellow worsted tape and bearing a white feather plume that extended 6 inches above the hat.

When contractors failed to produce the hats in sufficient quantities for the new artillery regiments, the commissary general proposed furnishing felt caps in lieu of hats. Izard, who thought the "cocked hats or Chapeaux . . . very inconvenient & unornamental Coverings for

Soldiers Heads," indicated that he would "be glad to receive instead of them felt or leather round Hats or Caps for my Regiment." By September 1812 the two officers agreed that the new light artillery cap should be the headgear furnished for the 2nd Artillery. This "Yeoman crowned" cap was 7 inches high, with a 2 1/2-inch-wide, leather-lined visor in front and widened to an 8 1/2-inch diameter at top—clearly an American attempt to copy the French "shako" widely used in Napoleon's armies. The cap was trimmed with a yellow worsted band and tassels, leather cockade with brass eagle, and a white feather plume.

To distinguish the regiment, a cap plate of stamped brass was to be furnished. The design selected by Izard was a rectangular plate with a central device consisting of a stack of cannonballs, surmounted by "Arty." It would be flanked by a "U." on the left and "S." on the right, with "II Regt." below. The 2nd wore this cap plate until 1814, when it and the two other foot artillery regiments were merged into the newly created Corps of Artillery, and a new cap plate was prescribed. Examples of the 2nd Artillery cap plate have been found at Fort Erie in Ontario, Canada (a post occupied by U.S. troops only during the summer-fall 1814 campaign), suggesting that its actual use extended well into 1814 among the former 2nd Artillery companies within the new corps.

American Militia Officer's Cockade, c. 1812

From the middle of the eighteenth century, cockades were increasingly used by military men to denote the nationality of the wearer. Spain had a red cockade, and France had, from 1789, a red, white, and blue national cockade. Great Britain had a plain black cockade, as did the early United States. The Americans naturally sought a distinction, which they found simply and efficiently by adding a small eagle at the center of the cockade. This could be a small metal eagle badge added on or, as in the illustrated example, painted in the center of a stamped leather or metal cockade. The type of cockade shown is called a "fan cockade" because of its high center section. This style was very popular with American militiamen of all ranks. The cockade illustrated was probably worn by a New York State militiaman.

PRIVATE, LIGHT INFANTRY COMPANY, THE 104TH OR "NEW BRUNSWICK" REGIMENT OF FOOT, SUMMER 1814

The 104th Regiment of Foot was raised during 1803 to 1805 as the New Brunswick Regiment of Fencibles. Fencible regiments were considered regulars but were required to serve only "locally," in this case, British North America (an added incentive to recruiting, considering the uneasy situation in war-torn Europe during this period). Serving as the garrison for New Brunswick and nearby Prince Edward Island, it became a standing regiment of foot on the British Establishment in 1811 and was numbered the 104th. In February 1813 it was ordered to Upper Canada (present-day Ontario) and performed an epic overland march during a particularly brutal Canadian winter, braving extreme cold and heavy snow while covering 350 miles during twenty-four days.

The 104th participated in the British attack on Sackett's Harbor, where it received its baptism of fire during the failed amphibious landing of May 29, 1813. The regiment was then ordered to the Niagara frontier in June, arriving in time to participate in the Battle of Beaver Dams. The light infantry and grenadiers were detached from the regiment (then quartered in Kingston) in July 1814 and ordered back to the Niagara Peninsula, arriving in time to fight in the bitter night action at Lundy's Lane. The remainder of the regiment joined them in time for the siege of Fort Erie, where the regiment suffered tragic losses in the 3 A.M. August 15 assault on the fort. Of the seventy-seven light infantrymen who were part of the column that had penetrated into a bastion, only twenty-three returned to British lines following the explosion of the bastion's powder magazine. The regiment fought, in the words of one of its officers, "the prettiest little affair any of us had ever seen" on October 20 at Cook's Mill—its last battle. The corps was dissolved three years later.

In 1814 the 104th wore uniforms made according to the 1802 clothing regulations, with minor modifications in cut and trimmings introduced during the subsequent decade. The coat was of madder red wool "Cloth, lined throughout ...with . . . Buff Serge . . . [without] lapels but made to Button over the Body down to the Waist." Cuffs, collars, and shoulder straps were of pale buff, the regimental facing color. The buttons and lace loops were sewn on "2 and 2," of white worsted tape edged with a blue and red stripe, with an additional yellow stripe placed against the inside edge of the blue one. This coat form was worn by all British infantrymen, but the flank companies were distinguished by their traditional shoulder wings, "with 6 darts of Lace on Each." The light infantry coats, or "jackets," also had pocket flaps that "slope[d] diagonally" and were trimmed with small buttons throughout.

This light infantryman wears dark gray trousers and short gaiters, officially adopted in 1812 for all foot regiments "on service." His felt cap is the new 1812 "Belgic" form, covered by its "cap case of prepared linen . . . worn in wet weather." The cartridge pouch is the new form adopted in 1806–8,

capable of holding sixty cartridges for the soldier's India Pattern musket. A cast-brass regimental plate bearing the regimental number and title is attached to his bayonet belt of buff leather. Rolled and strapped to his black-painted "Trotter" knapsack is the soldier's gray greatcoat. Thus uniformed and equipped, the 104th performed brave and hard service during the tough Niagara Campaign of 1814.

British Infantry Officers' Swords, 85th (Bucks Volunteer Light Infantry) and 1st (Royal Scots) Regiments, c. 1803–12

The 85th Foot was raised during 1794 in the estates of the Marquis of Buckingham and thus was known as the "Bucks Volunteers." Trained in the new light infantry tactics, and styled as such from 1808, it had already campaigned in Holland, Portugal, Spain, and France when, in 1814, it was sent to America. There the 85th served at Bladensburg, Washington, Baltimore, and New Orleans. Like other light infantry regiments, the officers adopted swords with curved blades, plain pommels, and steel guards. The sword shown here (left) is an excellent example of this unofficial but nevertheless accepted pattern that was worn until 1822. It has a sharkskin grip and a plain blade, and was made by "Tatham, 43 Charing Cross, London." Its scabbard is iron with dark sharkskin panels. The top mount is engraved with a hunting horn, the traditional insignia of light infantry units, and the Roman numeral "LXXXV," for the 85th.

From the end of the eighteenth century, many infantry officers wished for a sword with a curved blade, and in general, the army authorities agreed. In 1799 officers of grenadier and light companies were allowed to wear them, and in 1803 a new pattern sword was introduced officially for infantry officers. The 1803 pattern had a curved, flat-back blade with a gilt brass hilt, a lion's head pommel, and a guard with a crowned royal cipher. The grenadier company officers were distinguished by a small grenade above the cipher, the light infantry company officers by a bugle horn. The sword shown (right) belonged to a Light Company officer of the 1st Regiment. This was the senior regiment in the line infantry, and a most prestigious unit, which showed in the custom

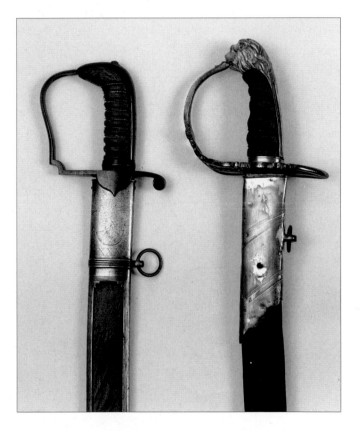

features on their swords. Not only did officers' swords have the features common to the 1803 pattern, but they also had regimental badges cast on either side of the guard with the words "The Royal." This is also seen on the high-quality blued and gilded blade. It most likely indicates that the sword was made between 1803 and 1812, when the regiment's title was "The Royal," until changed to "The Royal Scots" in 1812.

British Light Infantry Shoulderbelt Plates

Two regiments of British light infantry served in North America during the War of 1812. Differentiated from line infantry by uniform distinctions and special pattern arms, they became experts in their craft during the campaigns in Spain under the Duke of Wellington. Both of these brass shoulderbelt plates were found on a British campsite occupied after the Battle of New Orleans.

The 85th of Foot, later known as the "Bucks Volunteers," served in Holland and later fought during the arduous Peninsula Campaign. In August 1814 the regiment arrived in North America. As part of the expedition to the Gulf, it was successful in a difficult assault on the American batteries during the Battle of New Orleans on January 8, 1815. Owing to the utter defeat of the main army, however, the regiment was forced to retreat. It returned to England in May 1815, a shadow of its former self. Later that year it received the title "Duke of York's Own Light Infantry" and the motto *Aucto*

Splendore Resurgo in recognition of its excellent service and conduct.

The 1st Battalion of the 43rd (Monmouthshire) Light Infantry also came to America with a superb record of hard fighting on the Spanish Peninsula. The 43rd sailed directly from England to the Gulf, arriving near New Orleans on the morning of January 4, 1815. The men were only lightly engaged during the battle, forming the rear guard for the retreating British Army. Returning to Europe in April 1815, they reached Belgium too late to participate in the Battle of Waterloo.

British 60-Round Cartridge Pouch, 1804–15

During the Revolutionary and early Napoleonic Wars, quartermasters frequently attempted to "complete" each British infantryman with sixty rounds of ball cartridges for field service. Unfortunately, the pouches generally carried only thirty-six to forty rounds, necessitating the wear of a supplemental cartridge box or magazine for the remainder. Sometimes the men merely stowed the excess in their pockets or knapsacks. In 1804 a standardized pouch was adopted for the British infantry that was capable of carrying the entire sixty-round "combat" issue, and by the War of 1812, most of the British infantry had been reequipped with it. This example was found near the Canadian border and may have been an American war trophy. Its original leather sling has been replaced (possibly by its captor) with one of linen webbing.

Enlisted Men's Shoulderbelt Plates of the British 44th, 93rd, and 104th Regiments, c. 1810–20

The 104th (New Brunswick) Regiment was actually a Canadian unit raised on August 1, 1803, as the New Brunswick Regiment of Fencible Infantry. It was recruited in what are now the Canadian provinces of New Brunswick, Nova Scotia, and Quebec, and the proportion of French Canadians is said to have been substantial in the ranks. Officers, however, were mainly from Great Britain. The companies had buglers instead of drummers, but the regimental band did have drums.

In 1810 the regiment volunteered to serve anywhere in the world, and the offer was readily accepted. It was numbered the 104th Regiment in the British line infantry but remained posted in southern New Brunswick until the War of 1812. It was then sent to Upper Canada (now Ontario), where it fought bravely in many engagements. The regimental shoulderbelt plates were oval, silvered for the officers and cast brass for the enlisted men. From 1810 the name of the regiment in a crowned garter surrounding the number "104" appeared on the enlisted men's belt plate as shown in the illustration.

The 93rd (Sutherland Highlanders) was the only Scottish Highland regiment that served in North America during the War of 1812. It was a relatively new unit, its 1st Battalion having been raised in the Highlands in 1800 and sent to South Africa in 1806, returning to Britain in 1814.

The 1st Battalion embarked for America in the fall of 1814, part of the force heading for Louisiana, and was part of the doomed assault against General Jackson's American troops at New Orleans on January 8, 1815. In a desperate but unsuccessful attack, the battalion suffered 3 officers, 2 sergeants, and 58 men killed and 12 officers, 17 sergeants, 3 drummers, and 348 men wounded.

The regimental uniform was a red coatee with yellow facings. The dress headgear for battalion companies was a black ostrich feather bonnet with a white over red feather hackle on the left. In anticipation of an arduous campaign for the 1st Battalion in Louisiana, the tartan cloth for kilts was used to make trews (tight-fitting trousers) instead, and the blue undress bonnet, which had an unusually high red and white diced band, was worn at New Orleans instead of the feather bonnet. In 1810 a rectangular plate with the sharp corners cut off, as shown here, was introduced for all ranks. The enlisted man's was of cast brass and the officer's was silvered and engraved.

The 44th (East Essex) Regiment was raised in 1741. In 1814 its 1st Battalion then in Spain was sent to North America to participate in the British raids on the American coast. It was part of the force that beat the American forces at Bladensburg, captured Washington, and participated in the operations against Baltimore. In December the 1st Battalion, 44th Foot, landed in Louisiana and participated in the battle near Velere's Plantation and in the disastrous assault on January 8, 1815. Its final action was at the capture of Fort Bowyer, Alabama, on February 11.

Model 1813 Infantry Cap

On December 26, 1812, Callender Irvine, commissary general of purchases, wrote a memorandum to William Eustis, secretary of war, in which he recommended some changes in the clothing of the U.S. Army that would contribute to the comfort of the soldier while saving the government money. He proposed "to furnish Leather Caps in lieu of Felt Caps—the former being preferable as to appearance comfort, durability & on the score of economy," noting that leather caps "will last three or four years with decency, under any circumstances two Years, the latter [felt caps] but one Year & will not look decent half that time—the first wetting injures its good appearance." Irvine forwarded a sample of a leather cap proposed for the infantry, which was approved by Eustis on January 23, 1813, and sealed as a fixed pattern. The form of cap proposed was a leather copy of the felt "Belgic" cap that had recently been adopted in the British Army. An unusual departure from the flat-topped cylindrical felt cap that the Americans had earlier copied in 1810, it had a distinctive raised or false front. Today it is commonly known as a "tombstone shako" by collectors because of its resemblance to a headstone when viewed from the front, although this is clearly a twentieth-century term.

One month later, Irvine was already receiving proposals for "Leather Hats agreeable to pattern (with the addition of the two brass rings as in on the other Hat or Cap which is exhibited in the office)." By April 1813 the caps contracted for were to be "equal in goodness and workmanship to the pattern Cap exhibited, the edge of the front pieces to be painted white, and are to have one ring affixed on each side of the said Cap, to place the band & Tassels." That same month, Irvine directed that leather caps be furnished to the 6th and 15th Infantry Regiments if "there are a sufficient number of Infantry Caps (Leather) in store" and ordered that "leather Caps be packed for all the Infantry, stationed on the Niagara River, and at Buffaloe & Sackets Harbour." Besides cotton bands and tassels, worsted plumes or "Pompons" were ordered to trim the caps, as well as small cockades of stamped leather, with pewter eagles affixed in their centers.

Further documentation sheds some light on the appearance of the caps made up during 1813. In an August 12, 1815, report on "leather articles . . . now in store at New York and unfit for regular service," there is a discussion of 794 rejected "Infantry Caps . . . made on the old plan, that is with the fronts sewed to the crowns, Tho

well made and of good materials." The cap in this photograph is believed to be one of the 1813 contract caps based on its overall form and construction. It has a separate front "piece" sewn to the crown, which is edged with white paint and features the "two brass rings" referred to in 1813 proposals and contract documents. The original cotton band and tassels are still attached, although the cockade and pompon are missing. A cap plate was once attached in front; from the placement of the attachment holes, it appears to have mounted one of the oversized pewter cap plates issued to many infantry regiments in 1813. Finally, the front pieces rise only $1^1/2$ inches above the crown—closely matching descriptions of the 1813 contract caps still on hand in 1814, "the front pieces of . . . most of them not exceeding one & a half inches."

This "old plan" form of the model 1813 infantry cap was widely used during the war and besides this fine example, only two other caps of this form are known to survive—neither of which seem to have ever had a plate attached. Numerous examples of this second pattern model 1813 infantry cap do survive—distinguished by having the raised front made integral to the one-piece body, rather than being separately attached as on the 1813 contract caps. This "improved" cap is believed to have been first introduced in 1814 and, though a number of this form still survive, most show little evidence of having been worn and are probably part of the surplus stocks that appear in postwar inventories.

PRIVATE, BATTALION COMPANY, 5TH WEST INDIA REGIMENT, 1814–15

During the last third of the eighteenth century, European military theorists increasingly debated the issue of raising units composed of black men, an idea that was unacceptable to many who feared that arming blacks would lead to mutinies and slave uprisings. Nevertheless, the Republican French in the West Indies raised several black corps during the early 1790s. Black soldiers were much less prone to deadly fevers than European soldiers and they excelled in combat. British military authorities soon recognized the need to form their own regular regiments of blacks, and in spite of much opposition from the various island legislatures in the British West Indies, commissions were issued to colonels in 1795 to raise such regiments. Colonel Howe's regiment was authorized raised on May 20 and, in 1798, was numbered the 5th West India Regiment, later styled the "Duke of York's." Experience soon confirmed that, if treated fairly, the black troops made fine soldiers, as they were less prone to desertion and drink than the British soldiers.

From 1803 there were eight West India regiments in the British Army, all of them posted in various Caribbean islands as well as in Guyana and Belize. Some were deployed in the campaigns against the French Islands up until the last one fell in 1810, but the 5th missed seeing action, having been posted in Belize for many years until sent to Jamaica in 1812. Two years later, the regiment sailed with the 1st West Indian Regiment and several British regiments on Admiral Cochrane's fleet bound for Louisiana.

The regiment suffered considerably from exposure and the colder North American climate, and about 100 men became ill, some of whom died. From December 27, 1814, to January 5, 1815, five men were killed and four wounded in various skirmishes. On January 8, during the disastrous British attack on Gen. Andrew Jackson's American line, the 5th West India only had a sergeant wounded, as it was not seriously engaged due to delays in deploying its brigade for attack. The 5th West India Regiment was then taken to Dauphin Island, Alabama, and from there back to the West Indies. With peace at hand in America and Europe, the 5th West India Regiment was disbanded in 1817, and its men were offered land grants in Belize.

The compilation known as the "1802 Clothing Regulations," likely drafted between 1799 and 1802, gave the first extensive details on the uniforms of the West India regiments. It specified that the black soldiers would wear a red jacket with a red collar and shoulder straps, small "half" lapels, and pointed cuffs of the facing color. The jacket had very short skirts that sloped off behind, with no turnbacks. The regimental lace edged the collar all around as well as the shoulder straps and the top of the cuffs, and was used for the

buttonholes of the half lapels and collar. The 5th West India Regiment had green facings, the men's lace being plain white. The half lapels were initially squared at the bottom, but a watercolor of a soldier of the 1st West India Regiment, by Charles Hamilton Smith in about 1808, and his aquatint of the 5th West India Regiment, published in London on January 2, 1814, on which this illustration is largely based, show the half-lapels to have become angled below. Smith also shows the cuffs to have become like those of the rest of the line infantry: straight cut with buttons and buttonhole lace.

Soldiers of the West India regiments were not issued waistcoats but received two pairs of white duck gaiter-trousers every year. On July 7, 1810, this was ordered altered to blue serge gaiter-trousers. The West India soldiers were issued "Belgic" caps from about 1812 to 1813. Like the line infantry, West India regiments had distinctive insignias below the cipher. Those of the 5th had the Roman numeral "V," as did the pewter regimental buttons. The accoutrements were the same as for the line infantry with whitened buff belts in lieu of the earlier black ones. The 5th Regiment had a brass shoulderbelt plate with the "V" and "The Duke of York's" above and "West India Regiment" below, according to an actual plate found at a campsite occupied by British troops during the New Orleans Campaign.

British Royal Artillery Officer's Cap Plate, 1812–16

The Royal Artillery was a corps that gathered specialists trained in all matters pertaining to the use and deployment of artillery in the British Army. It was generally considered one of the finest corps of its type in existence, for both its scientific excellence and its battlefield performance. It consisted of marching battalions, which looked after the heavy guns and the field artillery serving on foot, and, from 1794, included the Royal Horse Artillery, which served the fast-moving light artillery.

The uniform of the foot artillery had generally the same cut as that of the line infantry, but it was blue faced with red instead of red faced with various colors. The men's lace was yellow and set in bastion shape, the officers' gold. The headdress also was generally similar to the infantry's, the "stovepipe" cap having been adopted by the rank-and-file artillerymen since 1800. The "Belgic" cap was introduced for the enlisted men in 1812. It had yellow cords, a white plume on the side, and a stamped brass plate. The plate, surmounted by a crown, had the "GR" cipher at the center surrounded by an oval garter bearing the name of the corps, and a mortar below with two flaming bombs, altogether forming an elegant design.

On January 14, 1812, the artillery officers were ordered to wear caps instead of bicorne hats. The officers' "Belgic" or "Waterloo" caps were generally like the men's but of better-quality felt with gold cords and a white hackle feather. The cap plate was gilded but otherwise similar to the men's. The officer's cap plate shown here is a fine example and was heavily gilded. The officer's early "Belgic" cap had, like those of the Foot Guards, gold lace edging the front panel's sides and top. On July 31, 1812, however, this gold lace was ordered removed and replaced by black silk lace. Further specifi-

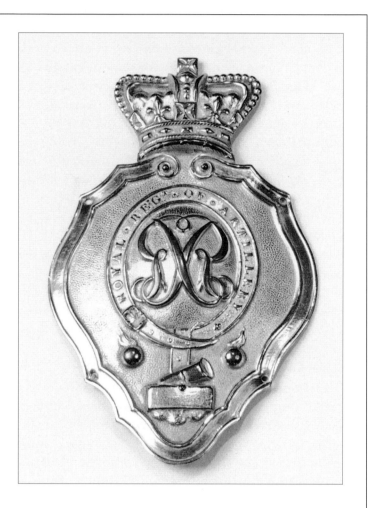

cations regarding the important matter of cords and tassels came on August 3, 1813, when the Royal Artillery General Orders directed, "The bottom of the Fringe of the lower, or longest Tassel, to be one inch from the extreme bottom of the Cap [shako], and the bottom of the upper, or shortest Tassel, to be two inches from the extreme bottom of the Cap, and each of the Tassels to be sewn to the Cap, three quarters of an inch above the head of the Tassel, to prevent them swinging about." So good of headquarters to think of the well-being and appearance of officers on the battlefields of Spain and Canada in such a way!

India Pattern Musket, 7th Regiment of Foot

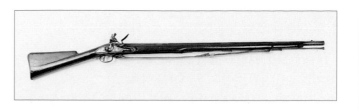

The rapid expansion of the British armed forces during the war with revolutionary France in the 1790s called for mobilization of vast bodies of troops. To meet the exhaustive demands for arms, the British government adopted the more simply manufactured "India Pattern" musket as an officially sanctioned pattern in 1797. By the outbreak of the War of 1812, most British infantry were armed with these well-made weapons.

The specimen illustrated here is regimentally marked on the butt plate to the 7th Regiment of Foot (Royal Fusiliers). In 1809 a reinforcing piece was approved to be added to the neck of the hammer for extra strength. This arm is unusual in that it still retains its original white buff leather sling.

As fusiliers, the men were entitled to wear bearskin caps, but on campaign this was rarely done, and in America they wore "Belgic" caps. The belt plates and cap plates bore the ancient regimental crest of a crown over the rose within the garter. The coatees were the usual red faced blue worn by all Royal regiments.

Enlisted Man's Cap Plate, 1st Regiment of Foot, or the Royal Scots, c. 1812–16

The 1st was the senior regiment in the British line infantry and arguably one of the finest units in the army. It was a Scottish unit raised in the Lowlands and thus generally dressed in the standard infantry uniform. Lowlanders typically wore the usual fashions prevailing in western Europe, although many of the badges and traditions in the regiment were distinctly Scottish.

By the early 1800s, the Royal Scots, as the regiment was commonly called, had four battalions (senior regiments tended to have several battalions), which were deployed in the West Indies, India, and Spain. In 1812 the 1st Battalion was sent from the West Indies to Quebec and moved to the Niagara Frontier during 1813. It took part in the capture of Fort Niagara and Buffalo; was part of the British force beaten at Chippewa on July 5, 1814; participated in the bloody battle of Lundy's Lane; and fought at the siege of Fort Erie in September. It spent the winter in Fort Niagara and returned to Britain in 1815. The 4th Battalion had meanwhile landed in Quebec City in June 1814 and stood guard there until sent to Britain in May 1815.

The cap plate illustrated here belongs to the "Belgic" model introduced in early 1812 but probably not in general wear until 1813 and 1814. It has an elegant brass plate with scalloped edges, surmounted by a crown. Many line regiments had the regimental number and perhaps a badge stamped in below the royal cipher, but that of the Royal Scots was in a class of its own. Indeed, two plate patterns with different badges were approved in January 1812, but only the example shown was actually produced and issued. Its cipher is surrounded by the Collar of St. Andrew, the badge of the Order of the Thistle below, the Sphinx commemorating its service in Egypt, and "The Royal Scots" in a scroll. The plate is surmounted by a crown—the small Maltese cross at its top being the only part missing from this rare example.

Two Militia Bell Crown Caps

Authorized by the U.S. Army in 1820, the leather bell-crowned cap replaced the Belgic-style cap of the War of 1812. Inspired by the flared-top shakos of the Russian Army and the Regency Shako (adopted in 1816) of the British Army, it reflected the latest tastes in military fashion. The caps of the regular army were trimmed with white metal fittings for infantry and brass for artillery. In 1832 a new felt cap was prescribed, and in 1834 all the remaining old-style leather caps were ordered to be turned in. The surplus caps were sold to the Marine Corps, which continued to use this style for quite a few years afterward. Slavishly influenced by the dress of the aristocratic armies of Europe, the American militia embraced this most fashionable style perhaps even before the regular U.S. forces did.

Left to right: This elegant example of a militia officer's cap is nearly identical in style to that of the regular infantry. The cap is of highly polished black leather with silver-plated fittings and tassels of silver bullion wire. The inside bears the maker's paper label, reading, "William H. Miller, Saddler, Harness, & Military Equipment Maker, 427 Broadway, New York." Mr. Miller's firm did business at this address only in the year 1821, which is a conclusive indicator of how quickly this style was adopted by the militia forces.

This slightly later cap of a militia or volunteer enlisted man lacks the elegant silk lining of the first specimen. It bears the handwritten name and address of its owner, "Geo. Storr, Cooperstown [New York]," on its interior. The insignia of a rifle company—an eagle with a hunting horn suspended form its beak—in the form of a large diamond-shaped brass plate is the only ornament. The original black feather plume towers over the smooth crown of this last reminder of Sunday militia drills on the local village green.

Infantry Officer's Sword Belt Pattern of 1819

The regulations of 1819 prescribed for regimental officers "a yellow oval plate (white for infantry) in front, one and a half inch wide, with an eagle in the center." The design for the artillery officer's belt plate was an eagle over trophies surmounted by a ribband with the motto "U.S. Artillery." Those of the infantry were silver-plated copper with "U.S. Infantry" substituted above, whereas those of the engineers were gilt brass and bore the device of that corps under the motto "Essayons." The earliest examples of these belt plates were meticulously fabricated and exhibit the highest-quality workmanship. In 1834 this plate was superseded by a new pattern that continued until 1851.

The belt and plate illustrated may be those of a militia officer, as regulations called for white buff, while this example is of Red Russia leather with chained straps. Although the militia of the period had a vast choice of extravagant belt plates from which to select, they occasionally preferred those of the regular army.

Model 1828 Embossed Eagle Infantry Cartridge Box

Without a doubt the most handsome accoutrement ever used by the U.S. Army, the embossed eagle box was proposed early in 1828 by the prolific nineteenth-century accoutrement vendor Robert Dingee of New York City. Although Dingee's first design for the flap of the box was considered "too figured," the Ordnance Department bought 2,000 anyway and issued most to state volunteer companies. None are known to have survived. The box shown here has the second, and more common flat design, produced by both Dingee and James Boyd of Boston as contractors and Allegheny Arsenal directly. Six hundred of a third flap design, which omitted the "US" letters, were produced just for the state of Virginia.

Except for the stamped flap impression, the box retains the characteristics of its predecessor, the model 1808 cartridge box, with twenty-six holes bored in a wooden block to hold individual paper cartridges; a tin tray with three compartments below the wooden block to hold additional cartridges, rags, and spare flints; a small opening in the front of the body of the box to provide admittance to the tray; two buckles on the bottom; and a varnished linen inner flap to help preserve the fragile cartridges. Suspension was provided by a 2¼-inch-wide whitened buff shoulderbelt, which this example retains. The cartridge box shoulderbelt did not have the familiar "round eagle" plate affixed until after 1841, so it is correctly omitted here. The flap design made it difficult to renew the appearance of the box, which required scraping the flap, according to regulations. Although the box was replaced by a significantly improved box as part of the 1839 accoutrement changes, stocks of the embossed eagle box remained in Federal depots until after the Mexican War.

Marine Officer's Fatigue Cap, 1834–39

Records of the Marine Corps quartermaster department are virtually nonexistent on the subject of the various styles of fatigue caps used between 1798 and 1852. The first fatigue headdress provided were referred to as "hats" or (sometimes) "citizen's hats." By the second decade of the nineteenth century, the terminology changed to "leather caps" and further reference was made in the late 1820s to caps with tops stiffened by whalebone or wire hoops. No further description of the fatigue cap followed until 1852, other than to note that fatigue caps were to be made "according to pattern." In the 1852 publication of uniform regulations, the officer's fatigue cap was shown, and quartermaster correspondence noted that officer caps differed from enlisted caps only in the use of a gold embroidered wreath and anchor device.

The officer's cap in the illustrated regulations is distinguished by having a narrower, almost Prussian-style top in place of the wide and relatively unstiffened crown of the army version. A photograph of a Marine lieutenant from about 1847 shows the officer wearing the fatigue cap. The cap is exactly as depicted in 1852, suggesting that the later illustration depicts the cap first prescribed in 1839. The question then becomes one of finding out what type of cap preceded it.

This cap consists of a grass green band edged top and bottom with ¼-inch wide gold vellum lace. Above the band is a narrow (almost vertical) crown of off-white or pale buff sides and a grass green top. The visor is black leather and the chin strap buttons are Marine Corps. Style of construction is consistent with caps of the period. The off-white or pale buff and grass green wool broadcloth, as well as the vellum lace, were elements of Marine officer's dress prescribed in 1834.

SERGEANT, U.S. MARINES, C. 1836

Among the colorful and well-designed uniforms of the 1832 to 1851 period, the green and pale buff Marine dress was one of the most distinctive. Its choice was more about presidential politics than any military necessity, and its manufacture and use were plagued with challenges for the small Marine Corps and domestic clothing industry of the United States. Problems with the uniform were not the fault of the Quartermaster Department of the Marine Corps. This department oversaw the design, procurement, and distribution for issue of all clothing, equipment, and weapons. All contracts were managed by the quartermaster of the Marine Corps in Washington, D.C., and the assistant quartermaster in Philadelphia inspected material received to ensure that it matched the pattern piece in every respect. Distribution to barracks and sea detachments was from the Philadelphia depot, and strict accounts were required of every commander for the items received, subsequently issued, and stored. This system was simple, effective, and contributed to a degree of uniformity throughout the Marine Corps that army units stationed across the continent could not hope to achieve.

The organization of the Marine Corps was based on army staff and regimental structure, but it differed in some fundamental ways. There were no regiments, as such, as the corps consisted of a number of barrack detachments permanently assigned ashore to guard naval installations at the major America seaports. These fixed detachments were commanded by a captain holding the brevet rank of major or lieutenant colonel. Ships' detachments, however, varied in size according to the ship, and the size of the detachment determined whether it was led by a captain, first lieutenant, second lieutenant, or a senior noncommissioned officer, commonly referred to as an orderly sergeant. These officers and orderly sergeants were responsible for ensuring that their men were always properly dressed and equipped. At the conclusion of a cruise, the commander's clothing records and individual marine records were closely scrutinized by auditors, and commanders were charged the costs of any missing or unaccounted-for items.

In 1834 Marines had three basic uniforms. Full dress, or "uniform" dress, consisted of a green-faced buff (off-white) uniform coat trimmed with yellow worsted lace and with yellow worsted epalets according to grade. The trousers were a salt-and-pepper gray, and a black leather bell-crown uniform cap completed the uniform. Accoutrements differed according to rank. The winter fatigue uniform consisted of a gray jacket of the same style as the contemporary army fatigue uniform. Marine jackets were trimmed with the same 1/4-inch-wide yellow worsted lace as used on army artillery jackets and in the same manner as on the shoulder straps and collar. Marine buttons completed the jacket. Summer or hot-weather dress consisted of a linen jacket and trousers.

The dress uniform in use in 1836 was originally adopted in 1834 and closely followed the army style in all respects except color. Green was not the color originally desired by Commandant Archibald Henderson or the quartermaster, Capt. Elijah Weed. When Henderson submitted a proposal for a blue-faced red uniform to President Andrew Jackson for his approval in 1833, Jackson rejected it and suggested that the Marine Corps resurrect the colors worn during the Revolutionary War, that is, green-faced buff. (Jackson slightly erred here, as the Continental Marines first wore green coats with white, not buff, facings.) At the time, neither Weed or Henderson felt green was suitable for military dress, as it was liable to fade from exposure to sunlight and salt water. The commandant, however, had just successfully stopped a move by President Jackson to merge the Marine Corps into the army and declined to protest the selection. The problems predicted in 1834 proved true. Finding suitable quality cloth from domestic manufacturers was extraordinarily difficult, and the green dye was so unstable that no two uniform coats matched after a single day of wear. As soon as President Jackson left office, the commandant received permission in 1839 to return to the traditional blue-faced red colors.

The grade of sergeant was indicated by three loops on the cuffs, the $^1/_8$-inch-diameter fringe on the epaulet, the buff trouser stripe, and the eagle-headed noncommissioned officer's sword manufactured by F. W. Widmann of Philadelphia. Equipment followed the army pattern except for the lack of a cartridge box plate, the use of a plain brass oval plate on the shoulderbelt, and a plain rectangular plate for the waistbelt. Musket slings were not used by marine units except during land campaigns of the Seminole and Mexican Wars. An orderly sergeant would have been dressed similarly to the sergeant, but without the cartridge box, shoulderbelt, bayonet, and musket. A red worsted sash further distinguished orderly sergeants from lesser-ranking sergeants.

Model 1833 Dragoon Waistbelt

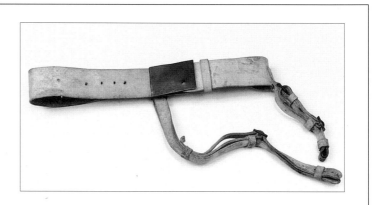

Although termed the model of 1833, that year has been used by collectors and historians only because it coincides with the reestablishment of a mounted branch of service for the U.S. Army, which had been disbanded after the War of 1812. It is likely that the style and construction details of this belt date back to that war, despite a sketchy archival record. It is known, through contracts made with Robert Dingee of New York City for the belts to be used by the new 1st Regiment of Dragoons, that they were to be made of whitened buff leather, initially in a width of 1$^3/_4$ inches, with the slings to support the sword in a width of $^3/_4$ inch. The belts also had a rectangular sheet brass belt plate. Cast brass slide buckles were part of the slings. This example corresponds to all of those characteristics.

After Col. Stephen Watts Kearney assumed command of the dragoons in 1836, minor changes were gradually made to the belt at his suggestion. The width of the belt was increased to 2 inches to better support the Ames sword used by the dragoons; single brass hooks replaced the buckles of the slings (although apparently their width was not changed); and a shoulderbelt was added to some examples. Despite these improvements, the belt was still deemed too weak for carrying the sword on horseback, and the Ordnance Board that began meeting in 1837 had a "more robust" belt that critics of the 1833 model wanted in place within a year. The belt would continue to evolve for several more years, however, until the model of 1841 belt achieved a degree of acceptance among the officers of the regiments of dragoons.

The "Cheesebox" Canteen

This style of canteen, with one piece of bent wood as the rim, is similar in construction to containers for cheese, hence the name. These canteens were made on round metal forms that were exactly the size of the sides, generally a little over 7 inches. The rim was secured by several copper tacks driven through the wood onto the form, which clenched the tacks. The rim was then secured to the sides by six to eight wooden pegs. No raised area was provided for the bung, or stopper.

According to those who have studied this construction, it is typical of New England coopers. Because several diameters for these canteens are known (all within $1/2$ inch of each other), it is likely that a number of different manufacturers were involved with their manufacture. Numerous examples are known, all painted dark blue-black, with vermilion "US" letters. A number of these canteens were overpainted with a second coat of dark paint and had the letters "MS," also in red, substituted for the "US."

Although much is known about the construction of these canteens, they remain one of the enigmas of nineteenth century accoutrements. The "US" letters suggest that they were made for the U.S. Army's Quartermaster Department, responsible for their procurement. The lettering, construction, and small leather strap retainers suggest early-nineteenth-century manufacture. Extensive reviews of the archival record of both correspondence and contracts has so far provided not one reference to their procurement or use by the regular army of the United States. Other accoutrements procured had a

"US" or "Public Property" on them, notably rifle flashes; these were clearly intended for state volunteer units, and that same explanation has been advanced for these canteens. Again, no documentation has surfaced that identifies their purchase and as being different from the stave-constructed canteen used by the regular army from 1812 until the 1840s. This is not a strongly constructed canteen, another argument against its being a regular army item. It has also been advanced that these canteens were made on speculation at the time of the Second Seminole War—hence the "US" letters—but enough stave-constructed and tin canteens were available that the army was not interested in them. They then may have been offered to the state of Massachusetts, which was very meticulous about marking state property, hence the "MS" letters. Possibly research in New England archives, particularly those of Massachusetts, will answer these questions. In the meantime, the cheesebox canteen will retain its mystery.

Private, 3rd U.S. Artillery Regiment, Spring 1836

The Second Seminole War erupted on December 28, 1835, when, faced with forcible removal from their homeland, Seminole warriors ambushed a mixed force of foot artillery and infantry troops under Maj. Francis Dade while on their march from Fort Brooke to Fort King in the Florida Territory. The 110 troops were wearing their overcoats over their accoutrement belts and were unable to get to their cartridges easily, thereby contributing to the loss of all but three men.

Until 1838 both regulars and volunteers from various states and territories served in the attempted subjugation of the Indians, but with little success. After that date, the war was principally conducted by detachments drawn from regular regiments in the U.S. Army, cooperating closely with mixed amphibious forces of sailors and Marines. Numerous, often futile, expeditions were conducted into the Florida wilderness of hummocks, bogs, and palmetto swamps in search of an elusive and talented foe—sapping the strength of men and challenging the talents of their officers. In 1841, however, Col. William J. Worth mounted the offensive during the summer—a season during which fever and dysentery was most prevalent, for which campaigning during that season was previously suspended. Destroying Seminole crops before the harvest in a "scorched earth" campaign, he succeeded in bringing about a closure to the drawn-out conflict, which officially ended by May 1842.

Although light field pieces were occasionally used during these operations, the men of the four regular artillery regiments fought mostly as infantry. A surgeon accompanying a fresh detachment as it marched into the Seminole lands "through a serpentine patch of the open pine-woods" noted the appearance of the men's "white cross-belts upon a ground of sky-blue—the colour of their fatigue uniforms—and black leathern caps glittering in the sun." The Florida terrain, a seeming Seminole ally, soon put an end to such martial spendor. Expeditions were often delayed for want of shoes and clothing, which "were torn to pieces by scrambling through the saw-palmetto," muck, and water. At the conclusion of the first campaign in May 1836, another observer described "a company drawn up, which could scarcely be distinguished by any uniform, except that of dirt, from the common militia; [although] their upright heads, and close touching elbows showed that they were regulars; their blue suits were bemired out of recollection, and their brightened belts were now all tarnished."

These two privates of the foot artillery are armed with model 1816 flintlock muskets and bayonets. Their winter fatigue uniforms of light blue kersey, trimmed with brass

buttons and yellow lace, are just beginning to show the wear of campaigning. Accoutrements consist of model 1828 cartridge boxes and bayonet scabbards, mounted on buff belting 2¹⁄₄ inches wide. After 1832 the foot artillerymen were issued brass-mounted "Roman" swords worn on buff waistbelts, although they usually left them behind while on campaign. Headgear is the collapsible or folding forage cap of leather, first adopted in 1833, which the troops wore while sleeping, "always buckled . . . under the chin . . . to keep out of our ears, ear-wigs, centipedes, cockroaches, etc."

1834 Pattern Officers' Uniform Cap and Epaulets, Lieutenant Edwin Rose, 3rd U.S. Artillery Regiment, 1833–37

A year following the release of the 1832 uniform regulations of the U.S. Army, patterns had been approved and contracts let for a new uniform cap for enlisted troops. Officers wore similar caps to the enlisted men but of better quality materials and trimmings. Described in 1834, artillery officers wore caps of

> . . . black beaver, seven and a half inches deep, with lackered sunk top seven and a half inches diameter, with a band of black patent leather to encircle the bottom of the cap; black patent leather peak, gilt eagle and cross cannons and number of regiment as at present worn; a strap of black patent leather, fastened to each side of the cap, to be worn under the chin. Plume-red cock-feather, falling from an upright stem, eight inches long, with a gilt socket.

The officers' model also differed in having a flat, horizontal "peak" or visor, rather than the enlisted cap's slightly convex, diagonally mounted visor. Unlike the rest of the 1832 uniform, which followed British military fashion, the cap's form was based on the French Army cavalry cap or shako. Although stylish in appearance, the cap was impractical and "much complained of . . . and with reason" by troops serving at western posts. It was but little worn, except for dress parade and guard mounts. This example belonged to Edwin Rose, who graduated from the U.S. Military Academy in 1830 and was commissioned as a second lieutenant in the 3rd U.S. Artillery Regiment. Rose was promoted to first lieutenant in August 1836, resigning in 1837. He later served during the Civil War as colonel of the 81st New York Volunteers during January–July 1862 and died in 1864.

Lieutenant Rose's epaulets are the pattern prescribed for artillery lieutenants in June 1832, with plain gold lace straps ending in a gold-plated metal crescent, from which hang a 2½-inch-long fringe of gold bullion fringe. Captains' epaulets were identical to lieutenants' epaulets, except that the bullion were of ¼ inch diameter, rather than the "smaller," ⅛-inch-diameter bullion worn by all lieutenants—there being no differentiation in form between junior and senior grade subalterns' epaulets. The regimental number on the strap is "silver embroidered where the bullion is gold" on both of Rose's epaulets, as appropriate for an artillery officer.

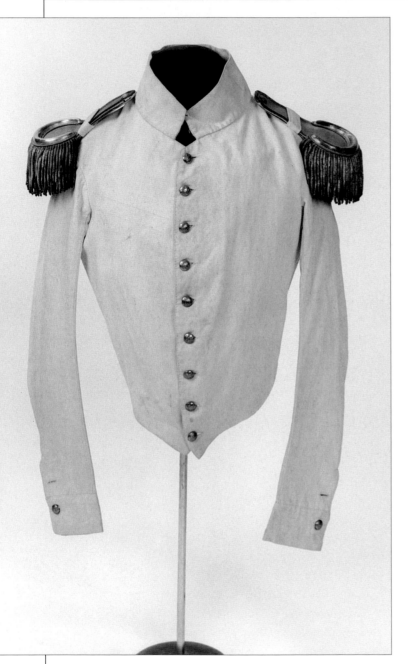

U.S. Infantry Officer's Shell Jacket, 1832–1840s

Although lightweight jackets for hot weather service had first been approved for issue to enlisted troops in the U.S. Army in 1802, it was not until thirty years later that such a practical garment was officially authorized for wear by commissioned officers. Such jackets had been worn by some army officers as a form of unofficial campaign or undress for decades. The 1832 uniform regulations stipulated that officers be provided with "Shell Jackts, to be worn in summer, during the extreme heat of the season," to be of "white cotton or linen, with standing collar, cuffs three and a half inches deep round the wrist, to open at the lower seam, where they will be buttoned with two small uniform buttons." The jacket was buttoned in front with ten small buttons (in contrast to nine buttons for enlisted men), and the front and rear of the jacket were to "come down in a peak." This style of jacket would remain in use virtually unchanged, with the exception of minor adjustments to the cut, through the Mexican War and until nearly the Civil War.

Although its wearer is now unknown, this infantry officer's shell jacket conforms almost perfectly to the 1832 regulations. Made of cotton and unlined, its long, exaggerated sleeves, cut to come down to the first knucklebone of the fingers, are characteristic of the style favored during the mid-1830s. The silver-plated buttons bear the device of an eagle and shield, with "I" superimposed for infantry officers. An unexpected and unusual feature of this jacket is that it is made to carry epaulets—normally worn with the dress uniform—rather than simpler embroidered shoulder straps were authorized for undress or fatigue duty. The epaulets are those authorized for a lieutenant, as the silver bullion fringe is smaller than that worn by captains or field-grade officers. Missing from the epaulets is the gold-embroidered regimental number, which was to be placed in the center of the crescent. Jackets of this form would be worn by officers serving in the summer months or on hot-weather stations and would have been typical wear during the Second Seminole War of 1835–36.

General Officer's Chapeau de Bras and Major General's Epaulets, 1830s–40s

Officially adopted during the War of 1812, the *chapeau de bras* was continued in the full dress uniform prescribed for U.S. Army general officers until it was finally dropped in the 1930s. During its more than 120 years of wear, it underwent a series of changes both in form and trimmings. This example conforms to the pattern first introduced in 1832, with its silk cockade surmounted by an elaborate, rather gaudy "loop," consisting of gilt braid ornamented with various trimmings of rays, buttons, horseshoes, silver eagle, and stars. Made of beaver felt, the hat in form appears to date to the early 1840s, being slightly smaller in overall size and with a pro-

nounced height and shape to its front and back fans. Similar though less elaborately trimmed *chapeau de bras* were to be worn by staff officers and field officers of the line when not serving with their troops.

The major general's epaulets that accompany this chapeau also show the continued evolution of military fashion. While the $^{1}/_{2}$-inch-diameter gold bullion fringe conforms to that prescribed for senior officers from 1832 to 1850, as do the small crescents and moillet-style stars of silver (two stars indicating a major general), the straps have a pronounced, rolled edging to the crescent that is rarely encountered until after 1851.

Lieutenant's Dress Coat and Epaulets, Corps of Engineers, 1845–51

Since 1802, the officers in the Corps of Engineers had been prescribed a uniform that included a dark blue, single-breasted coat with collar and cuffs of black velvet, and gilt buttons and trimmings. This selection was not arbitrary, as the color combination seems to have been a tradition long established for such scientific corps in many armies, including those of Great Britain, France, and Spain. Two devices, however, distinguished the American corps from their foreign counterparts: the placement of an embroidered star within a wreath on the coat's collar and the use of the gilt "Essayons" (a French phrase meaning "We Will Try") button. The button bore the device of "an eagle holding in his beak a scroll with the word 'Essayons,' a bastion with embrasure in the distance, surrounded by water, and a rising Sun." With the adoption of the U.S. Army uniform regulations of 1832, further distinctions were articulated, including a collar device of "gold embroidered wreath on each side near the front, of laurel and palm crossing each other at the bottom, encircling a star of gold embroidery" and the wearing of dark blue trousers during the cold months with 1 1/2-inch-wide black velvet stripes running down the outer seams.

With the publication of General Order No. 7 of February 18, 1840, specifications for engineer dress were now prescribed in depth, with further changes. New distinctions included a change from "plain skirts" to skirts with turnbacks of blue, united at the bottom of the coat by a similar wreath and star as on the collar, placed on a diamond-shaped piece of black velvet with gilt embroidered edging. The length of the cuff slashes and button placement conformed closely to the rank system used by the other corps, although instead of lace buttonholes, "against each button [was placed] united gold embroidered sprigs of palm and laurel."

This uniform has a cuff slash 3 inches long with two buttons, denoting that its wearer was a subaltern (first or second lieutenant). The gold epaulets bear within the crescent a silver castle, first prescribed in 1840 and increased in dimension in 1845; otherwise, they conform to those prescribed for a lieutenant of engineers in the

1839 uniform regulations. The epaulets are original to the coat, suggesting that the now-unknown officer wore this uniform sometime after 1845 and before 1851, when the army's uniforms were again changed with the publication of new regulations.

MARINE CORPORAL, 1847

The return to the blue-faced red uniform in 1839 was accompanied by a change in the fatigue uniform as well. Marine officers noticed that the sky blue kersey wool used by the army wore better than the gray and presented a smarter appearance. Consequently, in 1839, light blue kersey was adopted for fatigue dress and for the uniform trousers worn with the dark blue dress coat. The Marine enlisted uniform coat was almost identical to the army artillery coat except in its buttons and a slightly different weave to the yellow lace trim. With whitened buff leather belts, brass belt plates, black cartridge box, and bell-crown cap, the dress uniform was a showy outfit.

The fatigue uniform, by contrast, was almost devoid of ornamentation. Collar, cuffs, and shoulder straps were plain, and only the use of marine buttons identified the garment's service. Sergeants, however, wore jackets featuring two $^{1}/_{2}$-inch-wide half chevrons set into the front and back seams and trousers with a $1^{1}/_{2}$-inch-wide dark blue stripe in advance of the outer seam. The fatigue uniform for a corporal differed from the private's only in the use of a single half chevron on each sleeve. In 1849 a red welt was added to the edges of the dark blue trouser stripes.

Equipment followed the army patterns except that the cartridge box flap was plain, the shoulderbelt was oval and plain, and the waistbelt was rectangular and unadorned. Unlike the army, the Marine Corps continued to carry the bayonet from a shoulderbelt until the mid-1850s, and the only Marines who were provided musket slings and field equipment were those who accompanied General Scott's army in Mexico. The Marine Corps did not adopt the percussion system until the 1850s and were consequently still using flintlock muskets with brass picker and brush sets as a part of the uniform.

The marine fatigue cap was distinctive. Where the army cap was unstiffened and was normally trimmed with the company letter at best, the marine cap had a stiffened, almost Prussian-style crown and featured brass letters "USM" on the front. It is not clear in correspondence whether the letters were cursive or of the block form used by the army. An 1859 newspaper sketch, however, showed block letters, and that is how they are depicted here.

Uniform Coat of Lt. Mortimer Rosecrants, 5th U.S. Infantry Regiment, 1841–48

When Mortimer Rosecrants graduated from the U.S. Military Academy at West Point in June 1841, the army's uniforms were governed by the regulations of 1839 but were little changed from those first introduced in June 1832. At this time, the major general commanding the U.S. Army was Alexander Macomb, who demonstrated a strong predilection for English military cut and fashion. In fact, the head of the army's Clothing Bureau wrote to the inspector general, then on an official trip to Europe, to send home British uniforms and equipage, "for I perceive we have copied from the English in most of the [uniform] changes which have been made." Three cases of such British materials were shipped and presumably used as patterns for some of the new clothing then being made. President Andrew Jackson, who had no love for the British, "directed that the facings worn by the Revolutionary Army be restored" to the army of the democratic United States. Thus, the system of facing colors by branch of service was restored in dress uniforms and trimmings, with white or buff for general officers and staff, white for infantry, and red for artillery.

Newly commissioned 2nd Lt. Mortimer Rosecrants, therefore, found himself purchasing a coat with epaulets, among other uniform items, appropriate for an officer in the 5th U.S. Infantry Regiment. As an infantry officer, he wore a double-breasted coat of "dark blue cloth, lined with white serge; edged with white kerseymere . . . turnbacks and skirt lining of white kerseymere; skirt ornament [a] silver embroidered bugle; the [coat's] lace to be silver." To distinguish his rank as a subaltern officer in a company, Rosecrants's uniform had a slashed flap on the cuffs "three and a half inches long, with two loops and small buttons"—the higher the rank, the longer the flap and the more buttons and loops. Buttons were of convex, silvered brass with the raised device of an eagle with a shield on its breast, the shield bearing an infantry "I" upon it. The coat is heavily "wadded" at the breast with padding and cut tight in the sleeves and body, the wasp-waisted fashion then in vogue for gentlemen of fashion.

The rather plain epaulets are silver, in keeping with the infantry coat's prescribed button and lace metal and the underside is lined with white silk. The regimental number "5" is placed within the crescent of the epaulet in contrasting gold. Rosecrants's epaulets are a type known as "boxed;" that is, the silver bullion fringe is fixed in place around an inner frame. This form of epaulet was extremely popular during the 1830s and 1840s. Promoted to first lieutenant in July 1846, Rosecrants would continue wearing the same uniform and epaulets with his new rank—there being no differentiation in dress between the two grades. Breveted captain during the Mexican War on August 20, 1847, for gallant meritorious service at the Battles of Contreras and Churubusco, the young Rosecrants would die fourteen months later.

Model 1839 Forage Cap

Since 1833 the army had worn a collapsible leather model that the superintendent of the West Point Military Academy found "most unbecoming," although he believed it had "great merit on the score of economy and durability." Other officers clearly found fault with the leather cap and the numerous complaints concerning both its appearance and durability led the secretary of war in 1839 to approve adoption of a new form proposed by Maj. Gen. Alexander Macomb. Apparently based on the forage cap then commonly worn in the British Army, the new cloth cap had a round, flat crown of $10^1/_2$-inch diameter that tapered down 2 inches into a nearly perpendicular $2^1/_2$-inch-wide headband. It was finished with a $2^1/_2$-inch-wide, patent leather visor and a sliding chin strap of the same material that attached to the cap at the sides by small, brass "eagle and shield" general-service buttons. Made of dark blue, waterproofed broadcloth, it also had a cloth cape that attached around the rear of the cap from side button to side button, which could be let down in rainy or cold weather to protect the neck of its wearer. The blue cape was secured in front by black silk ribbon ties when folded up.

To distinguish the various branches of service, colored bands were to be worn around the cap's headband by noncommissioned officers and private soldiers, although this seems to have been implemented by only a minority of regiments and corps, judging from Mexican War photographs, artwork, and firsthand accounts.

The Company of Sappers, Miners, and Pontoniers wore black velvet bands with a brass castle device of the engineers in front, while red and white bands were worn, respectively, by a few artillery and infantry units. According to Theophilus Rodenbaugh of the 2nd Dragoons, "yellow worsted bands around the cap for ordinary noncommissioned officers and privates, and gold lace for the non-commissioned staff and first sergeants, were allowed and encouraged to distinguish the regiment from the First Dragoons." (A surviving cap worn by a member of the 2nd Dragoons still retains its original band of $1^1/_2$-inch-wide yellow worsted tape.) More common was the use of brass letters designating company affiliation, such as the "A" on this Schuykill Arsenal cap, marked inside with three dots to indicate that it is a Size 3. Stylish and popular, the model 1839 forage cap continued in service with only minor modifications well into the 1850s.

Trooper, 1st Regiment of U.S. Dragoons, 1846–47

Without regular cavalry for almost two decades, the U.S. Army was authorized to raise a regiment of dragoons in 1833. Critical to policing the overland trade and migration routes of the western territories, it comprised the backbone of Col. Stephen Watts Kearney's Army of the West, which marched from Fort Leavenworth to take New Mexico without bloodshed during the early days of the Mexican War. Kearney later pushed on to California with 100 mule-mounted dragoons, reaching San Diego on December 12, 1846. From New Mexico, part of the regiment proceeded into Mexico to join General Taylor's force, fighting at Buena Vista before linking up with Scott's army for the Mexico City campaign, where they charged with *élan* at the Battle of Churubusco.

The winter field uniform of the 1st Dragoons had changed little since 1833. It consisted of a dark-blue cloth jacket with a "stand up collar, trimmed with yellow worsted binding . . . single breasted, one row of buttons in front." The collar had two bound buttonholes and was framed all around with the same $3/8$-inch wide binding, as were the shoulder-straps and edges of the jacket body; the same yellow worsted tape was applied as piping to the back of the jacket's side seams. The jacket had two welted pockets set below the breast, one on each side. Trousers were of a light-blue mixture kersey trimmed with $3/4$-inch yellow binding "up each outward seam," placed "in advance of the seam." Sergeants had two similar stripes, with a $1/4$-inch spacing between the stripes. Laced ankle boots with spurs were worn underneath, with the trouser cuffs set snugly over by means of straps passing under the instep of the boot. Model 1839 forage caps were worn, with a brass company letter attached in front. The official specifications also provided for yellow bands around the crown for the dragoons, but this was not practiced in the 1st Dragoons. Instead, it remained a regimental distinction of the 2nd Dragoons through the war. A double-breasted greatcoat of light or sky blue kersey was provided, with a deep cape "to reach down to the cuff of the coat and to button all the way up." When not in use, it was rolled and strapped to the pommel of the saddle, as seen here.

This well-armed dragoon of Company B balances the butt of his model 1843 Hall carbine on his Ringgold saddle. It is attached to the trooper's buff leather shoulder sling by clipping the "swivel and hook" of the sling to the carbine's ringbar; normally, its nose would be inserted into the carbine bucket attached to the saddle just before the right stirrup to both relieve strain on the trooper's shoulder and to prevent the arm from swinging wildly about while riding. The Hall carbine was a breechloading arm with a percussion priming system. Although against regulations, its lock or breechlock could be removed and used as a pocket pistol, a fact not lost on at least one gallant dragoon who, "armed with a Bowie Knife and the chamber of my Hall's Carbine, visited the Fandangos and gambling rooms, danced, gambled, drank wine and Muscla, made love to the Senoritas and . . . staggered into camp at reveille."

In addition to this versatile weapon, he has a model 1840 "Wristbreaker" saber attached to his buff leather waistbelt, on which is also carried his carbine cartridge box (behind) and the leather percussion cap pouch, which came into use during the war. His saddle, bridle, and horse equipage are of the Ringgold patent of 1844, fitted with a cloth-covered valise, leather pistol holsters, a carbine bucket, and other fittings made in accordance with 1841 army specifications. In his holsters would be carried one or more model 1842 single-shot percussion pistols, although some members of the 1st did receive the repeating Colt "Walker" pistols before the close of the Mexican War.

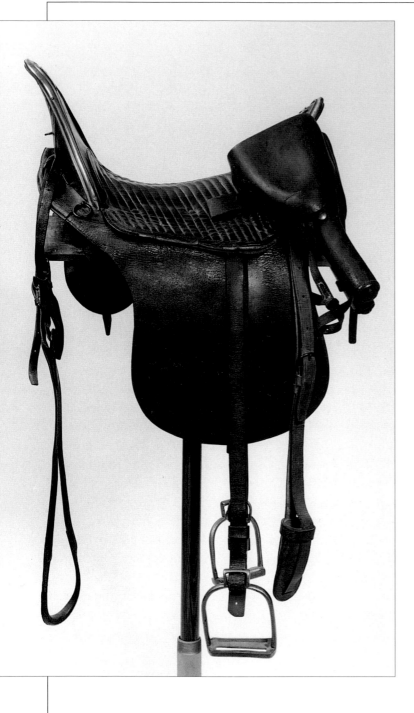

The Grimsley Dragoon Saddle of 1847

Thornton Grimsley of St. Louis, Missouri, received his first contracts from the U.S. government for dragoon saddles in 1846, and the pattern was adopted officially by the army on December 2, 1847. A review board of officers considered Mr. Grimsley's saddle, which was based on a French Hussar pattern, to be superior to any other at that time. Actually, Grimsley saddles were in use well before official recognition, as many had been privately purchased by officers and volunteers directly from the factory. In September 1846, Grimsley's saddles were being made for a company of the 1st Dragoons and being recommended for the Regiment of Mounted Rifles. One satisfied officer wrote in 1847, "I have used his saddle in the service, and consider it much superior to any we have ever used in our service."

The saddle itself was constructed of a wooden tree covered with rawhide with a high pommel and cantle. It was trimmed with a quilted leather seat and brass molding around the edges of the tree. Stirrups were of cast brass with a slotted bottom. Officers' saddles featured a more decorative molding and quilted seat. Personal belongings were carried in a cloth-covered leather valise strapped to the cantle, well off the horse's back, while the sky-blue overcoat was rolled across the pommel. The carbine was attached to a sling over the trooper's shoulder and the muzzle was inserted into a leather carbine boot slung from the saddle. Percussion pistols were mounted in leather holsters across the pommel.

Although this saddle was officially replaced by the McClellan pattern in 1859, it saw heavy use in the Civil War, especially among volunteer cavalry in the Western theater. Some Federal units still had these saddles at the Battle of Gettysburg in 1863. A favorite of many old regular army officers, the Grimsley pattern remained popular among numerous high-ranking generals, including Ulysses S. Grant.

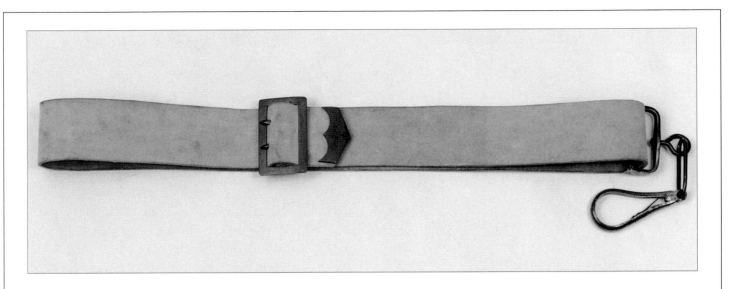

Pattern of 1839 U.S. Carbine Sling

The carbine sling has always been an indispensable part of a light horseman's equipage. When firing from the saddle, the horseman could drop the carbine if he needed to resort to pistol or saber in closer combat, and the sling would prevent it from falling to the ground. It also provided a means of slinging the carbine over the back and out of the way when dismounted.

The first official carbine sling adopted by the U.S. Army in 1835 was a simple affair of narrow black leather with a brass, horseshoe-shaped buckle for adjustment. Iron sling swivels appear to have been adopted a year or so later. In 1839 a much more robust pattern of white buff leather was adopted. It was first described in the ordnance manual of 1841: "CARBINE SLING, buff leather, length 56 in., width 2.5in.-1 buckle and tip, brass-swivel and D with roller, iron, bright, 2.62in. Wide-link and hook, iron guard-spring steel."

These slings were used by the U.S. Dragoons during and well after the Mexican War. After 1851 the sling color was changed to black, and during the Civil War slings had a brass tip that was wider and riveted to the belt. The addition of three copper rivets provided further strength to the stitching fastening the brass frame buckle to the belt. The iron swivel and snap hook remained basically the same.

During the Civil War, the 1st District of Columbia Cavalry was issued long, black leather boots for their Henry rifles that fastened directly to the saddle using the carbine sling swivel and snap hook. This change began the trend toward the carbine boot and the gradual obsolescence of the sling. In the latter part of the nineteenth century, rifles and carbines were usually carried in a boot attached to the saddle, and the over-the-shoulder sling was relegated to the realm of antique military curiosities.

Private, Company of Sappers, Miners, and Pontoniers, U.S. Army Corps of Engineers, 1846–47

From 1821 until 1846 there were no enlisted troops in the Corps of Engineers, although the need for such had been argued in vain by the chief of engineers. Finally, he succeeded in gaining approval to send a qualified engineer officer—with permission of the French government—to the French school for engineer officers at Metz, "for the purpose of having in the U.S. Army, an officer qualified to instruct and command a company of engineer soldiers in case Congress could be induced to authorize the enlistment of such a company." Capt. Alexander J. Swift was selected for this important assignment, after which he was stationed at West Point awaiting the passage of the Congressional Act authorizing such enlisted troops. The act was passed on May 15, 1846, which provided for a "company of sappers, miners, and pontoniers, to be called engineer soldiers; which company shall be composed of ten sergeants, or master workmen, ten corporals, overseers, two musicians, thirty-nine privates of the first class, or artificers, and thirty-nine privates of the second class, or laborers; in all one hundred men." The men were to receive better pay than those of their respective ranks in the line of the army, as befitting their position as technical specialists, assisting engineer officers in overseeing the construction of field fortifications, bridging operations, road construction, surveying, and reconnaissance.

Captain Swift was given overall command of the company, seconded by 1st Lt. Gustavus W. Smith. At Smith's suggestion, "Brevet Second Lieutenant George B. McClellan, who had just been graduated from the Military Academy, was assigned as junior officer of the company." The recruits "with two exceptions . . . were native born, and all but four of them were raw recruits." Three of the four veterans "were promptly made sergeants, and the fourth was a musician [bugler]." Swift managed the recruiting and gathering of proper engineer equipment, while Smith and McClellan supervised "the instruction of the company as an infantry command." Sailing from New York with seventy-one rank and file on September 26, 1846, the company was stationed on the Rio Grande that fall, where many men fell sick, including Captain Swift, who would die in early 1847. For the remainder of the Mexican War, Lieutenant Smith would command the small company.

Nicknamed "the pick and shovel brigade," the engineer soldiers were advised by officers to ignore the slur, and "endeavor to become *model* infantry, and engraft on that a fair knowledge of the duties of the engineer soldier." When they joined Gen. Zachary Taylor's army at Victoria in January 1874, the men of the company soon were able to reverse the joke, for, when the time came for heavy work, details were drawn from the line of the army "under the control of engineer officers, assisted by trained engineer soldiers." Marching 350 miles to Tampico and sailing from there to Vera Cruz, they joined Gen. Winfield Scott's army in the ongoing siege, where they destroyed the underground water aqueduct of the city, reconnoitered enemy works, and sited American batteries and siegeworks. At the Battle of Cerro Gordo, the men were finally able to prove their fighting abilities, when Smith and "his company of Sappers and Miners, joined Colonel Harney's command in the assault on the enemy's main work, and killed two men with his own hand." From that point on, the company marched in the vanguard of the advance division of the army and fought at Contreras and Churubusco, where "nothing seemed to them too bold to be undertaken, or too difficult to be executed." The engineer company's crowning achievement would take place during the capture of Mexico City. In the September 15 assault on the heavily fortified San Cosme Gateway, Smith recommended a method of attack that he believed would save lives. With approval from General Worth, Smith took his company and some supporting infantry and "broke through the walls from house to house" with pick-axes, crowbars, and axes until they reached the rooftop command of the Mexican battery and support, which they then enfiladed with "very deadly" musket fire, helping bring about the retreat of the enemy in whose pursuit they joined.

One week after the authorization of the Company of Sappers, Miners, and Pontoniers, their proposed uniform was submitted by the chief of engineers and approved by the secretary of war. For field service it consisted of a "Shell jacket —dark blue, with . . . a pocket for percussion caps covered by a flap on the right-side, in other respects to conform to the Artillery pattern," with the exception of the collar, which was to be of "black cotton velvet, with a single button and loop on each side $3^1/8$ inches long, of $1^1/8$ inch yellow worsted lace allowing the black facing to show through" and edged around with a narrow welt of scarlet. With this smart brass-buttoned jacket was worn light-blue mixture trousers trimmed with a black welt on the outseam. Headgear was the model 1839 forage cap of dark blue, with a band of black velvet upon which was placed the brass castle device of the Engineers. Made up at Schuykill Arsenal, this uniform was worn by the men throughout the war until the fall of Mexico City. During the city's occupation in late 1847, the quartermaster of the army was unable to provide the men with new engineer uniforms. "At their request," Smith "authorized them to purchase a better quality of cloth than that furnished by the government, and to have finer material for trimmings than the coarse cotton braid allowed by the regulations." The "handsome, well-fitting uniforms" were paid for by the men and made by "good" Mexican tailors.

That winter, the company also drew new firearms and accoutrements—the short model 1847 "Sapper's Musketoon," with its sword bayonet and sheath suspended from a buff leather waistbelt with a two-piece interlocking brass clasp. The company, which had been one of the first units in the regular army to receive percussion muskets, now turned in the model 1842 smoothbore muskets and bayonets with which they had fought during the war as well as their model 1839 infantry waistbelts and frogs. Percussion cap pouches of leather were also issued, thereby rendering obsolete the special pocket incorporated in the design of the original engineer jackets. Knapsacks, haversacks, and canteens were the standard forms issued to the infantry, and overcoats were to be the same as the foot artillery and infantry, trimmed with large, stamped-brass Engineer buttons.

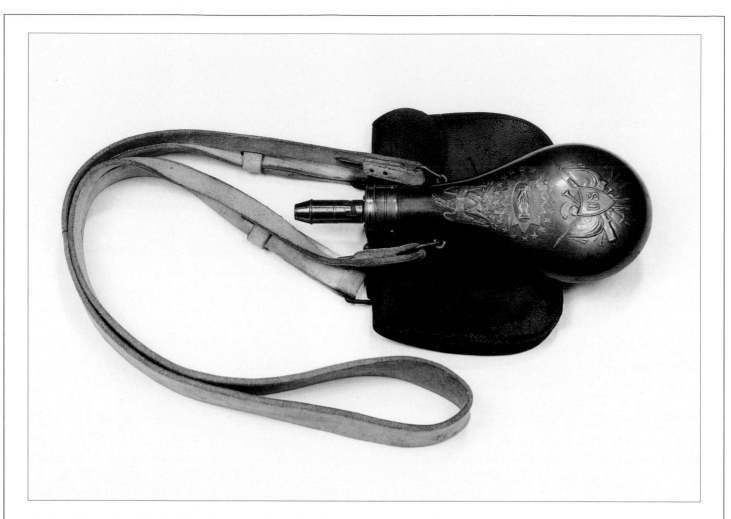

Model of 1839 Rifleman's Flask and Pouch Set

Incorporating improvements suggested by Maj. Rufus Baker of the Allegheny Arsenal in 1837, this is an example of the "new pattern" rifleman's flask and pouch set described to a limited degree in the Ordnance Department *Regulations* of 1838 and more completely in the *Manual* of 1841. The belt differed from its predecessors in the way the overall length of the set was established. The single oval brass belt plate on the belt was omitted in favor of individual brass hooks on each of the four ends of the belt. This necessitated japanned iron loops being sewn on the pouch for two of the ends, rather than the ends being sewn directly on the pouch itself, and wider loops (changing from round to triangular in shape) being put on the flasks as well. The belt remained 1¹/₂ inches wide and made of whitened buff leather until 1851, when it was blackened. Except for the iron loops already mentioned, the ball pouch remained the same, of black harness leather with two compartments inside. A bellowslike construction allowed considerable expansion of the pouch. A variety of powder flasks

were used as part of this set. This example was made by Batty, who supplied a slightly changed version of the Ames "peace" flask from 1847 through 1858.

An interesting aspect of riflemen's flask and pouch sets is that very few were ever used by the regular army. Indeed, the army had no rifle units from 1821 until 1842, when the Regiment of Mounted Riflemen was formed. All of the payment vouchers located to date for these sets indicate that the expense was to be charged to "Arming and Equipping the Militia." Contemporary illustrations confirm the fact that the overwhelming majority of these sets were used by state volunteer units. Regular army rifle units used a smaller cartridge box, with a single five-compartment tin, which was also adopted in 1839. After the addition of an implement pouch, it was used interchangeably by both mounted and rifle units. With the adoption of the elongated minié ball in the mid-1850s, the flask and pouch set was relegated to ceremonial use.

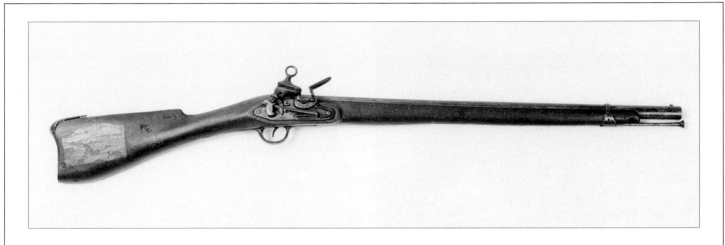

Mexican Cavalry Carbine, c. 1790–1847

This unmarked Mexican carbine was taken at the Battle of Churubusco and presented to Capt. John Jackson, according to the label pasted on the stock. John Henry Jackson was a lieutenant in the 9th U.S. Infantry in April 1847, promoted to captain on August 20 for gallantry and meritorious conduct at the Battles of Contreras and Churubusco. He was honorably discharged from the army on August 26, 1848, and later served as colonel of the 3rd New Hampshire Regiment during the Civil War.

The carbine presented to Captain Jackson was not of a particular Mexican model. Mexico had no arms manufactories and depended on imports, especially from Great Britain. This weapon, however, bears a marked influence from late-eighteenth-century Spanish Army carbines, although it does not conform exactly to any Spanish Army models. The Spanish regulation carbines, for instance, the model 1789, had two brass barrel bands, one in the middle and one near the muzzle. This Mexican carbine has only one near the muzzle. It also has, like its Spanish counterpart, the distinctive and very sturdy *miguelet* lock, the short barrel, and somewhat similar brass trigger guard and butt plate. The wooden stock itself appears to have been made fairly crudely in Mexico and the metal parts fitted on. The locks, barrels, and other vital parts would have been imported from Spain and assembled by Mexican gunsmiths, possibly for issue to frontier cavalry units or mounted militias, which needed, most of all, solid and dependable weapons that were almost indestructible. This carbine certainly had those qualities and was perhaps in service for half a century before its 1847 capture at Churubusco. It may have been crudely made, but it was a sturdy weapon to be reckoned with in the hands of a skilled cavalryman. And many of the Mexican cavalrymen were daring horsemen and excellent shots.

PRIVATE, GRENADIER COMPANY, 5TH OR *GUERRERO* REGIMENT, *PERMANENTE* INFANTRY, 1836

Characterized in the lore and pulp history of the Texas Revolution as a bloodthirsty barbarian or a base coward, the common Mexican soldier has, until recently, received little sympathetic treatment north of the border. The Mexican Army of 1835 consisted of two types of troops under the direct control of the Federal government: the regular army (*Ejercito Permanente*) and the provincial or territorial militia (*Militia Activa*). The *Militia Activa,* originally intended as a reserve or national guard force, had been on active duty for some years (due to revolts in various provinces) and could be considered nearly the equal of the *Permanente* troops when armed conflict first broke out in Texas in 1835.

The majority of the Mexican Army consisted of foot troops, mostly drawn from the Indian peasantry. Ideally, the infantry was issued a full complement of clothing and equipment in two allotments during its eight-year term of enlistment. This consisted, at least on paper, of a red-faced blue coat and matching trousers of blue or gray cloth, with white cotton duck used for summer. Also issued were cotton jackets, a leather shako, linen or cotton shirts, shoes or sandals, an overcoat, a blanket, and a cloth barracks or forage cap.

The most common "dress which the Mexican infantry and artillery troops of that day wore . . . was their fatigue suit, consisting of white cotton round jackets & trousers," according to one Texan eyewitness. The cotton duck jackets had small red cuffs and collars and were frequently worn in hot weather or tropical zones as a substitute for the heavier woolen uniforms. The jackets were cheap and easy to mass-produce, and most of the recruits for the standing regiments, as well as newly raised levies, were dressed in such garb. The leather shako or cap was made in the French style, wider at the top, trimmed with a brass frontplate and chinstrap scales, cotton cords and tassels, and a stamped metal cockade and worsted pompon, both colored in the Mexican national tricolor of green, white, and red. The black cap "often had drawn over it, a close fitting white cloth cover," to protect the cap and its trimmings from rain and dust, as well as to reflect the sun's rays, although the troops frequently wore some of the distinctive trimmings over the cover for show.

This private of the 5th, *Guerrero,* Regiment is dressed as he would have appeared at the Battle of San Jacinto on April 21, 1836. He wears a cotton cap cover over his shako, and his cotton jacket is trimmed with red worsted epaulets that signify his status as a member of the grenadier company. Following Mexican custom, his trousers are supported by a red sash wrapped around his waist and knotted behind, rather than the Anglo practice of using suspenders. Sandals are worn rather than shoes—practical footwear for a rainy spring campaign, especially for one whose feet are well inured to walking barefoot over rough terrain. His crossbelts are of blackened leather, commonly used in lieu of the more expensive, regulation buffed hide, and the cartridge box is copied from that used in the British Army. The regimental crossbelt plate of brass has a "G" cast into it; at least two examples of this *Guerrero* plate have been excavated from the San Jacinto battlefield site.

The infantry was generally armed with British-made muskets of the Short Land or India Pattern, although earlier Spanish models such as this model 1791, with its characteristic miguelet lock, were still employed. In fact, a Texan officer noted that most of the arms captured at San Jacinto were "old and useless" Spanish muskets, and the troops so armed preferred defending themselves with their bayonets on brass-mounted hangers, rather than risk having their own muskets explode in their faces when fired. This *soldado* carries a brass-hilted Spanish model 1816 hanger or short saber, copied from a form carried by French Napoleonic troops. A simple water gourd provides a cheap and readily available alternative to a canteen.

Mexican Staff Officer's Sword, c. 1825–50

The eagle's head pommel on this sword might surprise some, as it is an insignia strongly associated with American or French Napoleonic weapons, but it was, and still is, very Mexican. The eagle, perched on a cactus bush fighting a snake, is the national insignia of Mexico and appears at the center of the national flag. In addition to the eagle's head forming the pommel of this sword, the full Mexican eagle is shown on the sword's counterguard. Above the eagle, a French-style "Liberty Cap" at the center of rays is shown, a republican insignia adopted following the fall of Mexican emperor Augustin Iturbide in 1823. The small oval in the center of the knuckle bow appears to show the figure of an ancient Greek or Roman soldier and does not seem to represent the badge of a particular corps. The hilt is made of brass, and the grip of mother of pearl. The blade is straight with floral emblems etched, and the scabbard is of steel.

The general style of the sword is French, although this particular example could have been made in the United States or Europe. From the time of Napoleon up to the 1870s, the styles in vogue for swords and uniforms were predominantly French, and Mexico was no exception in this trend. As early as the 1820s, portraits of generals and staff officers of the Mexican Army show them wearing the generic type of sword illustrated, as indeed would some of their American opponents, with American insignias and perhaps even the same eagle's heads during the Mexican War.

Mexican Army Corps of Engineers, Coat Badge, 1847

This item, according to a note that came with it, was "cut from the coat of a dead Mexican at the battlefield of Buena Vista by Maj. J.C. Pattridge, P Master U.S. Army about three months subsequent to the battle of 22d July 1847." There was indeed a Joseph C. Pattridge of New York who was commissioned an additional paymaster on March 3, 1847, and discharged honorably on March 4, 1849, and there is little doubt that he was the souvenir hunter on the battlefield of Buena Vista.

The Mexican units at the battle of Buena Vista consisted of the Light Horse Regiment, the Jalisco Lancers, the 4th Regiment of Cavalry, and the Puebla Light Horse Squadron. A few men detached from service corps, such as the engineers, also would have been attached to the staff. This must have been the case, as the badge is that of the Mexican Corps of Engineers. The badge shows a flaming bomb under which are laid crossed pick and shovel and other insignias.

The Mexican Corps of Engineers had about 50 officers and a battalion of sappers of some 600 enlisted men. Officers and men were detached in small groups all over

Mexico. In addition, the corps was responsible for the Mexican Military Academy at Chapultepec Castle, near Mexico City. The uniform of the corps consisted of a dark blue coat with black collar and lapels; crimson red cuffs; dark blue cuff flaps; crimson red turnbacks and crimson red piping edging the collar, cuff, and pocket flaps; yellow lace on the cuffs; brass buttons; medium blue trousers with a crimson red stripe on each side; and black felt shako with brass plate and crimson red pompon. The officers had gold buttons, epaulets, and lace. The badge of the corps, embroidered in gold or yellow, was worn on the upper left sleeve of the uniform coat. This is illustrated in a portrait of nineteen-year-old Lt. Julian de Bavara, one of the "heroic children" who died fighting the Americans storming their military school at Chapultepec Castle. The other cadets who perished were younger and to this day at Chapultepec, sentinels in full dress stand guard around the clock at the castle to commemorate the heroic stand. The example illustrated is completely faded after three months' exposure on the battlefield of Buena Vista.

The Civil War
1861–1865

THE DOMINANT UNIFORMS, EQUIPMENT, AND FIRE-arms in both the Union and Confederate Armies during the American Civil War were for the most part conceived and developed in the decade prior to the war itself. That much of this equipage would have a distinctive European flavor was most certainly predetermined by world events. Since 1854 the generation that would constitute the armies had been indoctrinated by newspaper articles and books detailing the glory and adventure of the Crimean War. At the same time color lithographic prints showed the various armies in action with dashing uniforms and flags flying. American military observers, most notably Capt. George B. McClellan of the 1st Cavalry Regiment, were sent to Europe to report on the belligerent armies. All manner of technical data was gleaned by these military professionals, much of which was to influence equipment and uniform changes being contemplated by the U.S. Army.

It is likely that no aspect of European military splendor captured the American imagination more than the exotic French Zouave regiments. Comprised of some of the best soldiers that the French Army had to offer, the several regiments of Zouaves, before going to the Crimea, served in the French African colonies. They had adopted a uniform with a distinctive Middle Eastern flavor, and they were known for their bravery and skill in battle. Captain McClellan's report of his observations noted, "they are, what their appearance would indicate, the most reckless, self-reliant and complete infantry that Europe can produce." Within a few years Captain McClellan, now General McClellan, would have under his command several regiments of American-style Zouaves as his army advanced toward the Confederate capital of Richmond, Virginia.

The changes taking place in the U.S. Army uniform prior to the Civil War came as a result of decisions finalized in 1858. One of the most familiar results was the adoption of the French-style fatigue cap. This cap, with its sloping crown, would soon become symbolic of the Civil War soldier. Other less noticeable changes included the knapsack, the style of dismounted soldiers' dress coat, and a totally new pattern of canteen. After the Civil War began, the immediate needs of soldiers in the field brought other items of European influence into the army. The use of leggings for troops on the march and the adoption of the "pup" tent are two taken directly from the French. The Union Army even went so far as to purchase 10,000 complete French uniforms in a less than totally successful attempt to outfit several regiments of volunteers. Not to be outdone, the regulations adopted by the Army of the Confederate States called for a uniform that was strongly influenced by the Austrian Army. The use of sleeve braid to indicate rank of Confederate officers, which is evident in countless photographs, is a case in point.

As the Civil War ran its course, the uniforms of both armies would undergo changes dictated by both experience and necessity. By the closing year of the war, the Confederate soldier would largely be uniformed in a short, close-fitting jacket. His counterpart in the Union Army would most often choose to wear the looser fitting fatigue blouse but, contrary to common belief, some Union regiments would continue to take the field in the Zouave uniform until the final days of the conflict.

All of this is illustrated in the pages that follow, along with the story of the advances in weaponry seen in the Civil War, which came not from Europe but from the minds of innovative Americans. By 1865 Americans no longer needed to look across the ocean for military tradition or pageantry. Four years of war had established all that was necessary to last for generations to come.

8TH COMPANY, 7TH NEW YORK STATE MILITIA, 1861

The 7th Regiment New York State Militia was one of the finest regiments of its type in the entire country prior to the Civil War. Finely outfitted and armed with the best weapons, they were the ideal against which any other militia regiment could be judged. The 7th was organized and headquartered in New York City, and its ranks were filled with young men from some of the city's finest families. They frequently paraded in the city, where their expertise at drill was evident to all who saw them. When the war broke out in April 1861, the 7th New York immediately sprang to answer the call. On April 19 the regiment turned out 1,000 strong and marched down Broadway, headed to the nation's capital and to a war that was sure to be over soon. The 7th was one of the first regiments to reach Washington and was at the time widely credited with saving the city from Southern takeover.

The regiment was mustered into Federal service April 26 and remained in the city and in neighboring Arlington, Virginia, until ordered back to New York at the end of May, where it was released from Federal service. The 7th remained in its home city for the entire war, leaving only twice—once in 1862 and once in 1863—for brief duty in Maryland. Although this type of service may seem strange with a nation engaged in a war that most knew would determine its future, the security of the city was of paramount importance, and the regiment provided that. The skill and military knowledge gained by the men who served with the 7th was not wasted. Many of those who had spent long hours learning to be parade-ground soldiers used their expertise by serving in other New York regiments.

The uniform worn by the 7th New York State Militia was tailor-made of gray wool trimmed in black. Belts and straps were white leather. The knapsack worn by the soldier pictured here is the frame type, which was popular in the era prior to the Civil War. His firearm is the model 1855 rifle musket, which was the best military arm issued by the Federal government at the time. On a yearly basis, each state would receive a proportionate share of arms manufactured at the Federal arsenals. As a general rule, those coming from the Harpers Ferry facility were reserved for the various state militias. The few that came to each state were usually issued only to the very best regiments or those with the most political pull. The 7th New York would qualify on both accounts.

An Overcoat for a Volunteer of 1861

The necessity to clothe and equip the thousands of volunteer soldiers who answered the call created a crisis of unheard-of proportions for the U.S. Army Quartermaster's Department. Prior to the outbreak of war, one woolen mill, the Utica Steam Woolen Company of Utica, New York, was able to supply nearly all the woolen cloth needed by the army to make uniforms. Suddenly, with a need hundreds of times greater, it was necessary to call upon nearly every mill in the North to convert to the production of woolen cloth for the army. But even this was not enough. As the first winter of the war approached, tales of troops with little or no protective clothing began to pour in. At the same time, new regiments continued to be mustered into Federal service. To even begin to meet the demand, the quartermasters were forced to accept uniform items in colors and material that would have been unacceptable a few months before.

This overcoat is an excellent example of early-war emergency production. Made of gray felt rather than the sky blue kersey wool that was regulation, and with a red lined body, the coat violates nearly every standard. As the army was gradually able to get matters under control, items such as this would be placed in storage. Many would be issued to Confederate prisoners. That this coat was never issued is evident by the paper tag still affixed, giving its size as "1," or small. It is likely that this is the exact type of garment that prompted the following letter from the 18th U.S. (Regular) Infantry.

> *Camp Thomas*
> *Headquarters 18th Regt. U. S. Infantry*
> *Columbus, Ohio Dec. 10th 1861*
> *Col. G. H. Crosman, Q.M. Genl.*
>
> *Sir,*
>
> *The invoice of overcoats just received for this Regiment named these as "Gray" which is not the uniform of the Army and differs from those which one thousand of our men are now wearing.*
> *I beg most earnestly to represent that to use these overcoats will draw an invidious destination between the 18th and other Regiments—create dissatisfaction and seriously interfere with our recruiting by perpetually injurious comparisons between us and volunteers.*

> *I shall be greatly obliged if you will promptly furnish regulation blue overcoats and order the Regimental Q.M. to turn over the "Gray" to Capt. Myers who can easily find use for them. I respectfully request your immediate attention to this matter. Our men are suffering but I am not willing for the saving of a few days to furnish clothing so seriously objectionable.*
>
> *Very respectfully,*
> *Wm. A. Stokes*
> *Maj. 18th U.S. Inf.*

One of the unexplained army policies that continued throughout much of the war, but was particularly prevalent for the first two years, was the sending of odd or substandard items to the western armies. The practice was condoned from the highest levels, as attested to by the following instructions from Colonel Crosman, commanding officer at the Philadelphia Depot, in response to an order received from the quartermaster general:

> *2 Jan. 1862*
>
> *Pack and send to Maj. Allen, Q.M. St. Louis all the made up irregular clothing on hand and which may be delivered to you (except overcoats for mounted men). Irregular clothing means all black, or blue, or grays . . . and other woolen fabrics not regulation standard goods. Have this done immediately.*

An 1861 Forage Cap

One problem frequently encountered in the early months of the war was the receipt of poorly made garments from untried civilian contractors. Although most of those who received contracts from the army were honest, there were those who simply saw the chance to make a quick buck. One of the most common methods of cheating the government was the use of the much cheaper logwood dye instead of indigo dye for the dark blue uniform material.

Capt. George W. Lee, the assistant quartermaster in Detroit, wrote the following to Col. George H. Crosman, quartermaster at the main U.S. clothing depot in Philadelphia on September 24, 1862:

Colonel:

I am repeatedly called upon by officers in relation to the inferior quality of the caps furnished as regards quality and color the cloth seems in many of them to be of a very inferior quality being what the men call rotten. They come to pieces very soon and the color of a portion is only that known as Logwood or material which when exposed to rain and sun turns a dingy reddish brown.

The cap illustrated here was issued to and worn by Edward N. Whittier of the 1st Rhode Island Infantry at the First Battle of Bull Run. Originally dark blue, it has turned a rust color, which indicates the use of logwood dye. Whittier went on to a distinguished career commanding the 5th Maine Battery at Gettysburg and later winning the Medal of Honor. His cap's career ended after its first battle.

Rain Hat of a Southern Soldier

In the decade preceding the Civil War, the manufacture of rubber or rubber-coated cloth, based on Charles Goodyear's 1844 patent of a process to vulcanize rubber, was becoming a major industry. The army experimented with rubber buckets, inflatable pontoons, canteens, and even wagon springs, most of which were tried and abandoned as unsuitable. Prior to the Civil War, the 1st and 2nd U.S. Dragoons and the 1st Mounted Rifles were issued raincoats called *talmas,* made of rubber-coated linen. Just as hostilities began, however, it was decided that rubber-coated cloth ponchos or blankets would better suit the soldier in wet weather. At the same time, in the civilian market, rubber rain wear was rapidly becoming popular. It is certainly not surprising that a volunteer soldier leaving for service in the field, perhaps a member of one of the many elite militia companies, would outfit himself with gear designed to keep him dry and comfortable.

This rain hat marked "India Rubber Co." was found by a Union soldier on the battlefield of Corinth, Mississippi, in May 1862. It can be imagined that the finder considered himself fortunate. The fate of the original owner is not known, but chances are good that he no longer had any need of it.

PRIVATE, COMPANY I, 4TH VIRGINIA INFANTRY, CSA, "THE LIBERTY HALL VOLUNTEERS"

Civil War regiments, and the various companies that composed them, tended to be made up of men from the same general geographic area. Within early-war regiments, such as the 4th Virginia Infantry, the companies often bore names that told something of their origin, such as the 4th Virginia's Company C, the "Pulaski Guards," from Pulaski County, Virginia. Another company of the regiment took the process a step further by calling attention to a common heritage. The original company was comprised primarily of students from Virginia's Washington University, which from 1776 to 1798 was known as Liberty Hall Academy. With obvious pride in their school, the young men who volunteered for the great adventure did so as "The Liberty Hall Volunteers."

Before the end of the academic year, the company they formed had been receiving military training from cadets of neighboring Virginia Military Institute. By the time they were mustered into the 4th Virginia as Company I, on June 2, 1861, to serve for a period of one year, the men of Washington College were considered a well-drilled command, at least by 1861 standards. The young men learned quickly that war was serious business and that cannonballs and bullets had no respect for academic achievement. At First Manassas, the men from Liberty Hall saw six of their number killed and several wounded.

The Liberty Hall Volunteer shown here is dressed as his company appeared on the field at Manassas in July 1851. His uniform consists of a "battle shirt" instead of a jacket, accoutrements that were described as "old and indifferent," and a .69-caliber smoothbore musket altered from flintlock to percussion. When originally fitted, the company had no bayonet scabbards and no cap boxes, both of which were privately obtained and paid for by the company commander, Capt. James J. White.

By April 14, 1862, the company began to lose much of its academic flavor. On that date it was reorganized for the duration of the war, with the addition of forty-nine men from the militia and eleven transfers from other units. The 4th Virginia would serve with the Army of Northern Virginia until the end of the war. Along with the 2nd, 5th, 27th, and 33rd Virginia Regiments, they made up the famous Stonewall Brigade, a fact that the veterans of the Liberty Hall Volunteers most certainly boasted of in years to come.

DAVID RANKIN

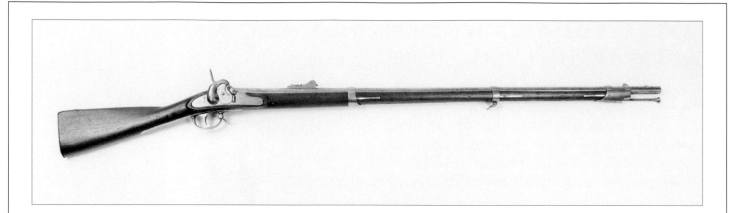

The Model 1816 Musket: The First to Fight

The battles of 1861 and early 1862 were largely fought with muskets that had begun life in the era of the flintlock. These arms, which were among the first truly mass-produced firearms in the world, were designated the model of 1816. They were smoothbore, firing a formidable .69-caliber round ball. Most, but not all, of those that would arm both the Union and Confederate volunteers who answered the first call to arms had been altered to some version of the percussion system of ignition. Their general use in the war would be short, but their significance cannot be overlooked.

In April 1861 the state arsenals of both North and South held thousands of arms of this model in various stages of repair. Some had already been given a thorough overhaul, which included rifling, the addition of a rear sight, and a breech that would fire the percussion cap. The very best of these were those that had been altered to the Maynard tape system under an 1854 contract with E. Remington & Sons of Illion, New York. Those units that were armed with the Remington rifled muskets were the fortunate ones. Others, most notably the Arkansas volunteers, went into battle at Shiloh in April 1862 with model 1816s still in the original flintlock configuration.

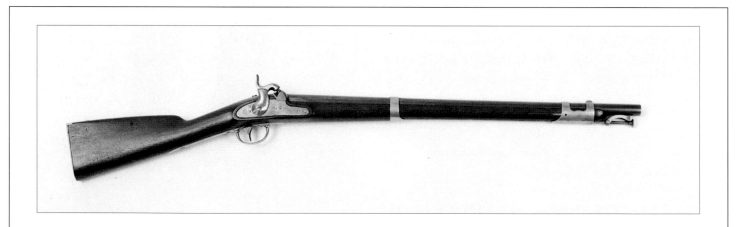

Model 1847 Cavalry Carbine

A similar arm to the .69-caliber carbine carried by the U.S. Dragoons in the late 1840s and early '50s was also issued to the artillery, but the carbine version featured the addition of a slide and ring for hooking to the trooper's carbine sling hook and a ramrod that was fitted into a loop attached to a small chain. This arrangement prevented the loss of the ramrod if the trooper was forced to try reloading while mounted. A serious drawback to the chain arrangement was the possibility that the arm would discharge while loading during rapid fire while dismounted. This was the last U.S. arm to employ this feature. Loading an arm like this while mounted was difficult at best, and on the move it was next to impossible. It can be imagined that when the breech-loading Sharps carbine was received by the Dragoons, it was a welcome change.

Major Nelson's Unconventional Overcoat

Maj. Hugh Mortimer Nelson served at First Manassas with the 1st Virginia Cavalry, later commanded Company H of the 6th Virginia Cavalry, and subsequently was a major on the staff of Gen. R. S. Ewell. Major Nelson was wounded at the Battle of Gaines Mill and a few months later died of disease.

Major Nelson must have presented an imposing figure, with this black woolen overcoat, tall boots, and black cap (both shown elsewhere, see page XXX). Although the coat is double-breasted it has buttons only on the left side. Oddly, these buttons are South Carolina state buttons, probably part of a very interesting story now lost for all time. The detachable cape of this coat was lined in red, which is generally associated with artillery and doubtless represents another intriguing bit of history. The shoulder straps of a Federal cavalry major add to the mystery of this coat, although it was not unknown for Confederate officers to favor this method of rank indication. Hugh Nelson had been a member of the Virginia Secession Convention prior to his entering the military service of his state and the South. All in all, his overcoat reflects the taste of an officer who served his country for just a short time, but gave all he could for the cause he believed in.

CLINCH RIFLES, GEORGIA MILITIA, APRIL 1861

DAVID RANKIN

The Clinch Rifles were formed in Augusta, Georgia, in 1852. Named in honor of a hero of the War of 1812, Gen. Duncan Clinch, the company was typical of the numerous elite militia organizations that could be found in the large cities of the United States in the decade prior to the Civil War. These companies were often composed of the best and the brightest young men of the urban areas, most of whom had sufficient financial backing to outfit themselves in the height of military fashion.

Membership in the Clinch Rifles was both an honor and a privilege that was not granted easily. A young man aspiring to membership would be voted on and was expected to pay dues, outfit himself in the company's uniform, and attend regular meetings. The purchase of one uniform was usually not enough; those wishing to remain members must be ready to conform to the decision of the majority regarding changes in style. The meticulously kept minutes of the meetings of the Clinch Rifles show that on May 30, 1859, a resolution was adopted to "change the uniform by making the coat a frock coat." This was followed just over a year later in July 1860 by a decision to discuss a design for a "new uniform," that would be tailor-made in Augusta.

In keeping with the European tradition of green for riflemen, and adding an elegant gold braid trim, the Clinch Rifles' uniform made them a distinctive and easily recognized company. The new uniform was based in style, if not in color, on the latest issue of the regular army. The French-style forage cap had been adopted by the regulars in 1858 for fatigue purposes. The frock coat for full dress had replaced a similar, less practical pattern the same year. Though the regulars would not wear the two items together, the decision to do so by the Clinch Rifles made for a smart and practical uniform by the standards of 1860.

Unlike many units raised in 1861 that bore the title "Rifles," the men of the Clinch Rifles were armed as a true rifle company. They carried the 1841 Mississippi rifle, modified to use the deadly looking saber bayonets. The Federal government, under a law dating from 1808, had issued the various states arms for their militias, and the Mississippi rifles were then issued to the company by the state of Georgia. The belt, the U.S. rifle belt model of 1855 with the attached frog to hold the scabbard for the saber bayonet, also stood out as unique to a rifle company. The cartridge box for the Mississippi rifle had no provision for a shoulder belt and was worn on the right side of the waistbelt. Although the saber bayonet had the appearance of a formidable arm, it was not well liked by the men who used it. One primary reason was that it made the arm difficult to load quickly when it was in place on the rifle. Another negative factor was the weight of the weapon, which, along with the weight of a full cartridge box, added to the soldier's already significant burden.

Confederate Frock Coat, 5th Louisiana Infantry

By late 1862 the vast majority of Confederate regiments were uniformed in the waist-length jacket. In 1861, however, many of the first units to take the field were also issued a long uniform coat similar in cut to that of the Federal Army. The coat pictured here belonged to a member of the 5th Louisiana Infantry. Research has shown that though this Army of Northern Virginia regiment was issued nothing but jackets after arrival in Virginia, at least one company left its home state fully uniformed with both a gray frock coat and a gray jacket. This company—Company E of the 5th Regiment—was raised in New Orleans, under the name 2nd Company Orleans Cadets in early May 1861. It was ordered into Confederate service on June 4 as part of the 5th Louisiana.

By late June, the 5th was on the Peninsula that extends below Richmond, Virginia. There the men spent the winter of 1861–62 and fought their first battle at Yorktown, a place many had probably read about when studying the American Revolution. The 5th Louisiana became part of the Army of Northern Virginia in April 1862. It would serve in this premier Confederate army for the entire war, except for six months in 1864, when it was detached with Jubal Early in Maryland and the Shenandoah Valley. The regiment fought in at least forty-two major battles.

One who left New Orleans with the Orleans Cadets in 1861 was twenty-one-year-old Pvt. Albert B. Cook, a native of the city who was working as a clerk when he enlisted on May 4, 1861. Cook's service to the Confederacy was tragically short. Five months after his regiment arrived on the Virginia Peninsula, he contracted dysentery. Cook was admitted to Seminary Hospital in Williamsburg on November 12, 1861, and four days later he died. A listing of his personal effects shows that like many young men from both the North and South who left for war, he was well equipped.

> *Inventory of the effects belonging to Pvt. A. B. Cook of Company E, 5th Louisiana Regiment, died November 16, 1861:*
>   1-grey uniform jacket
>   1-grey uniform coat
>   2-red, striped flannel over shirts
>   1-red flannel undershirt
>   1-pair red flannel drawers
>   1-double white woolen blanket
>   1-white cotton towel

1-pair shoes
One valise containing:
1-pair colored checked cotton pants
3-pair blue woolen socks
1-pair white woolen socks
1-towel
1-white cotton under shirt
1-red flannel shirt
2-comforters

Though it is unlikely this coat belonged to Private Cook, it is in all probability identical to the one sent home with his effects. The coat is made of gray wool and is trimmed in black. The buttons were obtained from the New Orleans military outfitters Hyde & Goodrich, which passed into other hands later in 1861. It is an excellent example of the type of uniform many Southern soldiers wore to the front in the first months of the war.

Uniform Jacket, 15th Pennsylvania Cavalry

Once Union volunteer regiments were mustered into Federal service, it became the responsibility of the Quartermaster's Department to supply them with clothing. Numerous infantry regiments received what were termed "special uniforms," but only a few Union cavalry regiments were supplied uniforms that deviated from the standard called for by army regulations. One exception was the regiment of Pennsylvania volunteers known originally as the Anderson Cavalry, but which was on Federal rosters as the 15th Pennsylvania Cavalry. From its inception in late summer of 1862, this regiment was granted the privilege of a distinctive uniform: a jacket trimmed in the orange of the prewar dragoons; dark blue trousers, also of the prewar army; red shirts; and specially ordered boots.

As appropriate to its uniform, the regiment began its organization at the prewar cavalry station, Carlisle Barracks, in south-central Pennsylvania. It had not completed filling its ranks when the Confederate Army entered Maryland in September. Although not fully equipped and numbering less than 300 men, the regiment was sent south. During the next few weeks, they rendered credible service but lost their colonel, William J. Palmer, when he was taken prisoner while scouting within Confederate lines.

Following this early action, the 15th was sent to join the Army of the Cumberland. They were not recruited to full strength until arriving in Tennessee, where they were rejoined by Colonel Palmer, who had been exchanged. The regiment continued its service with the western army, still wearing its distinctive uniform. When the war ended, the regiment had participated in battles and campaigns in both theaters of the war and could boast a war record equal to any.

The Rugged, Accurate Maynard

One carbine, often overlooked by students of Civil War cavalry arms, is the lightweight, rugged Maynard. This effective arm was the favorite of many Confederate cavalrymen, particularly in the western armies. The Maynard was the prewar invention of Dr. Edward Maynard, a Washington, D.C., dental surgeon. Although the arms trials of 1860 had given the Maynard a very favorable report, most purchases had been by Southern states, and it was here that they were to be found when the war began. Maynards, of the type shown here, were issued to troopers from Mississippi, Georgia, and Florida, and a few went to the Confederate Navy.

One distinct advantage the Maynard had for the South was the fact that the brass case cartridge it fired was not difficult to produce and could be reloaded. Early trials had shown that the Maynard cartridge could be reloaded as many as 200 times before splitting. During the first two years of the war, Confederate arsenals were able to supply Maynard cartridges with little problem; however, troopers were often admonished to take care of the used casings for reloading. But by 1864, as the Federal naval blockade became more effective, raw materials were beginning to run low. A bulletin circulated by Capt. William D. Humphries, depot ordnance officer for the Army of Tennessee, warned that "unless the troops take care of the thimbles [cases] of the Maynard cartridges . . . it will be impossible to furnish them again."

For unknown reasons, there were no substantial purchases of Maynard carbines by the U.S. government until June 1864. By then a second model had been produced that eliminated the long-range rear sight and the patch box. By the end of the war, just over 20,000 of the new Maynards were delivered to the Federal Army. Most of these were received too late to see active field service. Those that were issued ended up in the hands of troopers of the 6th, 9th, and 11th Indiana Cavalry, as well as the 10th and 11th East Tennessee Union Cavalry.

As a footnote to history, the Maynard carbine has been rediscovered over the last decades by modern shooters within the ranks of the North-South Skirmish Association. These marksmen know what the Confederate cavalrymen knew very well: the Maynard is a reliable, accurate arm.

Officers' forage caps from the Army of the Potomac

The two Union officers' forage caps pictured here represent two of many different styles worn by officers of the Federal Army. These caps both saw service in the Army of the Potomac. Officers have traditionally been required to purchase their own uniforms, and the items' style and quality reflect the officers' personal tastes and pocketbooks.

Many regiments that formed to fight for the Union were known by both an official numerical designator and a nickname under which the regiment was recruited. The 4th New York Infantry was raised in New York City in May 1861 as the "Scott Life Guard," named for the famous general Winfield Scott. It served initially in eastern Maryland and Virginia, until ordered to join the Army of the Potomac, on September 8, 1862. The regiment was assigned to the 3rd Brigade, 3rd Division, 2nd Corps.

Hardly had it reached its new command when the men found themselves in action at the Battle of Antietam. In this single action, they would lose more men than many regiments would in the entire war. The 4th was part of the Federal assault on the infamous "Bloody Lane." As the brigade moved to the attack, it was met with a devastating volley of musketry delivered by the North Carolina troops positioned in the lane. Almost instantly, 150 men of the 4th New York went down. Before the end of the day, thirty-seven more of the regiment would join them. The regiment would continue to serve until May 25, 1863, when its enlistment expired.

The cap worn by Capt. William B. Parisen was doubtless purchased by him from one of the well-established military outfitters in New York City when the regiment was forming. It is of high quality, its dark blue crown offset by a medium blue band around the base, to which is affixed an elegantly embroidered wreath inside of which is the regimental name. The flat, finely furnished

bill and chin strap are of a type only found on the finest officer's caps. Captain Parisen entered the service on April 22, 1861, as commander of Company E. He served until Company E was mustered out with the regiment.

The "McDowell" pattern forage cap also shown belonged to an unknown officer of the 17th Maine Infantry. Although this cap is very similar to that of the average issue to enlisted men, it is finished with much finer detail than those received under contracts with the Quartermaster's Department. The cap bears the Red Diamond Corps Badge of the 1st Division, 3rd Corps, and "17" in metallic figures that were stamped to resemble the embroidered cap devices often worn by officers. It is likely that the badge was placed on the cap when they were first issued to the army in April 1863, as this is the original die-cut style. The numbers were probably added in the fall of the same year, as the regiment was inspected on August 25, 1863, and the following report was forwarded to corps headquarters:

> The 17th Maine regiment with the exception of Company A is without designating numbers & figures & non-commissioned officers without chevrons. They have no cooking utensils. The cartridges of the Brigade are in poor condition, some having been wet & some being almost worn out by having been carried loosely in the box.

The 17th Maine had seen heavy action at Gettysburg in July, and the march back to Virginia had obviously taken its toll. It would continue service with the 3rd Corps until March 1864, when that corps was broken up and elements made part of the 2nd Corps. The veterans of the old 3rd Division were allowed to continue to wear their Red Diamond out of respect for the service of the gallant corps from which they came.

1ST MINNESOTA INFANTRY, JULY 1861

The story of the 1st Minnesota Infantry in 1861 could be used to illustrate the beginning of any number of regiments, both Northern and Southern, that answered the first call to arms in April 1861. Companies from various small towns along the Minnesota and St. Croix Rivers came together at Fort Snelling, which had not been used by the regular army since 1858. The state government put its best efforts forward to quickly arm and equip the regiment, which, after all, would represent the state itself in the short contest that was expected to follow to put an end to the Rebellion. The state sent forward the best arms in its arsenal, consisting of enough model 1855 rifle muskets to arm three companies and an assortment of model 1841 rifles and smoothbore muskets altered from flintlock to percussion. All except the 1855s were later exchanged for model 1842 percussion muskets.

In a scenario that was being repeated in varying degrees in nearly every state, the uniforms issued would conform to no particular regulation. Most of the men received clothing taken from the stock of a wholesale merchant of Indian trade goods: red and blue woolen shirts, blankets, rough shoes, and camp equipment. The same dealer had dark blue trousers quickly made up for the men. One company received gray uniforms made by the ladies of its hometown, and several other companies that were temporarily stationed near Fort Ridgely, Minnesota, received old U.S. Army uniforms. Army forage caps were procured and issued in June, before the regiment left the state.

During May and June, the 1st Minnesota drilled and received a continual flow of visitors to its camp, again scenes that were being repeated daily on both sides of the Mason-Dixon line. Finally, on June 14, orders were received to move the regiment south. The men were reported to be "frantic with joy" at the prospect of finally seeing action. The order prompted a local ladies aid society to put a concerted effort forward to produce havelocks for the men. These items of white cloth were made to fit over the army cap and were long in back to cover the neck from the sun. They were touted as being "indispensable to the soldiers comfort." By the time the main part of the 1st left the state, they had received 600 of the "indispensable" covers, along with a large quantity of needle books, towels, stockings, and other items from the women of the state.

As the 1st Minnesota moved east, the Chicago press reported that the men in their red shirts were "looked upon as heroes of romance, frontiersmen and Indian fighters." It was expected that the regiment would receive the regulation uniform when it arrived in the East. But when the army finally moved across the Potomac River to meet the Rebels,

DR. J. LINDSTROM

the men of Minnesota were still in the same basic dress that they had worn when they left home. Most would fight their first battle at Bull Run on July 21 in the red shirts that had marked them as frontiersmen.

During the general confusion, which was the hallmark of the first great battle of the Civil War, the 1st Minnesota shared the experiences of many of those on the field. The lack of uniformity and similar flags brought casualties on both sides from friendly fire. All told, the Minnesota regiment lost 160 killed and wounded on that hot July day. Soon after the battle, the regiment received the regulation army uni-

form, and for the remainder of its service, there would be nothing in the soldiers' appearance that would distinguish them from the majority of Union regiments. The 1st Minnesota was assigned to the 2nd Corps of the Army of the Potomac, where it served with distinction until the end of the war. At Gettysburg the regiment gained everlasting glory but again sustained heavy casualties. On the afternoon of July 2, 1863, when they were called upon to plug a gap in the center of the Union line, the gallant men of the northwest suffered a loss of 80 percent of those engaged in less than thirty minutes.

The Insignia of a Rifle Regiment

In the years just prior to the Civil War, the U.S. Army had only five regiments of mounted troops: the 1st and 2nd Dragoons, the 1st and 2nd Cavalry, and the Regiment of Mounted Rifles. The dragoon and cavalry regiments, armed with carbines, revolvers, and sabers, wore the familiar crossed-saber insignia on their headgear. The rifle regiment carried only the model 1841 "Mississippi" rifle, and its insignia was that which had long been associated with riflemen: the trumpet. This association likely grew out of the European tradition equaling military riflemen with hunters, who carried a trumpet or horn to signal the hunt. Riflemen also traditionally wore the color green as part of their uniform. The U.S. Mounted Rifles wore the same uniform as the other mounted regiments, but trimmed in green. In 1861 the Mounted Rifles became the 3rd U.S. Cavalry and traded their distinctive weapons, trim, and insignia for that of the cavalry.

During the Civil War, several regiments were formed that called themselves rifle regiments, although for the most part they were armed and functioned the same as other line infantry. One of these regiments was the 8th New York Infantry, the "German Rifles." When the war began, this regiment was one of the many regiments of Union volunteers who left for war wearing gray uniforms. The 8th had an iron gray uniform coat with green cuffs, trousers of the same gray with a double red stripe down the side, and a gray cap. For obvious reasons, the 8th, like other gray-clad Union regiments, soon traded its garb for the standard U.S. blue.

The insignia illustrated here has been passed down from the U.S. Mounted Rifles and the 8th New York "German Rifles." The plain brass trumpet would have adorned the shako of an enlisted man of the Mounted Rifles. The embroidered insignia are intended for wear by officers. Since there was but a single regiment of Mounted Rifles, the trumpet for that regiment needed no number affixed to it. It is embroidered of gold metallic thread on a black background. The "German Rifles" insignia has a green velvet background and bears the state-assigned regimental number.

"JACKSON IS WITH YOU!"

August 9, 1862. It was the moment of crisis at the Battle of Cedar Mountain, Virginia. A determined late-afternoon assault by the Federals of Maj. Gen. Nathaniel Banks had crumbled three successive Confederate lines and in hot, hand-to-hand fighting sent the left wing of Maj. Gen. Thomas Jonathan "Stonewall" Jackson's army reeling back in confusion. Jackson galloped forward through the wooded ground to try to stem what was becoming a rout and found himself in the midst of a battered and retreating army, among which was his own famous "Stonewall Brigade." Northern artillery shells screamed through the smoke-filled air and minie balls flew in from three sides. "It appeared for a few moments as though we had struck a full-grown tornado," one of Jackson's aides remembered.

Stonewall was a flash of electricity as he moved to rally his men. Riding among them, he tried to unsheathe his sword but discovered that it had rusted to the scabbard from lack of use. Jackson quickly unbuckled it from his belt and began to wave it, still sheathed. The charismatic Confederate warrior seized his personal battleflag in his other hand, then proceeded to shout, "Jackson is with you!" and "Rally brave men, and press forward! Your General will lead you!" The fleeing men halted, reformed, and began moving back to fight anew—first a few, then more. The superlative Jackson had turned the tide and soon would win further laurels as one of the South's foremost leaders.

Jackson, disdaining the finery of most military dress, was noted for his plain garb. He has often been described as appearing as dusty and drab as the foot soldiers of his command. The variety of dress and equipage among the soldiers was typical of Confederate forces during this period of the war.

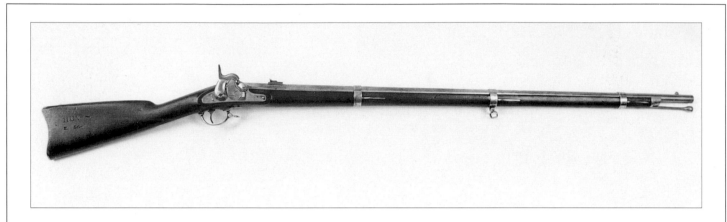

A Connecticut Model 1855

The model 1855 rifle-musket was the predecessor of the model 1861, which is considered the standard U.S. Infantry arm of the Civil War. The 1855 has the distinction of being the first rifled arm produced by the United States that was designed to fire the famous .58-caliber minié ball. Although designated the model 1855, deliveries of this arm did not begin until 1857. The model 1855 was produced at both of the U.S. government arms-producing facilities: Springfield, Massachusetts, and Harpers Ferry, Virginia.

The weapon employed the Maynard tape priming system. This system used a cavity cut into the lock plate, into which a roll of paper caps was inserted. This cavity was covered by a small steel door on which was beautifully stamped an image of a U.S. eagle. An intricate mechanism fitted within the lock fed the caps through a channel one at a time, each time the hammer was cocked. The action automatically aligned the cap with the nipple. When the trigger was pulled, a sharp edge on the hammer cut the paper roll, and the hammer at once forced the cap onto the nipple and caused it to explode, thereby firing the musket.

This mechanism worked surprisingly well. There were, however, two drawbacks: production time and money. With the outbreak of the Civil War and the taking of Harpers Ferry by Rebel forces, it was obvious that Springfield alone would never be able to meet the demand of the volunteer forces expected to be called to battle. It would be necessary to resort to the contract system to even attempt to meet the demand for rifle muskets. To expedite matters and ease the need for the additional manufacturing procedures necessary to include the tape primer, it was eliminated in favor of the standard percussion cap that had been in use since before the Mexican War. With this decision, the distinctive humped lock plate of the 1855 was done away with, and the famous model 1861 rifle musket was born.

It is interesting to note that when the Harpers Ferry arsenal was seized, the Confederate force removed the manufacturing equipment and moved it to Richmond. When production of the Confederate version of the model 1861 rifle musket was begun, the arm featured a humped lock plate but no cut or provision for a tape primer. This anomaly was necessary if the captured cutting machinery and gauges were to be used without time-consuming retooling. The lock plates of these weapons are stamped with the date of manufacture and "C.S. Richmond."

Prior to the war, it was the intent of the army that those arms manufactured at Springfield be sent to the regular army, reserving the Harpers Ferry production for the various state militia forces. It is likely that the Springfield production exceeded the demand of the regulars, and the overage was then sent to the states. This is borne out by the rifle musket illustrated here, which is marked "U.S. Springfield 1859" on the lock plate and bears property marks of Company K, 11th Connecticut Infantry, on the stock. The 11th Connecticut was organized and mustered in for three years of U.S. service at Hartford on October 23, 1861. The service of the regiment was varied. Its first action was at the battle of Roanoke Island, North Carolina, while serving with the 9th Corps, and the men were in the thick of the battle for "Burnside's" bridge at Antietam. Ultimately, the 11th would serve for four years.

A Historic Knapsack and Leggings

Army regulations of 1861 called for the U.S. soldier to have his regimental number painted on the back outer cover of his knapsack. On the side, the company letter and individual number assigned to the soldier were to be placed in such a manner as to be readily visible during inspection. Haversacks were required to be marked in a similar manner. It is important to note for today's student of Civil War equipment that each Civil War soldier would be given his own company designating number. Often, pieces of equipment are encountered that bear a letter followed by a number. This number is often taken to be that of a regiment. More often than not, however, the combination is the company letter followed by the individual, not regimental, number.

It was not unusual for volunteer regiments to add the state name to the number on the backs of the knapsacks of those within the regiment. Today, the survival rate for knapsacks with such regimental designation is extremely low. This can be explained by the hard use to which the knapsacks were originally put. Another factor is that postwar storage in hot attics caused rapid deterioration of the painted canvas.

Knapsacks such as the one shown here were originally issued with a wooden frame inside the bag. Early in the war, it was decided to remove the frame from those being made for the army, primarily because of the discomfort it caused the soldier while marching with the wooden frame against his back. Prior to the spring campaign of 1863, a board of officers conducted a survey of the weight and contents of the knapsack of the average soldier. It was found that the average knapsack, with contents therein and blanket rolled on top, weighed 15 1/2 pounds.

The knapsack illustrated here was carried by Pvt. Humphrey Moore of Company D, 26th Massachusetts Infantry. The leather leggings, which were found in the knapsack, are one of several varieties of this extensively issued item used during 1862 and 1863. Moore enlisted at Lowell, Massachusetts, on August 12, 1861. At the time, he was twenty-one years old and listed his occupation as machinist. The 26th left their home state on the steamer *Constitution* on November 21 and arrived at Ship Island, Mississippi, twelve days later. It was here that Private Moore was to spend his only service with his regiment, as he was discharged for disability on April 12, 1862. Moore continued in the service as part of the Veteran Reserve Corps, but his regimental knapsack and leggings, both of which were issued for field duty, were likely sent home.

The 26th Massachusetts saw hard service as part of the 19th Army Corps in the Department of the Gulf until July 1864, when it was transferred north. Moving once again by sea, the men landed at Fortress Monroe. By August they were part of Sheridan's Army of the Shenandoah. The climate likely was a welcome change from the heat of the Deep South. Had Moore not left his regiment when he did, it is unlikely that his knapsack and leggings would have survived the war. What the heat and dampness of the Deep South did not destroy, the arduous fighting in Virginia surely would have.

Private, 18th Massachusetts Infantry, January 1862

In July 1861 Gen. Montgomery C. Meigs, the newly appointed quartermaster general, contracted to purchase 10,000 complete uniforms of the pattern worn by the French Army's famous light infantry, the chasseurs à pied. The uniforms, along with all associated equipage, were to be obtained directly from the firm of Alexis Godillot, the manufacturer for the French Army.

The arrangements were made by the American legation in Paris, and by late November the complete order had been filled and the outfits were heading west. The overall cost of the individual uniform differed little from the established cost of production of similar items in the United States. Despite this, the Quartermaster's Department received heavy criticism for making such a large overseas purchase of items that could have been supplied by U.S. manufacturers. As received, the uniform consisted of the following:

1 uniform coat with epaulets
2 pairs of uniform trousers
1 fatigue jacket
1 hooded cloak
1 fatigue cap
1 uniform hat with plate, feather, and pom-pom
3 cotton shirts
2 pairs shoes
1 pair leather gaiters
1 pair linen gaiters
1 pair leggings
1 blue cotton cravat
2 pairs drawers
1 pair suspenders
1 cotton cap
1 pair cotton gloves
2 handkerchiefs

In addition, each soldier received a French knapsack, a superior item of leather finished with the hair still on to effectively repel water; a haversack; a drinking cup; and small bags for food. Also included were clothes brushes and a sewing kit. There was also an ample supply of pots, pans, and mess gear, designed so that each soldier of a squad would carry only certain pieces. At mealtime these pieces together made a complete outfit for cooking and eating.

By late December the uniforms had been received in New York and forwarded to the Washington Quartermaster Depot for issue. Three regiments of Gen. Fitz John Porter's division of the Army of the Potomac had been selected to receive the new outfits. These regiments were the 83rd Pennsylvania of Butterfield's brigade, the 62nd Pennsylvania of Morrell's brigade, and the 18th Massachusetts of Martindale's brigade. In true European fashion, representatives of the manufacturer had accompanied the uniforms to ensure that they were properly fitted and that the customer was satisfied. The timing could not have been better for the 18th Massachusetts. The uniforms they had received from the state in August were of inferior quality and by November had begun to wear out.

As the uniforms were distributed to the regiments, an immediate problem arose. Military uniforms, in the United States and abroad, were manufactured and shipped according to a tariff of sizes. That is, for every 100 uniforms, there would be a certain portion of each size from small to large, which careful study had determined would be needed in an average company of men. What had not been taken into account, and was perhaps not actually known, was that Americans tended to be bigger than their European counterparts. The 83rd Pennsylvania was quick to inform General Butterfield of the fact:

Hd. Qtrs. 83rd Regt. Pa. Vols.
3rd Brig. Porter's Div.
Brig. Gen. Butterfield
   Sir:
Of the new Zouave coats which the Regt. has lately received, the Frenchmen sent to fit them report, after a thorough trial, that one third of the whole are of too small a size. We have our proper proportion of the different sizes. One set of uniforms is yet undistributed in Washington. The Frenchmen state that of the large coats still there, sizes enough can easily be found to finish the equipment of both this Regt. and the 18th Mass. In no other way can the evil, in their opinion, be remedied, as it would clearly seem preferable that two Regiments should be entirely equipped, rather than that three should remain only partially so. I would respectfully suggest and request that permission from the proper source be obtained for an exchange of these small coats for the requisite number of larger ones.
   I am respectfully
   Jno. W. McLane, Col.
   83rd P.V.

French but Not Zouave

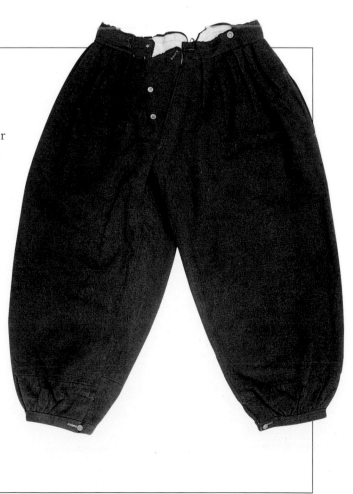

The 155th Pennsylvania Infantry was granted the right to wear the Zouave uniform in mid-1863. The style selected employed two distinct variations: the trim on the jacket was distinctly different from the original French version, and the full, baggy trousers were to be dark blue rather than the red worn by the French. At some point in the resupply of the regiments, a switch was made. Rather than receiving the very full trousers of the true Zouave cut, the 155th was issued the narrower, longer-fitting pants of the French light infantry, or chasseur à pied.

The explanation for the switch is probably very simple. Early in the war, the Federal government had purchased 10,000 sets of chasseur uniforms from the company that supplied the French Army. The color of the trousers was a slate blue-gray, and the material was nearly identical to that used by the Quartermaster's Department. If the war ended, the stock of these trousers that remained would be useless. The solution must have seemed obvious to an economy-minded army.

Evidently, some arrangement was worked out, as by January 22, 1862, the 62nd Pennsylvania had been issued the new uniform. Along with the uniforms, the regiment received the following translated document intended to accompany the original outfit:

Details for 8 days

For each man, empty entirely the knapsack, and refill it with small linen bags containing coffee, tea, sugar, rice, salt, pepper and chocolates, dissicated and compressed vegetables. Take plenty of lard or suet, in the small gamelle, or mess pan with which each man is furnished. Plenty of cartridges—60 in the knapsack, 40 in the cartridge box; each man must have besides 7lb. sea biscuit enclosed in a wrapper and placed in the knapsack under the cover, in place where the folded coat is usually carried. (See the drawings in the album of the packed knapsack and the instructions which has been given to every Sgt. and cpl. Of the regiments which have received the French equipment.)

Another benefit of the French equipment was the inclusion of the *tent d'abri,* the small individual shelter tent that would soon be adopted as an issue item for the entire army. Better known as a shelter half by today's student, the small tent was immediately popular, and by war's end most soldiers had spent time under one.

There is no direct evidence that the complete French uniform was ever worn into battle. By the time the Peninsula Campaign of 1862 began, the regiments that received them also had received regulation U.S. clothing. The French shirts and drawers continued in use until worn out. The commander of the 83rd Pennsylvania had in fact issued an order forbidding the wearing of any portion of the "Zouave" uniform without special permission. The 83rd, and probably the other two regiments, put their French uniforms in storage in Washington for use on some future occasion. When the Pennsylvanians went to retrieve the uniforms toward the end of their service, they found that they were missing.

The uniform worn by the 18th Massachusetts soldier pictured here is the complete outfit as would have been worn on dress parade. On campaign, the feather in the shako would have been removed and replaced by a pom-pom. The cartridge box, belt, and all accoutrements, except probably the bayonet scabbard, are French and were supplied as part of the complete outfit. The uniform is made of a heavier wool than found in U.S. garments, and unlike those of American uniforms of the period, the sleeves of the coat are of a narrow, close-fitting cut. The buttons on the uniforms supplied to the United States were made of cast white metal, rather than the regulation brass issued on American-made uniforms. The buttons have an embossed eagle on them instead of the regimental number that was standard in the French Army.

The 18th Massachusetts was organized in Readville and Boston and mustered into service on August 27, 1861. From the beginning, it was in the Army of the Potomac serving primarily with the famous 5th Corps. It fought in all the major battles of the army until mustered out on September 2, 1864, in front of Petersburg. After this, the veterans and recruits formed a battalion that was consolidated with the 32nd Massachusetts, in which they served until the end of the war.

The fact that the chasseur uniform was little used by the 18th is borne out in a letter sent by the regiment's commander, Col. Joseph Hayes, to the Quartermaster's Department in January 1864, claiming that his men never received the uniforms. The reason for the letter is unclear. Perhaps it was designed to avoid charges for uniforms they could not account for. In any case, the quartermaster's efficient bookkeeping was evident when a letter sent in reply reminded the colonel that "the clothing was regularly issued to your Regiment . . . through your regimental Quartermaster."

At a later time, some of the remaining French clothing was issued to the Excelsior Brigade. Toward the end of the war, the Quartermaster's Department offered the hooded cloaks for sale to officers. After the war, if any remained in store, they were likely sold on the surplus market. Thus ended the saga of what was most certainly the largest single purchase of foreign uniforms and equipment ever made by the U.S. Army.

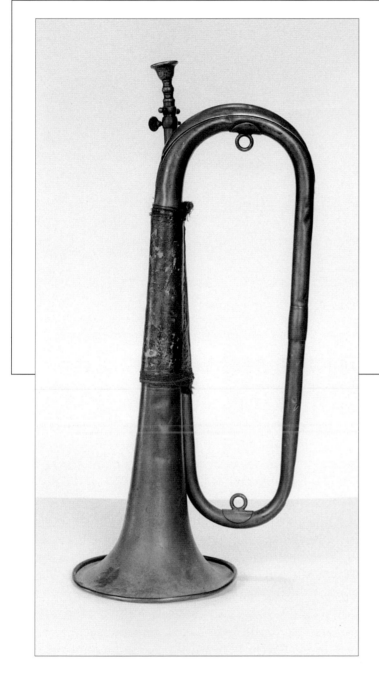

French Infantry Bugle of the 62nd Pennsylvania

The drum is usually thought of as the primary means of battle communication by Civil War infantry, and to a great extent this is true. An exception can be found within some regiments, particularly those outfitted in French gear, such as the 62nd Pennsylvania. Along with the complete uniform, the regiment also received French equipment, including bugles. The uniform was used primarily for dress occasions, with standard Federal fatigue uniforms issued for field service. Some of the French equipment proved to be very useful, however, and the French model 1845 bugle was one item that established its value on the battlefield. This example was carried and used by G. W. Freeman of Company H.

English Belt and Cartridge Pouch of the 44th Massachusetts

State sovereignty was not an exclusive trait of the states that formed the Confederacy. Massachusetts was one of several Union states that, when war broke out, immediately jumped into the arms market to ensure that her sons would be well armed and equipped. State representatives were sent to England to secure arms and accoutrements on the open market. The competition from other states, as well as the Federal government and, of course, representatives of the Confederacy, made it a seller's market. Massachusetts was backed by the world-famous financial house of Baring Brothers & Co., who were staunchly pro-Union and would also underwrite the financial dealing of the U.S. government in Europe.

Before the U.S. government got control of things, Massachusetts had purchased thousands of Enfield rifle muskets and related accoutrements. One of the regiments that would receive a full outfitting of English gear was the 44th Massachusetts Infantry, a nine-month regiment. The 44th were issued Enfield rifle muskets and leather accoutrements of the style carried by English militia units.

When the regiment left home bound for Beaufort, North Carolina, on October 14, 1862, Pvt. T. W. Leighton of Company I wore this very serviceable belt and pouch. The buckle is the distinctive snake pattern used by the British Army well into the twentieth century. The area of service of the 44th Massachusetts was to be the coastal region of North and South Carolina. The regiment, along with Private Leighton, returned home and was mustered out on June 18, 1863.

BURNSIDE'S BRIDGE

On September 17, 1862, two regiments of Union infantry forced the crossing of Antietam Creek by charging across a narrow stone bridge under fire from Confederate infantry on the hillside beyond. The two regiments both bore the regimental number 51: the 51st Pennsylvania and the 51st New York, part of the 2nd Brigade, 2nd Division, 9th Corps. The 9th Corps was commanded by Gen. Ambrose Burnside. It was he who, under pressure from the army commander general George B. McClellan, ordered the taking of the bridge at all costs. After the battle, the bridge would forever bear the name Burnside's Bridge.

The regiment depicted here in the initial dash across the bridge is the 51st Pennsylvania. The 51st had been organized at Harrisburg in November 1861 and had served first as part of Burnside's coastal operations. It would remain associated with the 9th Corps for its entire term of service. The regiment was armed with pattern 53 Enfield rifle muskets. Brigade quartermaster returns show issues of the standard Federal four-button fatigue blouse and forage caps to the regiments. The 51st Pennsylvania was unique in that it carried three flags into battle: the Pennsylvania state color and two flags presented to the regiment by the citizens of Norristown, Pennsylvania. All three went across the bridge together. Because of the intensity of the fire facing the Pennsylvanians, two of the three flags were badly shot through and were retired from service a few weeks later. The regiment itself also took a heavy loss: of the less than 400 officers and men who went into the fight, 125 were listed as casualties.

An Officer's Jacket of the 13th New Jersey

The use of the short jacket as a battle uniform during the Civil War was by no means confined to enlisted men. As the war progressed, more and more officers discovered the comfort and practicality of a waist-length jacket as an undress uniform. Col. Ezra Carman of the 13th New Jersey was typical of many who had such items tailor-made for them.

This stylish example of an officer's battle jacket is adorned with a single row of officer's small eagle buttons and black galloons (braid) on each sleeve. The galloons are similar to those found in gold braid on the coats and jackets of Confederate officers. A handy outside pocket had been included on the left breast. The shoulder straps of a full colonel of infantry are found on each shoulder. At a distance, it would have been hard for a Confederate sharpshooter to distinguish the exact rank of an officer wearing such a jacket—a distinct advantage for a field-grade officer, who may have been in command of a regiment and thereby presented a very tempting target.

The first action seen by the 13th New Jersey Infantry was the battle of Antietam, Maryland, on September 17, 1862, under the command of Colonel Carman. Newly assigned to the 12th Corps of the Army of the Potomac, the men were thrown into battle in the famous Cornfield, having never before in their short military experience even loaded their muskets. Colonel Carman would, in the postwar years, become the historian of the famous battlefield where his regiment received its baptism of fire.

Identification Badges

From the very first battles of the Civil War, the possibility of dying in battle became an unavoidable reality for every combat soldier. Visions of an unmarked grave, or one simply marked "unknown," had a disquieting effect on even the bravest of men. In early battles of the war, men were known to write their names and regimental designation on pieces of paper and pin them to their clothing. But paper falls off or is easily destroyed.

By 1862 enterprising Union Army sutlers and even Northern mail-order houses had begun to sell metal pins and medallions with the purchaser's name and regiment permanently engraved or stamped on the surface. The idea caught on quickly, and metal identification tags soon became a common sight within every combat unit. Because they were not an item of government purchase, Civil War identification badges exist in an endless variety of shapes and patterns, although they are generally about the size of a quarter and usually made of silver.

Sadly, in some cases, well-meaning friends removed identification badges from the bodies of comrades to place them with their personal effects. If the regiment was forced to move on before the body could be properly attended to, another grave would be filled and marked "unknown."

Badges:

Shield of sheet silver worn by Corp. Cornelius W. Parker, Company I, 112th New York Infantry. This type of badge was commercially made. The company letter was highlighted by being cut out in the center. These were then engraved to individual specifications.

Shield of silver with raised letters identifying the wearer as a member of the Veteran Reserve Corps, worn by Henry A. Smith, who served with Company I, 5th Vermont Infantry, before being wounded at Fredericksburg on December 13, 1862. The wound was serious enough to incapacitate him for further field service, and he was transferred to the Veteran Reserve Corps on July 1, 1863. His pride in his original regiment is evidenced by his decision to recognize that fact as well as having the corps badge of the 6th Corps engraved on his new badge.

Flattened silver coin made into an ID badge. Not all badges were made from scratch. Some were fashioned from coins by sutlers and others. This badge was worn by William R. Adams, a drummer with Company I, 33rd New Jersey Infantry.

Silver identification badge of a cavalryman. This badge clearly marks its wearer as a mounted soldier. It was the property of Lt. Clark M. Pease, Company H, 5th New York Cavalry. This regiment was one of the hard-fighting regiments of the Army of the Potomac Cavalry Corps and also served under Phil Sheridan in the Shenandoah Valley.

The Gillmore Medal

During the nineteenth century most European nations awarded medals to members of their armed forces for specific acts of bravery or for other notable achievements. Until the Civil War, with only minor exceptions, the U.S. government awarded no medals. Soldiers deserving special recognition might be mentioned in special orders read before the command but had little tangible evidence of their moment of glory.

On July 12, 1862, Congress approved the awarding of 2,000 Medals of Honor to enlisted men who "shall distinguish themselves by their gallantry in action, and other soldier-like qualities." On March 3, 1863, the original act was expanded to include officers, and no specific number of medals was designated. While this was certainly well received, the number of those who received the medal was very small in comparison to the total number serving in the Federal Army.

To offset this, several commanding officers had medals struck that would be awarded to men under their command who, in specific circumstances, were felt to deserve special recognition. These were the Ely Medal, commissioned in December 1863 by Col. John Ely of the 23rd Pennsylvania and limited to 100 for gallantry in the charge on Marye's Heights in May 1863; the Kearny Cross, authorized by Gen. David B. Birney on March 13, 1863, for enlisted men of the 1st Division, 3rd Corps, "that have distinguished themselves on the fields of battle that this Division has participated in"; the Butler Medal, 197 of which were purchased and awarded by Gen. Benjamin Butler to black troops distinguished for courage at the Battle of Chaffin's Farm, Virginia, on September 29, 1864; and the Gillmore Medal, adopted on October 28, 1863, by General Orders No. 94, Headquarters Department of the South, by command of Maj. Gen. Quincy A. Gillmore.

The Gillmore Medal was intended for enlisted men and was to be awarded for "gallant and meritorious conduct during the operations before Charleston." The award was to go to not more than 3 percent of the men serving who had been in action or on duty in the trenches or batteries. Company officers were to nominate men of their unit who were felt to be deserving of the award. The medal had on its face a representation of Fort Sumter in ruins and was produced by the firm of Ball, Black & Co. of New York City. The Gillmore Medal pictured here was awarded to Corp. Elisha F. Soule, Company K, 7th Connecticut Infantry. Soule was twenty years old in September 1861, when the 7th Connecticut was formed and he volunteered for service. After mustering in, the regiment was sent immediately to the area of Hilton Head, South Carolina. It was for his conduct during the summer 1863 siege of the Confederate Fort Wagner that Soule earned his Gillmore Medal. Years later, he wrote of the circumstances that resulted in his receiving the award:

After the assault on Fort Wagner Company K was detailed to take charge of the Battery of Cohorn mortars nearest Fort Wagner, and our duty was the first thing in the morning to knock the sandbags off the fort, that had been placed during the night. We had a small hole through the breastworks to watch the effect of our shots. One morning the gunners were F.O. Jaques, Andrew Taylor and myself. The night before going to the front to man the gun Taylor asked me to take his money and send it home as he was detailed to go to the front and would not come back alive. I laughed at him and told him I expected to come back all right. Within one hour after we commenced firing he was killed by a sharpshooter. My hand was on his shoulder when he was shot. Word came one morning to dismount the corner gun on Fort Wagner. We had not been firing long when it was dismounted.

The regiment spent the next year campaigning in the coastal area of South Carolina and Florida, moving as far south as St. Augustine. In April 1864 it was moved to Virginia and served in the operations against Petersburg. The 7th was there when Corporal Soule took his discharge and returned home, proud of his medal and his service to his country.

THE INDIANA ZOUAVES

Although the Zouave craze that swept the United States started in Chicago in 1859, the only Union regiments to fight in the Civil War dressed in the true Zouave fashion came from states east of the Allegheny Mountains. While the romance of the French Zouave continued to capture the imagination of many in the western states, the desire to go to war in red baggy trousers and a turban seems to have been lacking in this predominantly agricultural region. Those regiments who chose to call themselves Zouaves also chose to interpret the uniform as they saw fit. One of these was the 11th Indiana Infantry, the Indiana Zouaves, also often called the "Wallace Zouaves" for their first commander Lew Wallace, later famous as the author of *Ben Hur.* In his postwar autobiography, Wallace wrote of the 11th Indiana's first uniform:

> *There was nothing of the flashy Algerian colors in the uniform of the Eleventh Indiana; no red fez, no red breeches, no red or yellow sash with tassels big as early cabbages. Our outfit was of the tamest grey twilled goods, not unlike home made jeans—a visor cap, French in pattern, its top of red cloth not larger than the palm of one's hand; a blue flannel shirt with open neck, a jacket Greekish in form, edged with narrow binding, the red scarcely noticeable; breeches baggy but not petticoated; button gaiters connecting below the knees with the breeches, and strapped over the shoes.*

Before anything else could be done, the war began. It was immediately evident that little help could be expected from the Federal government. With the loyalty of Kentucky, her neighbor across the Ohio River, in doubt, the legislature passed another bill May 1 to provide for the defense of the state of Indiana. This act directed the governor to immediately procure a supply of first-class arms sufficient for 20,000 men. Acting upon this authority, Governor Morton sent an agent to visit the eastern states and Europe to purchase arms. Despite competition from other states and from both the U.S. and Confederate governments, from May 1861 to February 1862 the state's representative is reported to have purchased and delivered to Indiana the following: 30,000 English Enfield rifles; 2,731 carbines; 751 revolvers; and 797 cavalry sabers.

The sabers were purchased from the Ames Manufacturing Company in June 1861, and many of the Enfields were obtained from the well-known military outfitters Schuyler, Hartlry & Graham.

In addition to arms, the state was responsible for clothing and equipping the six regiments enlisted for three months' service, two one-year regiments, thirteen infantry and two cavalry regiments enlisted for three years, plus two independent companies of cavalry and three batteries of artillery—a Herculean task for a state that only months before could not find over 5,000 of the arms she was supposed to have.

Whereas most of the arms came from outside the state, most of the accoutrements and uniforms were purchased from Indiana merchants. On August 3, 1861, 3,036 sets of infantry accoutrements were purchased from Watkins & Slaughter, and on August 22 another 3,803 sets were obtained from Fishbank & Sulgrove, both located in Indianapolis.

Out of deference to the five Indiana infantry regiments that had served in the Mexican War, the state began numbering her Civil War volunteer regiments with number six. The 11th Regiment was thus the sixth regiment of the three-month volunteers, organized in late April 1861. At the end of their term, these regiments were all then reenlisted for three years.

The uniform shown here is the first uniform worn by the Indiana Zouaves. It was designed by Colonel Wallace for the three-month regiment and retained when they were remustered for three years. Because there were few large shoe companies, each company of the 11th obtained its footwear from a different maker. The distinctive caps were manufactured by the firm of Meyberg & Hellman, and at least part of the uniforms by G. W. Geisendorff & Company, both Indiana contractors. This soldier is armed with one of the Enfield rifles with saber bayonet purchased by the state agent. He also carries a bowie knife, which was a favorite side arm of many early volunteers.

The Essential Ingredient: Army Shoes

Throughout history, no item of army issue has been more important to the soldier than his footwear and this held true among the fighting men of the American Civil War. The campaigns of the Civil War often called for soldiers to march for miles over rough-surfaced roads or, worse yet, on roadways with no surface at all—roadways that in wet weather would also seem to have no bottom. A single campaign, such as the march from Virginia to Gettysburg in 1863, could be expected to wear out even the best-made shoes. Shoes issued for that campaign were reported to have worn out in sixteen days. The resulting continual necessity to resupply this vital article taxed the ability of the Quartermaster's Departments of both the Union and Confederate Armies.

Before the outbreak of the Civil War, shoes and boots for the small peacetime army were supplied by the Federal clothing depot in Philadelphia. With strict attention to detail and a steady supply of quality material, the prewar soldier could expect to receive comfortable and well-made footwear. During this period, the Quartermaster's Department easily filled orders coming from even the farthest posts on the western frontier.

In April 1861 all of this changed. Suddenly the army quartermasters were faced with a workload literally a thousand times greater. Volunteers came from all parts of the North, and they all needed shoes.

The Quartermaster's Department had no choice but to turn to the contract system to try to fill the desperate need. This system, which had served well in the Mexican War, would in the next four years be put to the supreme test. Nearly every establishment capable of, or claiming to be capable of, producing footwear received an army contract. Going from a tightly controlled system to one that relied on the honesty and ability of often unknown manufacturers produced results as varied as the marketplace itself. Fortunately for the Federal Army, the states that remained in the Union contained the vast majority of the prewar shoe industry. One of the very lucrative markets for the Northern manufacturers had been the slave-holding South. A plain, sturdy shoe was needed to supply the slave population, and except for the few made on the plantations, these had come from Northern factories. The shoe, termed a Negro brogan, was very similar to the army shoe. In addition the vast numbers of immigrants moving to the American western frontier needed ready-made shoes, which also came from the Northern states. But even all of this production capability was not enough.

The army shoe was usually referred to in official documents as a "bootee." It had a high top that covered the ankle, laced with four eyelets, and had a squared toe.

It quickly became evident that the wearing of gray uniforms by Union troops was definitely a problem. On August 31 the Quartermaster's Department issued an order to make up and distribute 4-inch-wide red, white, and blue armbands to be worn by those in gray uniforms. This was quickly abandoned when it was found that the Confederate government had also issued similar armbands to distinguish its troops. Finally, on September 23, the War Department sent a request to Governor Morton:

This Department respectfully requests that no troops here-after furnished by your State for the services of the Gov-ernment be uniformed in gray, that being the color generally worn by the enemy. The blue uniform adopted for the Army of the United States is recommended as readily distinguishable from that of the enemy.

By October the gray uniforms had begun to wear out. When a new uniform was issued, not only the gray was gone but so were the baggy trousers. The new issue consisted of a black jacket with a blue button-up front that gave the appearance of a vest and regulation trousers. The regiment went on to see active service in both theaters of the war, serving first in the west, with actions against Forts Henry and Donelson, the Battle of Shiloh, and the taking of Vicksburg. After reenlistment in 1864, the men were assigned to the 19th Corps and served in the Shenandoah Valley under General Sheridan. The veteran Indiana Zouaves were mustered out on July 26, 1865.

Normal sizes ranged from 5 to 12. In the prewar era, the soles were normally attached with wooden pegs. During the war, both hand- and machine-stitched shoes were accepted. When properly made, these shoes were very serviceable. Unfortunately, however, the lure of government money led to contract fraud. In a letter dated October 9, 1862, the U.S. quartermaster in Detroit reported receiving bootees that had a life span of two days and that the men "refused to wear to Dixie." A quartermaster in St. Louis described shoes that lasted four days on the march. He also discovered that some had old pieces of plate iron sewn between the outer and inner soles. As the war progressed, the government tightened control on contractors, and things improved greatly. By 1864 there were few complaints.

The army bootee was made of tanned leather, finished with the rough side out. The soldier was expected to purchase blacking from the sutler and keep the outer surface well blackened. An order issued by the 3rd Brigade, 1st Division, 2nd Corps, on January 2, 1865, stated: "The troops of this Brigade will be in readiness for review at 11 am tomorrow. . . . The troops will appear with knapsacks, haversack and canteens. Overcoats will be neatly rolled and strapped on the top of the knapsack, buttons and brasses, arms and accoutrements will be neatly cleaned and shoes blacked."

Supplying footwear to the Confederate soldier was a problem of monumental proportions. With the Northern manufacturers no longer at its service, the South was forced to rely on both its own resources and the skill of the blockade runner to keep her soldiers ready for service. Ironically, many of the shoes that made their way from England to Southern ports were superior to those worn by the Northern soldiers. In a report dated August 16, 1863, a Union Army quartermaster stated that he had examined English-made bootees captured from the blockade runner, *I Suppose.* He found them to be "made of well tanned leather very well curried, but not blacked the grain side is as usual high in the ankle and confined by straps and buckle instead of string." He concluded that the shoes "appeared to me the best I have seen for Army use." Confederate soldiers were not always fortunate enough to receive such footwear, however, and they were commonly reported to have taken the shoes of fallen Unionists. By late 1863 some Confederate regiments were being issued tanned hides to be made into shoes by those in the command with the skill to do so. Confederate property returns also show a large number of shoes being issued with the upper portion made of canvas instead of leather. In a few instances, shoes with wooden soles, nicknamed "rockers," were worn by hapless Southern soldiers.

Private, 53rd New York, "D'Epineuil's Zouaves"

The 53rd New York Infantry came as close as any regiment to exactly copying the uniform of the French Zouaves. This was most certainly because both the regiment's colonel, Lionel J. D'Epineuil, and its lieutenant colonel, J. Vigneur de Monteil, had been officers in the French military, D'Epineuil in the navy and de Monteil the army. The regiment was organized in New York City between August 27 and November 15, 1861, but included companies from other parts of the state. There was some hint of trouble with the 53rd from the very beginning. The regiment took a long time to recruit, even after D'Epineuil received permission from Quartermaster General Meigs to outfit them in a very close copy of the uniform of a regiment of the French Zouaves of the Imperial Guard. On August 13 Maj. David Vinton, in charge of the New York Quartermaster Depot, received the following from General Meigs:

Major:

Col. D'Epineuil has written here in regard to his Zouave uniforms. While I advise all officers to adhere to the regulation uniform some regiments can only be raised on conditions of having a peculiar dress. This appears to be the case with the French Zouave Regt. of Col. D'Epimeuil. He states that the coat of the model which he has made is $29 and that he thinks upon contract it can be reduced to $25 or $26. You will aid him by making contracts on the best terms possible but will provide the uniform in the French style as he desires. Subject them to careful inspection as to the material and work.

M.C. Meigs
QM Genl.

The New York City newspapers seemed to take a particular interest in the uniform of the 53rd. On August 18 the *New York Times* reported that "the uniform is that of the Blue Zouaves of France, which consists of dark blue jacket, trimmed with yellow braid, vest of the same, and full pants of light blue, red fez, with blue tassel and duck leggings. The cloth will be of the best quality, as good, in fact, as is used in the French army, and not the cheap flannel that has hitherto [been] given some of our Zouaves." An update by the *New York Tribune* on September 12 correctly stated that "the uniform of the men is an exact copy of the 6th Regiment Imperial Zouaves of France, and is to be completed by Messers Brooks Bros., by special contract with the War Department. It consists of red fez cap with long yellow tassel, dark blue jacket trimmed with bright yellow braid, blue sash, and yellow and black leggings and duck gaiters."

When they finally completed organization, the 53rd consisted mostly of men of French descent but also included one company of American Indians from the Tuscarora Reservation. The regiment was armed with the Enfield rifle musket and standard accoutrements. They left New York on November 18, after being presented a stand of colors by the French ladies of the city, and moved to Annapolis, Maryland. In January they became part of General Burnside's expedition to Hatteras Inlet.

It was at this point that things began to go seriously wrong. It is apparent that the officers of the regiment had been in the habit of ignoring the condition of the men under their command. Desertions had been a continual problem, and it was only with great difficulty that 900 of the 1,500 men who had enrolled were kept together for service. The entire regiment was placed on a ship headed for Hatteras on January 5, 1862.

The trip was supposed to last only a few days, but the ship was so heavily laden that it was unable to land at Hatteras Inlet. A small vessel was sent out, and a few of the officers and a small detachment were able to reach shore. The rest of the regiment was ordered back to Fortress Monroe to await a steamer to transport them to Hatteras. Here, too, they were unable to land, and the ship was ordered to return to its starting point, Annapolis. After thirty-four days, the men finally set foot on land. By this time, the damage to morale and the conditions of the regiment were beyond repair. Desertions, which had been bad before, were now rampant. Within just a few days, the number of men present was reported as 541. Extracts from an inspection report dated February 19, 1862, are sufficient to tell the story:

Arms and Accoutrements: Enfield rifle muskets in bad order generally. Some considerable number excessively rusty and being, if not already, rapidly destroyed from this cause. Bayonets . . . very rusty. Several men had no bayonets or accoutrements, and apparently lost them.

Clothing: Uniforms of the Zouave pattern, and was generally, very dirty, and in very many cases, filthy. Bodily cleanliness was neglected to a considerable extent. [While onboard ship] the troops became very badly infected with vermin-body lice, with which they are still afflicted. The [uniform] pants from their baggy form and heavy plaits inside and outside are of the most unfavorable style for getting rid of the lice—on several cases in different tents where I examined them, underneath the plaits, the nits were in countless numbers soon to develop into life, and the large white body louse which was seen crawling about the person or clothing of the men. Some forty of the men had thrown away or burned their uniforms and were in drawers thirty of whom I inspected in this condition with arms at their tents. A large heap of uniform clothing which had been thrown away by the men, had been gathered up and was exposed near the guard tent.

The officers have been in the practice of sleeping out of camp, absenting themselves for days without authority, and of grossly neglecting their command.

On March 21, 1862, the 53rd New York was disbanded. Company A was transferred to the 17th New York as Company G. Those who wished were allowed to enlist in the regular army, and the rest of the men were transferred to other New York regiments. Lieutenant Colonel de Monteil and a few of the men who made it to shore at Hatteras served with the 9th New York at the battle of Roanoke Island, North Carolina. Lieutenant Colonel de Monteil was killed in this action. Colonel D'Epineuil was largely exonerated by General Burnside when the regiment was disbanded. The blame for its condition was generously placed on the "unfortunate appointments of officers under him." He was given a job as a clerk at the Treasury Department. In 1870 he returned to France to help his native country in its war with Prussia.

The uniform of the 53rd New York shown here is that received from Brooks Brothers. Even though it existed for only a short time, it was well documented by contemporary accounts and photographs. It is probably not surprising that no known examples exist today.

The Forage Cap of a Brave Lieutenant

Lt. J. C. White of the 1st New York Infantry was cited for bravery at the Battle of Chancellorsville, Virginia. Although he was with the regiment for only a short time, his service as an aide-de-camp put him close to headquarters and in the forefront of action at Chancellorsville. Lieutenant White joined the regiment just as the Army of the Potomac was receiving the initial issue of the legendary Corps badges. In addition to the embroidered wreath of a staff officer on the front, his officers-style cap has the badge of the 1st Division, 3rd Corps pinned in the center of the top, exactly as prescribed in army orders. The 1st New York was mustered out of service before the Gettysburg campaign, their term of service having ended. Had Lieutenant White remained in service, he would have been required to "securely fasten" the Corps badge to the cap. Experience quickly showed that badges pinned on were easily lost or removed.

The first Corps badges were cut from layers of material by steel dies supplied to army quartermasters.

The dies were placed on top of several layers of material and struck with a mallet. Due to the extremely hard service of the months following their initial issue, few examples of this first-issue badge have survived.

Chevrons of Sergeant Major Worn by William A. Smith, 17th Michigan Infantry

Chevrons have served to indicate military rank for noncommissioned officers of the U.S. Army since 1821. During the Civil War, both Union and Confederate armies used the same design and color arrangement as those worn by the regular U.S. Army prior to the war. By regulation, privates wore no chevron, corporals wore two, and sergeants three. Color was dictated by branch of service, with red for artillery, yellow for cavalry, and light blue for infantry. The chevrons of sergeants varied depending upon the duties of the wearer.

The chevrons of William A. Smith of the 17th Michigan Infantry, with three stripes and three connecting arches, indicate that he was the regimental sergeant major, the highest-ranking NCO in the regiment. They are light blue and are machine sewn to a dark blue background to match his uniform coat. Chevrons were issued in pairs, and the soldier himself was responsible for their attachment to the sleeves of his uniform. The pride of rank was such that initially most men were quick to see to this duty. By midwar, however, it was frequently necessary for regimental commanders to publish orders demanding that all NCOs who had

not done so put their chevrons on immediately. One such order, dated August 12, 1863, was issued by the commander of the 1st Brigade, 2nd Division, 1st Corps. It read in part, "Every nco will be required to wear the stripes and chevrons due to his rank, and Regimental commanders will cause the present neglect to be remedied in the shortest practicable period of time." It is probable that in the minds of no-nonsense volunteers, outwardly identifying oneself as a person of authority had, in combat, become a health hazard.

Smith had enlisted in Company A of the 17th at Adrian, Michigan, on August 4, 1862. The regiment's service with the famed 9th Corps would take it from South Mountain, Maryland, to Petersburg, Virginia, by way of Knoxville, Tennessee. During this time, Pvt. William Smith saw his share of battle and had been wounded once in December 1863. His promotion to sergeant in February 1865 was followed quickly by promotion to sergeant major on May 12. With the war over and muster out only a month away, it seems certain that the new top sergeant was more than happy to wear these chevrons home.

A Jacket of the 72nd Pennsylvania

Many of the volunteer firemen of Philadelphia were among the first to answer the April 1861 call for three-month volunteers. When these young men returned home after their short service, many were still eager for a try at the Southern foe. When the call went out for troops for three years' service, the natural place for them to enlist was a regiment of "Fire Zouaves" being formed by DeWitt Clinton Baxter. The regiment was to wear the popular Zouave uniform and be drilled in the picturesque Zouave manual of arms.

The uniform selected by Colonel Baxter was a dark blue jacket of French Zouave cut. Instead of having the characteristic trim associated with the French Zouave, the jacked was edged in red piping and had a row of rounded brass buttons down each side of the front. A dark blue forage cap, also trimmed red, a sky blue vest, and white canvas leggings 11 inches high and closing with six black buttons completed the outfit. The uniform was used as an inducement to join the regiment, which was mustered into Federal service as the 72nd Pennsylvania Infantry on August 10, 1861.

The original uniform was not government issue but had been made on special contract in Philadelphia. In November new recruits were beginning to arrive, and it was necessary to make arrangements for them to be uniformed as Zouaves. It was also anticipated that if the regiment was to remain Zouave, after the initial issue wore out, plans would need to be made to resupply the unique uniform. These concerns prompted the following correspondence, which is typical of other regiments who wore what the army termed "Special Uniforms:"

Head Quarters, 72nd Penna. Vol.
3rd Brigade, Corps of Observation
November 22nd, 1861

Brig. Gen. W.W. Burns
Com. 3rd Brigade
    Dear Sir-
    I have recruits coming forward, and have not the Zouave Uniforms, such as worn by this Regiment, to issue them. I shall need at present about two hundred to completely uniform the Regiment, and as the Government does not issue such as I require, I have to request that you will make some arrangement by which I can procure them, and also that I may be able to reuniform my Regiment in the same manner, as often as it may be requested to do so while we remain in the service.

    This Regiment having been recruited, and thus far uniformed as a Zouave Light Infantry Regiment, it is my desire, participated in, by my entire command, that such an arrangement may be effected. I would therefore respectfully suggest that you forward this application through the proper channel, to the Quarter Master General.

    It is understood, that the uniform shall cost the same as the U.S. uniform, to be manufactured under contract to be made by the Quarter Master of the Regiment with parties in Philadelphia and be subject to inspection by, and delivery to the U.S. Qr. Master in charge of clothing in Philadelphia.

    I have no hesitation in saying, that the men enlisted under the promise of this uniform, are not excelled by any troops, either in drill, appearance, or efficiency, and by careful training, and just dealing the service will secure them. Hoping this may meet your approval, and that some arrangement of the kind alluded to may be practicable, I am Dear Sir, very respectfully,
    Yours, etc.
    D.W.C. Baxter
    Col. Com. 72nd PV

As requested by Colonel Baxter, the request was forwarded for approval by General Burns, and went up the chain of command, receiving additional approval. On December 5, Quartermaster General M. C. Meigs sent forward to the Philadelphia Depot the following order:

Lt. Col. Geo. H. Crosman
Depy. Q.M. Genl.
Philadelphia
　Colonel:
　Enclosed is a copy of a letter from Col. D.W.C. Baxter, commanding the 72nd Regiment of Penna. Volunteers, dated November 22nd, with the endorsements thereon, asking that arrangements may be made to keep their Regiment furnished with Zouave uniforms.
　You will at once carry out the recommendations of Brig. Gen. Burns except that you will make the contracts for the uniforms yourself.
　M.C. Meigs

The 72nd Pennsylvania continued to wear the Zouave uniform, or at least parts of it, throughout its term of service. In July 1862 the men decided to switch to the much cooler standard-issue fatigue blouse during hot weather, but by the time the regiment was thrown into action with Sumner's 2nd Corps at Antietam, they were once again wearing the jacket of a Zouave.

The jacket shown here was the property of Edward A. Fulton of Company N, Baxter's Zouaves. It is probably part of the second issue made to the regiment in mid-1862. Fulton was shot in the leg and received two other wounds at the Battle of Antietam on September 17, 1862. He went three days without medical attention and was finally sent to Smoketown Hospital in Philadelphia. He was discharged and sent home in 1863. The bullet had not been removed and continued to bother him for years. Finally, in 1880, doctors decided to remove it. Ironically, he died shortly thereafter, on May 30, 1880.

33RD NEW JERSEY VOLUNTEER INFANTRY, FALL 1863

By late summer 1863 much of the romanticism associated with the war had been lost. Returning veterans missing arms or legs, or word of those who were never to return, had dampened some of the spirit that had filled the ranks of new regiments forming in 1861 and 1862. Special inducements were often used to bring new volunteers forward. Bounties in the form of cash were offered, and in some cases, as with both the 33rd and 35th New Jersey, the offer of a special uniform was used to enhance recruitment. The system evidently worked, as the two regiments filled and were mustered into U.S. service in September and October 1863.

The uniform of the 33rd New Jersey was dark blue trimmed in red, cut in a similar pattern to that worn by the famous 9th New York, Hawkins' Zouaves. Instead of a fez, the headgear selected by the regiment was a kepi of the style worn by the 95th Pennsylvania, Gosline's Zouaves.

The regiment left the state on September 8 and was almost immediately shipped to the western Army of the Cumberland. For several months, the men were employed guarding bridges and in varying details, all of which took their toll on the bright uniforms that had prompted some to enter the life of a soldier.

As spring came on, the army began preparations for what would be one of the major operations of the war, the campaign under Sherman that would result in the taking of Atlanta. All regimental commanders were ordered to make necessary requisitions for needed clothing and supplies. In January the 33rd's German-born Col. George W. Mindil ordered uniform items to replace those worn out in the four months prior. This order included 300 pairs of pants, 196 pairs of leggings, and 240 sashes. As the time to begin the campaign approached, the order had not been filled, and it was necessary to draw regulation items from the brigade quartermaster in their stead. Once Sherman's army started south and became actively engaged, the possibility of obtaining the replacement items diminished with each passing day. On August 22, 1864, after nearly four months of continual fighting, Colonel Mindil wrote the following letter to the quartermaster general:

H.Q. 2nd Brigade
2nd Div. 20th Corps
near Atlanta, Ga.
   General:
   The Zouave clothing ordered for my regiment last Jan-
uary and which was needed to complete its outfit for the
spring campaign only arrived in Chattanooga a little over
a month ago, at a time when the regiment was actively
employed in Georgia, and too late to be of service even if
it could have been obtained.

   Had these articles of clothing arrived in April or
sooner, as expected, they would have been all needed, but,
owing to their non-arrival the regiment was compelled to
take the field in mixed dress, and as the campaign pro-
gressed the wants of the men were supplied from time to
time with the regulation uniform, until now no other is in
use. Hence the 300 pants, 196 leggings, and 240 sashes
invoiced to the regiment and now said to be in store with
Capt. C.K. Smith A.Q.M. at Chattanooga, would make
but an incomplete outfit as no jackets, vests, or caps of the
corresponding Zouave pattern are left, having all been
issued and worn out this year.

   Under these circumstances I would respectfully ask that
this clothing be passed over to some other regiment wear-
ing this especial dress, say the 35th New Jersey or 17th
New York of the 16th Corps of this Army.

   Or if the Government would relieve us of the leggings
and sashes we could use the pantaloons for issue to the
men.

   But if there is no way of disposing of these goods then
as a last resort, enough of Jackets (300), vests (300), caps
(350), pants (50), leggings (100), and sashes (60) would
have to be sent in addition to make an entire outfit.

   Requesting an early reply
   Yr. Obt. Servant
   G.W. Mindil, Col.

Colonel Mindil's letter must have been music to the ears of the Quartermaster's Department, which had continued to do its best to maintain regiments issued special uniforms in the clothing they had been promised. The following letter from the quartermaster general to Colonel Mindil sums up what must have been the prevailing feeling of those responsible for supplying the army with uniforms:

September 5, 1864
   Colonel:
   Your communication of August 22, has been received.
In compliance with suggestion therein contained, Col.
Easton, QM at Nashville, Tenn. Will be instructed to
hold the clothing intended for your regiment for issue to
one of the other regiments equipped with similar
uniforms.

   The Quartermaster General is glad to learn that you
have now adopted the regular uniform of the United
States Army, and, trusts that you will from previous expe-
rience perceive its advantages.

   Not the least of these is the facility with which troops
can always be equipped. Whereas when special and irregu-
lar uniforms are adopted, considerable delay must neces-
sarily ensue in filling requisitions, as the uniforms must be
specially made up to order and difficulty is sometimes
experienced in obtaining the necessary material.

   If all troops would adopt the regular uniforms no such
delay would ensue, and, it is believed that they would be
as comfortably clothed.

   By Order, QM Genl.

The 33rd New Jersey stayed with Sherman's command until the surrender of the Confederate Army in North Carolina. They participated in the Grand Review in Washington in May and were mustered out on July 17, 1865, no longer Zouaves, but certainly battle-hardened veterans.

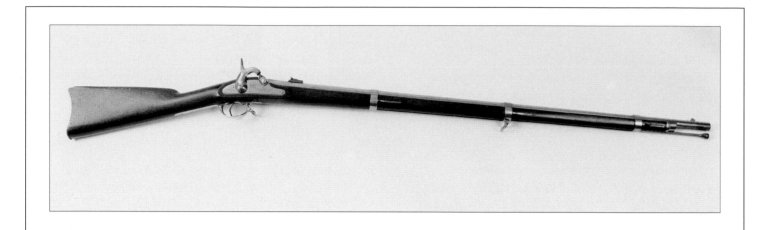

Model 1861 U.S. Rifle Musket, Schubarth Contract

The .58-caliber model 1861 rifle musket was the standard by which all other arms in the hands of Civil War soldiers were judged. As the U.S. Army, and indeed the armies of the world, stood balanced on the edge of the era of the breech-loading rifle, the model 1861 represented the zenith of the development of muzzle-loading military weapons.

The model 1861 had hardly gotten into production when the firing on Fort Sumter in April precipitated the war that many had feared was inevitable. To meet the huge demand of thousands of volunteers, the government was forced to turn to the numerous production facilities in the Northern states capable of arms production. With only a few exceptions, these facilities were not in the arms-manufacturing business, but most had the machinery and power source to allow their conversion to war production. A prime example was the Bridesburg, Pennsylvania, firm of Alfred Jenks & Sons, which began 1861 as manufacturers of textile machinery and ended the year as makers of the model 1861 rifle musket.

Several contractors lacked any actual manufacturing capability but were nonetheless able to secure contracts to manufacture the model 1861. One such individual was Mr. C. D. Schubarth of Providence, Rhode Island. Mr. Schubarth had invented a patent breech-loading arm, but when he approached the War Department, he was told that there was no time to look at such arms. It appears that Mr. Schubarth then turned to one of the senators from his home state, who obliged him by arranging a contract to produce the rifle musket desperately wanted by the army. As a consideration for his assistance, the senator was to receive 5 percent of the money paid to Mr. Schubarth. Needless to say, this was not included in the actual written contract. Lacking actual manufacturing capability, Mr. Schubarth subcontracted with other firms, including Alfred Jenks & Sons to supply the parts he needed to assemble rifle muskets. With this inauspicious beginning, it should not be surprising to learn that after receiving contracts for 10,000 arms, Mr. Schubarth is recorded to have delivered only 9,500.

A Hawkins' Zouave Jacket
9th New York Infantry

In April and May 1861 no fewer than five infantries were raised in New York City that were to go to war wearing the Zouave uniform. The 9th New York, Hawkins' Zouaves, was one of these. The regiment was raised by Rush C. Hawkins, a lawyer and a native of Pomfret, New York. Hawkins had served in the Mexican War, and early in 1861 had raised an independent Zouave company that became the nucleus of the 9th New York. The uniform of the 9th consisted of a dark blue Zouave-style jacket trimmed in red, a dark blue false vest with a red stripe down the front, and dark blue chasseur-style trousers with red trim. Headgear was a red fez with a dark blue tassel and cord. White canvas leggings were worn, later replaced by similar ones of black leather. The regiment was also issued a wide red sash. Officers of Hawkins' Zouaves wore an elegant uniform that consisted of a gold-trimmed jacket and trousers and a scarlet kepi trimmed in gold. Officers also were issued a dark blue frock coat.

The initial uniforms of the regiment were supplied by the state of New York and were tailor-made by Brooks Brothers of New York City. The 9th was first mustered into state service on April 23, 1861, followed quickly by muster into Federal service on May 4. It was sent first to the vicinity of Newport News, Virginia, and in January 1862 the regiment became part of Burnside's North Carolina Expeditionary Corps. In this command, the men saw action at the Battle of Roanoke Island. Evidently the rigors of service were taking a toll on the uniforms, prompting the following letter from Colonel Hawkins:

> Steamer Virginia
> off Roanoke Island, N.C.
> Feb. 27, 1862
> Col. Crosman
> A.Q.M. U.S.A.
> Phila. Pa.
>> Dear Sir
>> I wish that you would do me the favor to send me, one thousand blouses, and one thousand pairs of pantaloons, the latter to be made of Army cloth the lot you sent me before, had about one hundred pairs of miserable satinet, smuggled in among them, and possessed but little warmth and less wear.
>> I would not trouble you, but I find that I cannot depend upon Depot QM's they promise everything and do nothing, and the consequence is that the sol-

> diers have suffered greatly for the want of what is allowed them by regulations.
>> I am, Dear Sir, with great respect most faithfully your obed. Servt.
>> Rush C. Hawkins, Col. 9th NYV

This issue was doubtless to save the Zouave uniforms for active field service, for the regiment continued to wear and receive the Zouave dress for its entire length of service. The jacket shown here was the property of Sgt. Latham A. Fish, originally in Company C and later transferred to Company K. The metallic device used to close the top of the jacket bears the "C" of his original company. Fish wore this jacket in action at Roanoake Island and Antietam, where the Zouaves were part of Burnside's 9th Corps on the Union left.

5th New York Veteran Volunteers, 1864

On May 11, 1863, the highly recognized Duryea Zouaves, the 5th New York Infantry, were mustered out of service, their term of enlistment having ended. By fall of that year, the decision had been made to recruit a new regiment with the veterans of the old 5th as its nucleus. These men filled four companies and the remainder of the regiment was filled with men recruited from the reorganized 31st and 37th New York, veterans and recruits of the 94th New York, and a battalion consisting of men of the 12th New York Infantry whose term of enlistment ran beyond that of the remainder of the regiment.

The new 5th New York was to be outfitted in a uniform that closely resembled that of the original regiment, except for the jacket, which was to be light rather than dark blue. The first contract, made with John Boylan & Co. of Newark, New Jersey, called for a light blue jacket. As received and issued, the jacket was a medium blue, several shades darker than the army's sky blue used for trousers and overcoats. The rest of the uniform consisted of red Zouave trousers, a gray shirt, white canvas leggings, and leather gaiters. This was all topped off with a red fez and white turban. All this was much to the liking of the veterans of the original regiment, but some of those being transferred were less than enthusiastic. One veteran of the 12th New York wrote the following when faced with the prospect of becoming a Zouave:

A present source of annoyance lies in the fact that the Fifth is a Zouave regiment, and we fear we may be compelled to adopt its uniform, which consists of crimson zouave pants, buff leather gaiters, light blue zouave jacket with scarlet braids sprawling fantastically over it, a variegated waistband wound round half a dozen times, and horror of horrors, a crimson skull cap with a yellow tassel, or else a crimson and white turban. I suppose I would be permitted to continue the detailed duty uniform, but we cannot tell, one thing is certain, I will not wear the other without a fight.

It can be presumed that the disgruntled writer learned to live with his new outfit, as the 5th New York Veteran Volunteers received a continual supply of the Duryea Zouave uniform until they were mustered out August 21, 1865. The soldier shown here is armed with a model 1861 rifle musket. He is wearing leather leggings rather than the white canvas originally supplied the regiment. As was favored by regiments wearing the Zouave jacket, his cartridge box is worn on the waist belt instead of being suspended from the regulation cross belt. After formation, the regiment had initially served in the defenses of Washington, but it was ordered to join the Army of the Potomac in May 1864. From that time until the war's end, it served and fought as part of the 5th Army Corps

Zouave Jacket of the 155th Pennsylvania

The 155th Pennsylvania infantry is one of only a few Union regiments that reversed the process by entering the service wearing the regulation uniform, and then switching to the Zouave dress. The Zouave uniform jacket pictured here was worn by Sgt. William D. Porter of Company K. The slate blue-gray wool body is trimmed in pale yellow, using a highly Americanized version of the front ornamentation, or tombeaux. The complete uniform called for the soldier to wear a red fez with a blue tassel and cord rather than the regulation forage cap. This change from standard led Sergeant Porter to place his red (1st Division) 5th Corps badge, a Maltese cross, on the left breast within the tombeaux.

The change to the Zouave uniform was authorized in mid-1863 and was considered an honor. The uniform was produced by the Philadelphia Quartermaster depot by altering some of the French chasseur uniforms purchased in 1861, many of which had been found to be too small to issue. The regiment wore the uniform for the remainder of its term of service. Despite the early authorization and the usual efficiency of the Philadelphia depot, the new outfits had not been delivered by December 1863, prompting the following letter from the Quartermaster General's Office, dated December 11:

> Col. Geo. H. Crosman
> Asst. Q.M. Genl.
> Philadelphia
>   Colonel
>   You are respectfully requested to inform this office whether uniform (Zouave) for the 155th Penna. Vols, Gel. Garrard's Brigade, is made. It was asked for by Genl. Garrard at the same time as that for the 140th N.Y. Vols. to be made of the dark blue French chasseur uniform trimmed yellow, that of the 140th N.Y. red.
>   Please answer as soon as possible and also state how much of the Chasseur uniform has been altered, and how altered, trimmed, etc.
>   It was the intention to use this clothing for the uniform of "Garrad's Brigade" (Zouave).
>   Very respectfully;
>   By Order of the Q.M. Genl.
>   Alex J. Perry, AQM
>   It is presumed as it is not taken up on your last weekly report that the uniforms for the 155 Pa. Have not yet been made. Your reply to this will be awaited before further action. A.J.P.

Shortly after this rather direct letter, the regiment received its uniforms. It is evident that the change in uniform was not received by every man of the regiment in the spirit in which it was intended, or perhaps the passage of several months dimmed the initial enthusiasm. Whatever the reason, the following regimental order was issued September 12, 1864:

> The commanding officer has heard with surprise and mortification that some of the men of this Regiment have been guilty of selling or trading portions of their Zouave clothing to persons belonging to other Regiments. He is sorry to see that the men of this Regiment have so little pride in their uniform—a uniform so universally known as one worn generally by none but good Regiments. This gross dereliction of duty will not be permitted.
>   A.L. Pearson
>   Col. Cmdg.

Union Army Corps Badges

One of the most distinctive—and enduring—innovations to be handed down from the Civil War is the use of special badges or patches, to identify various military organizations. Although these were not introduced into service until the spring of 1863, they became a cherished part of the memory of every soldier who wore one. The original circular, which was distributed from the Headquarters of the Army of the Potomac, clearly illustrates both the purpose and the intended design of the first badges:

March 21, 1863
Circular

For the purpose of ready recognition of Corps & Divisions in this Army & to prevent injustice by reports of straggling & misconduct through mistake as to the organizations, the Chief Quartermaster will furnish without delay the following badges to be worn by the officers & enlisted men of all the Regiments of the various Corps mentioned. . . .

1st Corps A Sphere (Red for 1st Div. White for 2nd Div., Blue 3rd Div.)
2nd Corps A Trefoil " " "
3rd Corps A Lozenge " " "
5th Corps A Maltese Cross " " "
6th Corps A Cross " " "
(light Div. Green)
11th Corps A Crescent " " "
12th Corps A Star " " "
The sizes & colors will be according to pattern.
By command of Maj. Genl. Hooker

5th Corps Badge, worn by Edwin J. Baker, Company H, 42nd Pennsylvania Infantry.

6th Corps Badge, worn by a soldier of the 21st New Jersey Infantry.

19th Corps Badge, worn by a cannoneer of Nim's Massachusetts Battery.

10th Corps Badge, an extra-fancy badge of officer quality, worn by Maj. Edwin R. Smith, 169th Regiment, New York Infantry.

3rd Corps Badge, worn by A. Woods, Company I, 2nd New Hampshire Infantry. This sutler-sold badge has raised letters that identify its wearer as a member of the "3rd Corps, Hooker's old Division, Army of the Potomac." His name is engraved on the back.

20th Corps Badge (originally the 12th Corps), worn by Arthur Presant, Company K, 102 New York Veteran Volunteer Infantry. This badge is engraved with the names of hard-fought battles in both the eastern and western theaters of the war.

A Confederate Officer's Caps

As a general rule, the caps worn by the Confederate Army were similar in construction to their Union opponents. Usually the Confederate cap had a lower crown, and the style more closely resembled the cap worn by the French Army. Some Confederate caps have a colored band around the outside lower edge, about the size of the inner sweatband, designating the various branches of service. But expediency of manufacture made this a rare luxury. There are instances of extra-fancy caps being issued to Confederate units. One such unit, the Pee Dee Artillery of South Carolina, received red forage caps in mid-1863. Confederate officers often obtained caps with a trim of gold cord on the sides and top as a further designation of rank. Although Confederates are often known to have favored the soft or slouch hat, the image of Confederate soldiers always wearing a soft, wide-brimmed hat is belied by the extensive num-

ber of caps now known to have been worn by both Southern enlisted men and officers.

These two Confederate forage caps were both the property of Maj. Hugh Mortimer Nelson, who commanded the Floyd County Troop of the illustrious 1st Virginia Cavalry at First Manassas. He was later to command Company D, 6th Virginia Cavalry, and go on to be an aide-de-camp to Gen. R. S. Ewell. Major Nelson was wounded at the battle of Gaines Mill and died of disease. One of Major Nelson's two caps is the style much liked by Confederate officers: gray with gold cord trim. On the top, his rank is indicated by three concentric gold rings instead of the three-cord quatrefoil often seen. The major's second cap is black with a high crown that falls forward to the bill, and two small, brass buttons with a flower design to secure the chin straps. A cap very similar to this was worn by none other than Gen. T. J. "Stonewall" Jackson.

PRIVATE, 88TH NEW YORK INFANTRY, SUMMER 1863

The 88th New York Infantry was one of three regiments of the hard-fighting Irish Brigade, which served in the 2nd Corps of the Army of the Potomac. The regiment was formed in New York City in the fall of 1861 and bore on its guidons the title "Fourth Irish." The 88th could almost be considered a veteran unit from the start. Fully a third of those in its ranks were former British soldiers, many of whom had seen service in the Crimean War and the Indian mutiny. The regimental officers were nearly all ex-officers or noncommissioned officers of the 69th New York State Militia who had served at First Bull Run. Comparatively few of the men of the 88th were U.S. citizens by birth. It was said that some of those recruited were fresh from the old sod and when they enlisted spoke nothing but Gaelic.

The veteran qualities of the regiment were first evidenced during the Peninsula Campaign. At Malvern Hill, on July 1, 1862, after bitter fighting during the day, the regiment got into what they termed "a regular Donnybrook" at night, where clubbed muskets were the primary weapon. The following day, Gen. Edwin V. Sumner, their corps commander and himself a longtime army veteran, inspected the men and was invited to inspect a pile of broken muskets and asked to order new ones. Sumner was outraged until he found out how the weapons had been broken. As explained to him, "the byes wint for the Rebs in the way they wor used to." And so they fought throughout the war, winning glory in the attack on the Bloody Lane at Antietam, on Marye's Heights at Fredericksburg, at Gettysburg, and on to Appomattox. It has been said that the men of the 88th were known to play cards under fire and make jokes while in line of battle.

The soldier illustrated here is wearing the New York State jacket, which was adopted in 1861 by the state for issue to her regiments. Not all regiments got the jacket, and many New York troops wore the standard Union infantry four-button fatigue blouse. Those who did receive the jacket, which included all of the New Yorkers of the Irish Brigade, received reissues of them at least into early 1864.

During the Gettysburg campaign in the summer of 1863, the 88th New York was part of the 2nd Brigade, 1st Division, 2nd Corps, along with the 28th Massachusetts, 63rd and 69th New York, and 116th Pennsylvania. The entire brigade, except for the 28th Massachusetts, which had Enfields, was armed with the .69-caliber model 1842 smoothbore musket. This weapon had originally been favored by the brigade's commander, Gen. Thomas Francis Meagher, who in 1861 had believed that most of the fighting would be done at close quarters, where the buck-and-ball load in common use in the model 42s was particularly deadly.

This soldier is wearing the canvas leggings that had been widely issued to the Army of the Potomac in the spring. Most of his surplus clothing had been sent for storage until the fall, as dictated by division orders. His accoutrements are regulation army issue, and he wears the newly issued red trefoil corps badge of the 1st Division, 2nd Corps, although a similar badge of green probably would have been more to his liking.

The Shirt of a Rebel from England

This Confederate shirt, along with its owner's Confederate jacket, were until recently part of the collection of the Royal Artillery Museum in Woolwich, England, where they had been placed by their owner in 1905. Confederate sentiment was high in many circles of English society, and numerous young men made the journey to the American South to join the Confederate Army. It is little wonder, then, that the jacket and shirt were found so far from the land its original owner fought for.

Unlike the Union Army, which usually issued shirts of white or gray wool, the Confederate issue was often based more upon the availability of materials suitable for the purpose. While many Southern soldiers simply wore civilian shirts, the military cut of this example makes it likely that the shirt was quartermaster issue. Certainly the blue and brown stripes of the shirt material would not have prevented its purchase by any Confederate clothing facility. An interesting note is the documented issue of "138 striped shirts" to the 20th Battalion Virginia Artillery on December 2, 1862, and the issue of checked shirts to the Army of Tennessee in 1863.

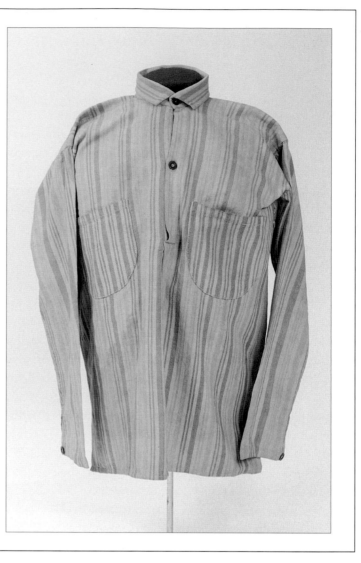

A Hand-Carved Pipe of a Connecticut Volunteer

Most of a soldier's time was spent in camp or on duties other than combat. Tobacco was not only a popular item at the sutler's stand, but also a prime trade item. Accounts abound of Union and Confederate soldiers meeting while on picket to exchange news and such luxury items as tobacco and coffee.

During time spent in camp, maybe over the long hours in winter quarters, items such as this fine, regimentally marked, carved smoking pipe were often produced. The regiment spent the winter of 1862–63 encamped near Stafford Court House, Virginia. The pipe may well have been produced then. As part of the hard-fighting 12th Corps, and later the 20th Corps, the 5th Connecticut saw action in both the eastern and western theaters of the war. As a constant companion, this pipe must have shared the quiet of many a campfire and long night on the picket post. Packed securely in a pocket or knapsack, it surely heard the fury of many battles.

A Confederate Jacket Found in England

This fine example of a Confederate-issued enlisted man's jacket was placed in the Royal Artillery Museum in Woolwich, England, in 1905 along with a Confederate shirt. The items were likely worn by an English citizen who had cast his lot with the American South and returned home when his chosen country was no more. The jacket, which has Louisiana state buttons, is typical of the type produced in Southern clothing depots and issued to soldiers serving in the western Confederate armies. The material, which is now a light gray-brown color, is that known as "wool jean." Jean was woven with both cotton and woolen yarn and gave the initial appearance on the outer surface of being entirely made of wool. The simple cut says that this jacket is probably a product of late-war manufacture. It is likely the color was originally gray, as many of the dyes used for producing gray during the nineteenth century are known to have turned brown with use and exposure to the elements.

It is a popular misconception that Confederate soldiers were in rags toward the end of the Civil War. Numerous photographs, as well as correspondence in Confederate Quartermaster records, such as the following Army of Northern Virginia report, tell quite a different story:

Office Chief QM 2nd Corps
Feb. 2nd, 1865
Col. Jas. L. Corley
Chief QM, ANV

Colonel:

From an examination of the Inspection Report, I find that the troops of this Corps are represented as still requiring a large amount of clothing. This is an error, which I have corrected upon the report by an

endorsement. With the exception of a few pants & shirts the estimates forwarded on the 1st of January '65 have been very nearly filled.

From the quality of clothing issued during the past two months the troops ought to be well clothed.

G. D. Merce
Maj. & act. Corps QM

SONS OF ERIN

MARYANNE TRUMP BARRY

It was midmorning on September 17, 1862. The Battle of Antietam had been raging for more than four hours, as a brigade of New York infantry moved toward its objective: a road with its bed several feet below the level of the ground on either side. This road now served as a natural trench for the veteran Southern troops of Gen. D. H. Hill's Division. As they advanced across an open field of clover and up a slight incline in perfect formation, their emerald green flags, emblazoned with the gold harp of Ireland, proclaimed to all that this was the famed "Irish Brigade." In front of them, mounted on a magnificent bay horse, rode their flamboyant commander, Brig. Gen. Thomas Francis Meagher.

Within minutes they had pushed aside a Rebel skirmish line and reached the crest of the field. Less than 100 yards ahead, Hill's Confederates waited. Almost immediately they received a crashing volley from the Confederate line. It was here that the Sons of Erin stood and returned fire. General Meagher's horse went down, and the flagstaff holding the proud green flag was shot in two. The Irishmen stood and

slugged it out until their ammunition was exhausted and they were forced to withdraw. Filling their cartridge boxes, they soon returned to continue the fight. But this time there was no stopping. They charged forward with a loud cheer. Within minutes, the road was cleared and the Confederates were in retreat. The gallant action had taken a fearful toll. This struggle for a small section of Maryland country road cost the brigade 113 killed and 422 wounded.

The regiment that is the focal point of this dramatic painting is the 69th New York. The Irish Brigade also included the 63rd New York and 88th New York, as well as the 1st Division of Maj. Gen. Edwin V. Sumner's 2nd Corps. Of particular note is the use of the waist-length eight-button jacket issued by the state of New York to many of her regiments. The dark blue jacket with light to medium blue trim was adopted in April 1861 as a substitute for the army regulation frock coat. In reality, it was a much more practical garment than the long coat and was greatly liked by the troops who wore it.

Some accounts of the Antietam fight have mentioned a few of the Brigade going into battle barefoot. Since supplies of footwear were not a problem on this campaign for the Federal Army, it can only be assumed that the feel of clover under bare feet, perhaps for the last time, was just too much to resist for young men who had likely spent many happy hours that way.

General Meagher and his staff were well known for their stylish, even elegant uniforms. Meagher, the son of a wealthy merchant, an adventurer, and Irish revolutionary, is shown here wearing a yellow silk sash and mounted on the magnificent bay horse that within minutes will become a casualty of battle. It has been said that Meagher considered his brigade a symbol of Irish glory. If this is the case, that glory indeed shone brightly at Antietam on September 17.

Caps with the Infantry Insignia

A bugle, more reminiscent of a French hunting horn, was authorized as the insignia for infantry in the U.S. Army in 1863. Originally the device was worn only by officers, but in 1858 with the adoption of the new army hat, a brass bugle that measured about 3 inches across was authorized for enlisted men, to be worn on the front of the hat along with the regimental number and company letter. It was not the intention of the army to have the insignia, except for the company letter, worn on the enlisted man's forage cap. Since many volunteer regiments never received the army hat, however, it was a fairly common sight during the first half of the war to see all the issue brass worn on the cap. The cap of Leveret Lynn, a wagoner of Company B, 24th Connecticut Infantry, is an excellent example of the way the infantry device was affixed along with the company letter and regimental number. The brass bugles were made with two small brass wire loops soldered to the back. The

letters and numbers each had two small brass wires affixed to their backs. It was necessary for the soldier to punch holes in the crown of the cap and push the loops or wires through. The wires would simply be bent over, and the loops had a thin strip of leather passed through them to secure them in place.

The officer's forage cap worn by Capt. Charles Barton, Company H, 7th Connecticut Infantry, is made in a style that was worn early in the Civil War. The curved, narrow bill was made popular by Gen. Irvin McDowell, who commanded the Federal Army at the First Battle of Bull Run. As McDowell's image faded, so too did the desire of many officers to wear this style cap, although the "McDowell" cap was still favored by some at least through 1863. On the front of Captain Barton's cap is a metal infantry bugle stamped in a pattern to look like an embroidered insignia.

Four-Button Fatigue Coat Worn by First Sergeant Frank Fitz, 44th Massachusetts Volunteer Militia

One of the most practical and widely worn uniform items issued to the Union soldier was the dark blue short coat originally intended only for fatigue purposes. The garment known officially as a "sack coat," was patterned after a popular item of civilian casual wear and was adopted by the U.S. Army in 1858. It was made of loosely woven wool and came in two styles, lined and unlined. It was described by the Quartermaster's Department simply as "extending half way down the thigh, and made loose . . . [with a] falling collar, an inside pocket on the left side; [with] four coat buttons down the front."

Every Federal soldier received a sack coat, even if he was issued a dress coat. In practical terms, the volunteers would often requisition the lined coats for winter wear. The intent of the army was that the men would wear the dress coats on campaign. In fact, during the first two years of the war, the dress coat could be widely seen in the ranks, although it saw the greatest use in the eastern armies. By 1864, however, the comfort and lower cost to the government of the sack coat made it the accepted norm for the Federal armies fighting in all theaters of service.

The sack coats were made and issued in only four sizes. They would be sent from the army supply depot in bales of 100, which was enough to outfit a company at full strength. The bales were securely wrapped in canvas and contained what the army considered an appropriate mix of sizes. Careful studies conducted during peacetime made this system work fairly well, although unfortunately, companies of eager volunteers often contained an overabundance of muscular farm or factory workers, who were not recruited by size. This fact gave birth to the many tales of ill-fitting uniforms. Resourceful soldiers soon learned to trade, alter, or otherwise make do.

The coat of Sgt. Frank Fitz is a fine example of the Federal-issue sack coat. With the exception of the Massachusetts state buttons, which probably replaced the standard issue as a show of state pride, not a soldier who served the Union would fail to recognize it immediately as one exactly like he wore.

Kepis for Officers

These two officer's caps are of the style more closely associated with the French Army's cap. They have a lower crown than the caps usually issued by the Federal Army and have a flat, straight bill, which is also associated with this style cap. They represent superb examples of the type of cap often purchased from military outfitters by army officers.

The regulation dark blue kepi that belonged to Lt. Green Smith, son of the famous abolitionist Gerritt Smith, is adorned with ornate black cord trim and has the wreath insignia of a staff officer, as well as a red 9th Corps badge, on the front. It is obvious that he shared his father's convictions, as the young lieutenant was cited for bravery for attempting to rally the black troops at the tragic Crater at Petersburg, Virginia, in July 1864

The kepi of Maj. Elliot C. Pierce, 13th Massachusetts, is typical of that worn by many officers. Major Pierce commanded the 1st Army Corps ambulances at Gettysburg and had a position on the corps staff. His status as a staff officer is reflected in the corps badge, which can be seen on top of the cap. It is the sphere of the 1st Corps but is divided into three colors representing the three divisions of the corps. The elegant embroidered bugle on the front of the major's cap proudly designates his original regiment as the "13th."

1ST SOUTH CAROLINA VOLUNTEER INFANTRY, U.S. COLORED TROOPS

WILLIAM GLADSTONE

The 21st Regiment South Carolina Volunteers was officially organized January 31, 1863, making it the second black unit to be mustered into U.S. service. The lineage of the regiment can be traced to a company of black soldiers formed at Hilton Head, South Carolina, in May of the previous year by Maj. Gen. David Hunter. This company was largely composed of runaway slaves, but as word of the probable issuance of a Proclamation of Emancipation by President Lincoln began to spread, other black men eager to serve the Union came forward.

On November 24, 1862, Boston minister Thomas Wentworth Higginson, a fervent abolitionist, assumed command of a new regiment that had grown from the single company. As Colonel Higginson worked to bring the regiment to full strength, he also began a strict program of drill and instruction. The skill gained by the men of the 1st South Carolina filled both the soldiers and their white officers with a great deal of pride, which was elevated even further when on New Year's Day of 1863, as the anticipated Emancipation Proclamation took effect, they received a set of regimental colors confirming them as U.S. soldiers.

The 1st South Carolina was also one of the only regiments, black or white, to see service before it was officially recognized as a military unit. The men had been on an expedition along the coasts of Georgia and Florida in November 1862. Their first real service as a regiment came in a weeklong expedition up the St. Mary's River on the Georgia-Florida border in January 1863. It was here that they saw their first action in a skirmish with Confederate cavalry at Township, Florida. The men of the new black regiment acquitted themselves well and received praise in the Northern press. In February 1864 the regiment was redesignated the 33rd Regiment United States Colored Infantry. They continued to serve in the area of South Carolina, Georgia, and Florida until mustered out on January 31, 1866.

The soldiers depicted here are wearing the first uniform issued to the 1st South Carolina. Except for the red trousers, it is the regulation U.S. Army pattern. The trousers are similar to those worn by the French Army and were probably an inducement to enlist. Such inducement was not needed, however, and the different color made the men of the regiment feel that they were being set apart from the white regiments, who all wore the regulation sky blue. Colonel Higginson petitioned General Hunter to have a second issue of trousers, and by mid-February 1863 blue trousers had been received.

Throughout 1863 there were at least five types of firearms carried by the 1st South Carolina. These were a mixed lot of Springfields and Enfields, as well as .69-caliber foreign-made arms of different types. By January 1864 these had all been replaced with the latest Springfield rifle muskets.

With this, the last physical hurdle had been overcome. There were many more social hurdles, some of which would far outlive the men of the 1st South Carolina Infantry, but a start had been made.

Frock Coat of General Edward Bouton

U.S. Army regulations of 1861 specified that all officers wear a frock coat of dark blue cloth, a skirt extending two-thirds to three-fourths of the distance from the hip to the knee. A brigadier general's coat was to have two rows of eight buttons placed in pairs. That of a major general was to have two rows of nine buttons each arranged in groups of three. This distinctive button arrangement allowed for easy recognition of a general officer at a distance, a fact that was both an advantage and a disadvantage. If such an officer had the misfortune to fall within the sights of a Confederate sharpshooter, the marksman had no trouble picking a target of certain importance. One officer, Col. Adrian R. Root of the 94th New York, commanding the 1st Brigade, 2nd Division, 1st Army Corps, recognized this problem and on December 5, 1862, issued an order that stated in part, "No officer of the 1st Brigade will be permitted to enter battle with a uniform coat or shoulder straps, or with any distinctive badge or rank upon his person, that can attract the attention of the enemy." Unfortunately for many officers, Colonel Root's visionary order was not appreciated by those in higher command. This order was countermanded by the commander of the 2nd Division, 1st Corps, on May 25, 1863.

General Bouton's coat is an excellent example of that required in 1861, and for the rest of the war. In addition to the button arrangement, the coat bears shoulder straps with a single star, which regulations specified also as a mark of rank for a brigadier. General Bouton did not receive his promotion to the brevet rank of general until February 1865. Prior to this promotion, he had served first as a captain commanding the 1st Illinois Light Artillery battery and later as colonel of the 59th U.S. Colored Troops. When General Grant recommended him for promotion, he declared Bouton to be "one of the best officers in the Army."

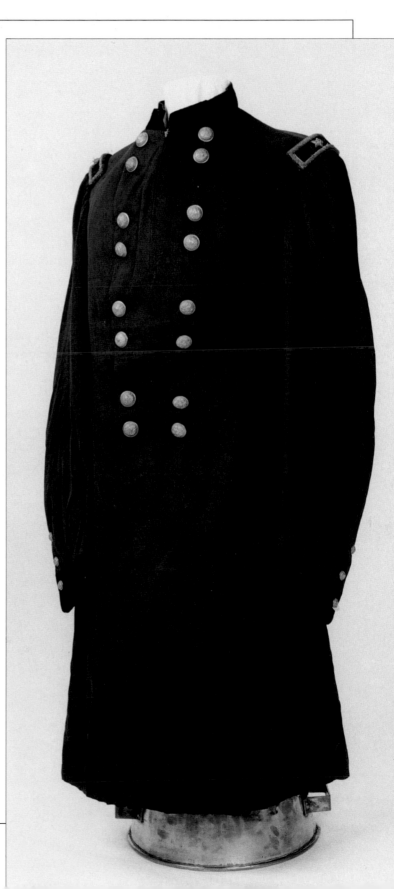

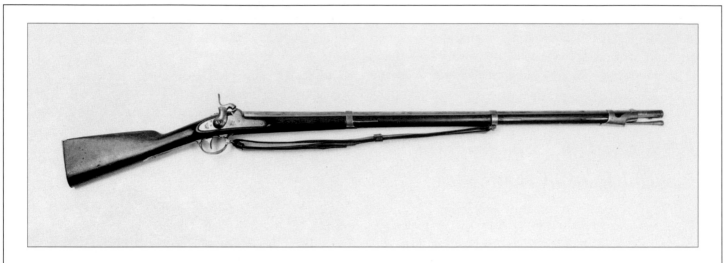

The Model 1842 Musket

Even after the regular army had been armed with the model 1855 rifle musket, the model 1842 was still the predominate arm in the hands of the numerous militia units of both the Northern and Southern states. It only stands to reason then, that when war broke out in April 1861, many units leaving for the front were armed with this weapon. As the war progressed, both the Union and the Confederacy made a concerted effort to rearm their front-line regiments with the state-of-the-art rifle musket. Before the war, many 1842s were taken into the Federal arsenals and had rifling cut into the bore and a rear sight added. These arms fired the .60-caliber minié ball.

Despite the longer range of the rifle musket, many regiments armed with the '42s only reluctantly gave them up. One of the rounds issued for use in the arm was called "buck and ball," which consisted of the standard .69-caliber round all surmounted by three .32-caliber buckshot. The combination more than made up for the long-range inaccuracy of the smoothbore. At close range (under 200 yards), where much fighting in the Civil War took place, the .69-caliber ball packed a devastating punch, and the buckshot could be lethal. One Union regiment, the 12th New Jersey, was still armed with the '42 and buck and ball at Gettysburg. As part of the 2nd Corps, Army of the Potomac, they were on the famous inner angle near the Bryan barn during Pickett's Charge. Little needs to be said of their feeling toward the arm in light of the fact that they chose to represent the buck-and-ball load in granite on top of their monument, which stands there today. By 1864 the '42 had all but disappeared in the hand of Union regiments fighting with the various armies. A few Confederate regiments would continue to use the arm until the very ending months of the war.

Private, Company K, 3rd Battalion, 8th U.S. Colored Heavy Artillery, Late Summer 1864

WILLIAM GLADSTONE

The struggles and triumphs of such regiments of black troops as the 54th Massachusetts are well documented. Today they are beginning to take their rightful place in the annals of Civil War history. As always, in the writing of military history, there are others who have escaped the documentation of the historian's pen. These men served in places with names most students of the war have never encountered. The 8th U.S. Heavy Artillery is one that deserves particular note. The regiment was raised in Rhode Island as the 14th Rhode Island Colored Heavy Artillery from August 1863 to January 1864. Its designation was changed to the 8th U.S. on April 4, 1864, and again to the 11th U.S. Colored Heavy Artillery in May. They continued to be carried on army rolls as the 8th Regiment until the fall, however.

Almost all of the men who enlisted in the 14th Rhode Island had been brought up free in their native state and had never lived under the yoke of slavery. An inspection report dated August 10, 1864, had the following to say:

The Battalion, as a whole, is a superior one. The men are almost all free, and not freed men. There is hardly a contraband [runaway slave] in the organization, and the majority of the command can read and write, and are usually well informed. Their superiority . . . is marked.

These men were putting both their lives and their freedom on the line by volunteering to serve in the South. The 3rd Battalion of the regiment was sent to garrison the defenses of New Orleans, where they were later joined by the full regiment and where they spent their entire service. They were mustered out on October 2, 1865.

Despite the fact that this regiment was designated and served as heavy artillery, the uniforms issued were the regulation for light artillery. The soldier shown here wears the jacket of the light artillery but as is proper for heavy artillery, is wearing the accoutrements of an infantryman. He is also equipped with a maneuvering, or "shod," hand spike, which was used later to lever the heavy cannon found in fortifications back into position after firing. In addition to infantry accoutrements, regiments of heavy artillery were also armed with infantry weapons. The 8th was armed with both Springfield and Enfield rifle muskets.

Cannoneer's Cap

This cap was worn by an Irish volunteer, Daniel P. Doyle, who served with the famous 9th Massachusetts Battery. The battery gained everlasting glory by the desperate delaying action fought by them on July 2, 1863, at Gettysburg. Here on the Union left, the battery, commanded by Capt. John Bigelow, was ordered to delay the advance of the Confederates of Barksdale and Kershaw's brigades long enough for a Union defense line to be formed in their rear. In the action that followed, the battery suffered a total of twenty-eight casualties.

The brass crossed cannon artillery insignia and battery number 9 are affixed to the top of the cap. The Maltese cross of the 5th Corps has been painted above the brass devices. This cross is tinted red, white, and blue, likely dating from the battery's service with the Reserve Artillery Brigade of the 5th Corps from May 1864 to June 1865.

Maj. Hugh Nelson's Boots

These are the boots of a Confederate mounted officer with an eye to rakish style and perhaps to history. Maj. Hugh Nelson, whose overcoat and caps are also included in this book, may have had these boots made after seeing engravings of officers of the French Army under Napoleon, or even paintings of the famed commander himself. The extra-high cut, covering the knee, would not have been out of place in any of the battles of the French Army of the First Empire. To hold the top of the boot in its proper position, a strap was affixed that passed around the leg above the knee. Major Nelson died early in the conflict, so he probably purchased these boots in 1861. At that time they may well have been imported from Europe. As the war progressed, the shortage of leather in the South made footwear such as this nearly impossible for any but the highest-ranking officers to obtain.

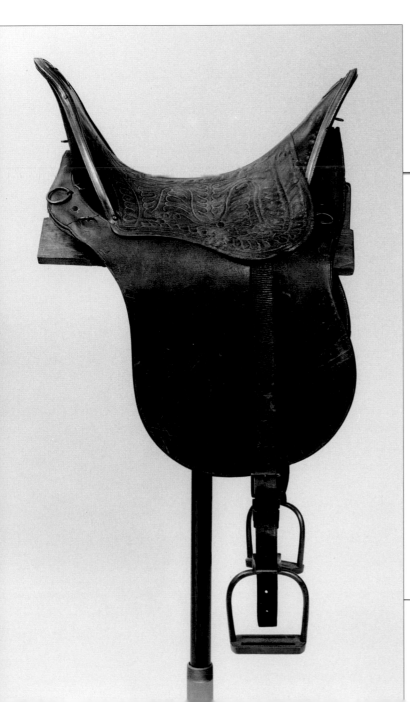

The Grimsley Saddle

The army-issue saddle of the decade prior to the Civil War was known by the name of the man who held several patents on it, Thornton Grimsley. The Grimsley was in general use by the regiment of U.S. Dragoons and the Mounted Rifle Regiment from about 1851 until the adoption of the model 1859 McClellan saddle. The Grimsley had a high pommel and cantle, which gave it a graceful appearance. Many officers who served with the mounted units on the western frontier favored this saddle and continued to use it in both the Union and Confederate Armies during their service in the Civil War.

Although it has no verifiable history, it is very likely that the saddle pictured here is one that carried its owner to war. The fancy tooled leather seat and extra-high-quality black leather are evidence that it belonged to an officer. It is one of the finest examples of its type to have survived.

A Nonregulation Revolver That Went to War

One of the greatest advances in firearms development in the decade prior to the Civil War was the
advent of the self-contained metallic cartridge firing
revolver, patented by the Smith & Wesson arms company. No longer did its user have to bother with easily
damaged paper cartridges or spend precious moments
placing percussion caps on six cylinder chambers. It is no
wonder that the popularity of such arms, combined with
the outbreak of the Civil War, led other companies to
quickly copy the idea. The Moore's Patent Firearms
Company, located in Brooklyn, New York, was one such
company. The Moore's revolver was a particular favorite
of Union officers who were willing to accept its smaller
.32 caliber for the quick-loading cartridge it offered.
Although it was produced only between 1861 and 1863
due to a patent infringement lawsuit brought by Smith
& Wesson, many were sold.

Capt. C. Maynard, Company A, 26th Connecticut
Volunteers, was obviously popular with those he commanded, as they gave him this Moore's revolver to show
their admiration. It is suitably engraved on the backstrap

between the polished wooden grips, "Capt. J. C. Maynard Co. A, 26th Regt. C.V. by his company." The
respect shown for Captain Maynard was obviously well
founded. The 26th Connecticut was recruited for nine
months' service in September 1862. They were well
drilled for the next two months, during which time
Captain Maynard probably received his revolver. On
November 13 the regiment left camp bound for the
operations in Louisiana. It was not until May at Port
Hudson, which, like Vicksburg, stood heavily fortified
overlooking the Mississippi River, that the regiment saw
its first action. On May 27, after several days of preparation, a column that included the 26th was ordered to
assault the Confederate works. Charging over an open
field, the men took an advanced position, but at great
cost. When the 26th called its rolls after the battle, 107
were dead or wounded. Among the latter was Company
A's beloved captain, shot through the chest. His wound
was not mortal, but the brave captain, who had carried
his fine revolver into battle, was disabled for life.

"FOR GOD'S SAKE FORWARD!"

The gallant men of the 2nd Wisconsin of the famous Iron Brigade are shown here moving to engage the advancing Confederates of Archer's brigade on the morning of July 1, 1863. The regiment had just completed a twelve-mile march and was only arriving on the field when a staff officer galloped up to the regiment's colonel, Lucius Fairchild, with urgent orders to move his regiment forward. Union cavalry had been fighting since early morning holding off a superior force of Rebel infantry, and they were running low on ammunition. Infantry of the Army of the Potomac's 1st Corps were only now moving to replace the hard-pressed troopers. A Confederate force was observed moving around the Union left; it was up to the 2nd to stop them. The 1st Corps commander himself, Gen. John F. Reynolds, rode to the regiment to lead it on, calling out, "Forward men, forward for God's sake and drive those fellows out of the woods!" Within minutes General Reynolds would lie dead and the 2nd Wisconsin, along with the entire Iron Brigade, would be engaged in a desperate struggle.

It is certain that General Reynolds knew exactly what troops he was ordering forward, but as the Confederates came on, they were ignorant of exactly who they were facing. Some believed they were going to meet only a hastily formed Pennsylvania militia. They fired a devastating volley into the oncoming Federals, but the Northerners kept coming. It was then that Archer's men saw the black hats that had become the Iron Brigade's badge of honor and they knew what General Reynolds had known: this was not militia; this was the Army of the Potomac.

The hats worn by the men of the Iron Brigade were the pattern 1858 army hat. Along with several other 1st Corps regiments, the men had elected to continue to wear this headgear rather than the forage cap most of the regiments of the famed eastern Union army were wearing. Readily visible on the front of the hat is the red disk corps badge of the 1st Division, 1st Corps. On the badge are the brass numbers and letters identifying the regiment and company. The 2nd Wisconsin was armed with the .54-caliber Austrian Lorenz rifle,

with its unique quadrangular bayonet. A few of those depicted are wearing the white canvas leggings that much of the army had been issued before the Battle of Chancellorsville.

It should be noted that the men of the regiment are wearing their knapsacks into battle. This practice was being strongly promoted within the army because a high percentage of knapsacks were lost when regiments removed them before moving into action. At Gettysburg both the 1st and 2nd Divisions of the 1st Corps retained their knapsacks in battle. The 3rd Division removed them outside of town and they were lost.

Full Dress for an Officer

The pattern 1858 army hat was intended for wear with the dress uniform of the army until the early 1870s. This hat belonged to an officer of an unknown 22nd Infantry regiment. It is army regulation in every respect. The regimental designation is a bugle fashioned of gold metallic thread, as is the eagle that holds up the right side of the brim. The gold and black cord and the black feather are the finishing touches. The black silk

edging around the brim is also typical of hats made for officers. The fact that there were only nineteen regiments of regular infantry during the Civil War makes it likely that this was the hat of a volunteer officer. Its excellent condition leads us to believe that the officer this hat belonged to probably chose the much more comfortable cap for wear on campaign.

The Controversial 1858 Army Hat

The hat adopted as part of the 1858 uniform change was almost universally disliked by the regular army from its first day of issue. Made of stiff black felt, the hat was heavy, hot, and uncomfortable. Although it was originally intended for general wear, the adoption of the pattern 1858 forage cap for fatigue purposes soon relegated the hat to use on dress occasions. The enlisted version such as seen here was embellished by the addition of a woolen braided hat cord; a brass device indicating branch of service; a company letter and, if called for, a regimental number, both of brass; and a brass-stamped American eagle intended to loop up one side of the brim. In addition, a single black ostrich feather was affixed to the front, sweeping rakishly around the side. The hat cord, like the uniform trim, was to be the color of the "facing of the corps."

If the hat was unpopular in the regular army, it was initially more so in the volunteer army enlisted to fight in the Civil War. The hat was laughed at and equated to that worn by the Pilgrim fathers. Strangely enough, however, some regiments seemed to wear the hat as a badge of honor. Most notable among these was the Army of the Potomac's famed Iron Brigade. The hat became symbolic of the regiments of this brigade and was readily recognized even by the Rebel units who faced them in battle.

The hat gained popularity in the Union armies fighting in the western theater, but not as the Quartermasters Department would have preferred. The western soldier liked the broad brim worn down on all sides and soon found that if the crown was pushed in and reshaped to a more stylish configuration, the hat made up in protection from the elements what it lacked in comfort. As the war progressed, the hat all but disappeared in the eastern armies. The forage cap was felt to give a more soldierly appearance, and orders exist, beginning in 1864, that actually forbid the wearing of any other headgear.

The hat pictured here may well have been the exception when it came to being worn as intended. The brass castle and yellow cord are the insignia of an enlisted man of the engineers. These elite troops, often serving under the best officers in the regular army, could be expected to present a proper appearance when on parade. Only a single battalion of regular engineers existed during the war years, along with two regiments of volunteer engineers from New York State.

Army Leggings

Most students of Civil War uniforms today don't look upon the use of leggings as having been prevalent within the ranks of non-Zouave infantry regiments. Within the Union Army of the Potomac, however, production and supply records paint a somewhat different picture. These utilitarian items, copied directly from those in use by the highly regarded French Army, were purchased in quantity by the Quartermaster's Department and issued principally to the eastern army from early 1862 to early 1864. They were intended especially for use on campaign, which most certainly explains their low survival rate.

The use of leggings within the Federal Army can be traced to a letter written on December 5, 1861, by Quartermaster General Montgomery C. Meigs to Lt. Col. George H. Crosman, commanding the Philadelphia Quartermaster Depot. In this letter, General Meigs talks of both leggings and gaiters, both of which were produced. The gaiter, a low leather spat, was primarily an item of issue to units dressed as Zouaves. In Civil War correspondence, these terms are often used interchangeably.

Quarter-Master General's Office
Washington city Dec. 5,1861
Lt. Col. Geo. H. Crosman
Deputy QM Genl.
Philadelphia
 Colonel:
The General-in-chief calls for the issue to the troops of gaiter.
 . . . legging and leather gaiters are made of russet leather, soft and pliable; the leggings having black leather straps at the upper and lower edges.
 For our troops wearing the common uniform trowsers a gaiter [legging] covering the foot and ankle, as high as the uniform Cavalry boot leg seems desirable.
 You are requested to procure samples of such as you think suitable both in linen and in leather, and send them here for examination and approval as soon as possible.
 There are some leggings now in use by Zouave Corps. Please send specimens of such of these as you find in the market with appropriate prices.
 The experience of the Army in the late muddy roads has shown that for a winter campaign in our climate, something of this kind is necessary to enable the troops to make a day's march in comfort and health, and without destruction of their shoes, socks and trowsers.
 Very respectfully
 M.C. Meigs
 QM Genl.

The above was followed on January 8, 1862, by another letter from Meigs to Crosman, detailing the decision made in Washington. The legging was to be "of sufficient height to reach the lower part of the calf. To be made of cotton or linen duck—stout. To be secured by looped leather . . . passing through metallic eyelet holes & a strap of black leather . . . around the upper edge of the [legging] with a iron buckle."

On March 31 General Meigs further directed that "the leggings were ordered to be sent to the Army of the Potomac for issue to troops in campaign, and should be issued to no others." General Meigs's command must have been carried out, for by June 19, 1862, the 6th Wisconsin Infantry of the Iron Brigade reported the need for twenty-three pairs of leggings to replace those worn out.

By the spring of the following year, the use of leggings, at least under the conditions described above, must have been generally accepted by the Army of the Potomac regiments. As they emerged from winter quarters and began preparation for the spring campaign, orders and requisitions for securing and wearing leggings were issued at all levels of command.

The extent to which leggings were worn on the march is not documented. That they were used at least until 1864 is certain. On March 26 of that year the 3rd Brigade, 2nd Division, 5th Corps, complained of receiving leggings that wrapped around the leg the wrong way, were too long, and did not fit properly.

The leggings received by Pvt. James Boisbrun, Company A, 115th Pennsylvania, a regiment of the 3rd Corps, upon which he carefully placed his name, were certainly included in those issued as a result of this order. Private Boisbrun was wounded at Chancellorsville. The regiment was hotly engaged on May 3, losing their colonel but capturing nearly 400 Confederate prisoners.

LITTLE ROUND TOP

DR. RICHARD E. KRAUS

Rocks, boulders, and small hills, which at times seem to pop up out of nowhere, abound in southern Pennsylvania. Except in extreme cases, if any of these are ever named or noted, the fame does not go beyond the local community. A small, rocky hill south of the town of Gettysburg was just such an extreme case. On July 2, 1863, the blood of brave men baptized it, and today it is known worldwide as Little Round Top. It was the anchor on which the left flank of the Army of the Potomac rested, and its defense or capture was of supreme importance. The defense was left to men of the Union Army's 5th Corps; its capture was up to soldiers of Confederate general John B. Hood's division, among them the 5th Texas Infantry.

The 5th Texas, along with the 1st and 4th Texas, had come east in 1861 and had been a part of Lee's Army of Northern Virginia ever since. They had fought in most of the major engagements of the famous Confederate command and had marched north in June on the campaign many hoped would end the war and gain Southern independence. Much of the army had been engaged on July 1 and had gained some success. Now, on the afternoon of the second day of battle, it was the Texans' turn.

They had moved quickly forward, passing an outcropping of huge boulders that would later be known as Devil's Den. Ahead lay their objective: a steep hill strewn with large rocks. Along with their sister regiment, the 4th Texas, the men of the 5th stormed the hill straight on. For more than an hour they struggled ahead, losing for every inch of ground gained. Finally they reached a plateau within reach of the heavily defended summit. Three times they tried to reach

Confederate Officers' Sword Belts

Confederate officers, like their Union counterparts, usually purchased their own equipment. It was particularly true in the Confederacy, however, that items such as saddles, belts, holsters, and boots would be fabricated for officers in government facilities upon special request. Unlike enlisted men, the officer was expected to pay for the item. Though there is no way to tell exactly where, or by whom, these belts were made, they serve to illustrate the declining resources of the Confederacy. Both belts employ the two-piece interlocking belt buckle of the type often seen on belts dating decades before the Civil War. They proudly bear the letters "C S," which stands for Confederate States, as a distinguishing device. The different styles of lettering employed on the two buckles indicate that they came from two different manufacturers. The real significance, however, is the materials the belts are made of. The belt that appears white is made of sewn canvas instead of leather. As the war progressed and such essential items as shoes and boots quickly ate away at the leather supply, the South was forced to turn to other materials and to make do. By 1863 shortages were already starting to become evident. It was truly a dark cloud on the horizon of the young nation.

their goal, and three times they were forced back. Finally, with darkness coming on and many of their officers down, the Texans who remained fell back to the shelter of Devil's Den. The hill remained in Union hands, and so it would.

The regiment depicted here is the 5th Texas Infantry. It is shown as it most certainly appeared during one of the attempts to reach the summit of Little Round Top. The men had received both new Enfield rifles with saber bayonets and rifle muskets during the first week of November 1861, shortly after their arrival in Virginia. During their time of service, they continued to be well supplied with clothing. In the first quarter of 1863, the regiment had received a substantial number of jackets, pants, cotton shirts, shoes, socks, and drawers, which would be resupplied as needed in the field during July and August.

The regiment had initially been issued caps, but issues of clothing throughout the remainder of the war show only an occasional reissue of this item. It can be assumed that many of the Texans preferred to acquire their own hats from other, unnamed sources. Worn with doubtless pride on the hats and caps of the gallant men of the Lone Star State is the star that identified them as Texans. These emblems were most certainly fashioned by hand from materials available. It is known that the zinc tops of ration cans were used by Civil War soldiers for this purpose.

An important factor in the supply of the Texas regiments serving in Virginia was the maintenance of a Texas depot in Richmond. Here uniforms were gathered and held for issue to the Texas troops. It would appear that the uniforms were received from the Richmond Quartermaster Depot run by the Confederate government. But whatever the source, the Lone Star troops were assured of an adequate supply. In operation throughout the war, the depot was manned by one or more disabled soldiers from three regiments, who acted as agents for the rest of the command. On November 4, 1864, Pvt. A. N. Vaughan of the 5th Texas was placed in charge. He was probably the last to administer the operation. Vaughan had been wounded in the leg at the Wilderness in May and was unfit for field service. He was replacing Sgt. W. U. Bayless of Company K, who was killed while temporarily on duty with the 5th Texas.

A Confederate "Beehive" Hat

The Confederate soldier is often portrayed wearing a wide-brimmed hat. It is well known that most Southern soldiers preferred this type of headgear. The fact is, however, that at least an equal number of forage caps were issued to soldiers, particularly those who served under General Lee in the Army of Northern Virginia. While the Federal Army of the Potomac did all it could to uniformly put its men in either the forage cap or the pattern 1858 army hat, their Confederate opponents were satisfied to issue whatever could be obtained, be they caps or hats, and not always of any uniform pattern or color. Confederates were also known to requisition civilian hats as they passed through various towns and villages, particularly on Northern soil.

The following report from Confederate quartermaster general Alexander R. Lawton to Secretary of War Seddon details some of the difficulty the South had with obtaining supplies, including headgear.

> QM Gen. Office
> Richmond, Aug. 5, 1864
> Sir
> I enclose herewith the estimate recently requested by you for the Secretary of the Treasury showing the amount of Sterling funds required to meet the wants of this Bureau abroad for the next 6 months.
> The great scarcity of wool compels me to rely upon drawing from abroad fully one half of the cloth required for Army purposes & the difficulty of obtaining leather especially such as is well tanned increased the demand for shoes. Our entire supply of Blankets has to be drawn from abroad. The same is true as to Hats for which a cap is but a poor substitute. The necessities of the officers have become so great that I feel compelled to do all in my power to relieve them & it really concerns the efficiency of the service that some facilities be extended to them for clothing themselves.
> Major Waller at Nassau reports an indebtedness of £15,000—which is included in this estimate.
> I will add that to the extent that means can be provided, I believe it to be expedient to purchase abroad. The high prices at home & the inflation of currency consequent upon purchasing at these rates is thereby avoided.

Cloth for soldiers jacket & pants	$787,000
Hats (300,000 more)	450,000
Blankets (200,000 pair)	600,000
shoes & leather	400,000
Flannel for shirts & linings	125,000
Thread & buttons	20,000
pay & trans. for officers abroad	12,410
Uniform cloths for officers	120,000
Boots for officers	60,000
Stationery for Army at large	75,000
Field glasses to be called for by the Signal Bureau	10,000
Maj. Waller's indebtedness	67,500

> This estimate looks to a preparation for next winter. It might be reduced if existing contracts could be relied on to produce a material proportion of the supplies they call for.

The Confederate hat pictured here is of medium brown wool and is similar to ones known to have been imported from England. Its high crown was reminiscent of farmer's beehives of the period, hence its nickname. This hat is thought to have been picked up on the battlefield at Gettysburg and therefore would predate General Lawton's request for funds.

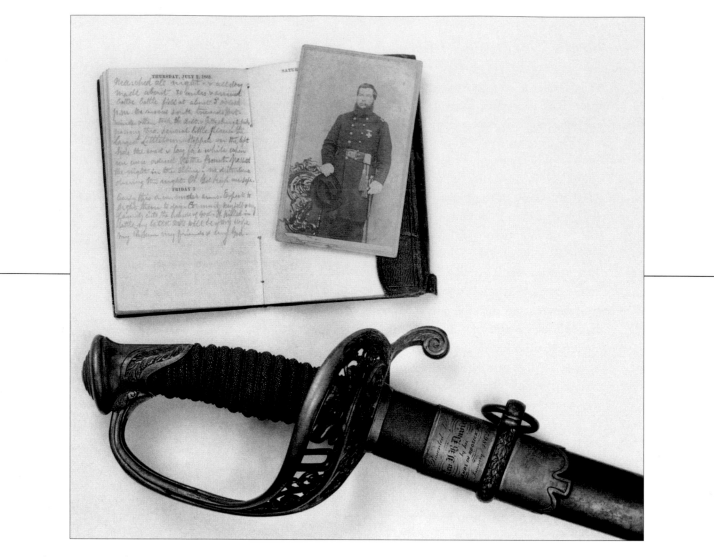

The Sword and Diary of a Chaplain-Turned-Warrior

Although chaplains are considered noncombatants, many chose to carry an officer's sword as a badge of rank. Others, like Chaplain Joshua B. Davis of the 7th New York Cavalry, received such a weapon from friends who, by its presentation, hoped to show their respect for one called to do the Lord's work where it was badly needed. The presentation inscription upon its scabbard reads, "Present to Rev. J. B. Davis, by his friends in Hoosick N.Y., Jan. 1862." The 7th New York Cavalry, which consisted only of seven companies, would serve just two more months before being honorably mustered out of service. Within four months, Reverend Davis once again answered his country's call. This time his sword would serve its intended purpose as an instrument of battle. Reverend Davis was now Major Davis of the 122nd New York Infantry.

On July 2, 1863, the regiment, along with the 6th Corps, had been rushed forward from Maryland to the rear of the Federal Army desperately engaged at Gettysburg, Pennsylvania. That night they rested behind the army's left flank near Little Round Top. They were aroused before daylight. In the few minutes he had before the regiment moved, Major Davis made a short entry in his diary that goes far to tell us of the spirit of this chaplain-turned-warrior:

Friday, July 3-1863
   Early this a.m. under arms. Expect to fight them today. Commit myself & my family into the hand of God. If killed in battle my last thoughts will be of my wife, my children, my friends & my God.

The 122nd, along with the other regiments of its brigade, was moved quickly to the Federal right flank on Culp's Hill. As it arrived, a regiment of the 12th Corps then holding the line was forced to fall back, having run out of ammunition. The 122nd was thrown in to plug the gap. Here Major Davis received the wound that removed him from further service with his regiment when a Confederate bullet smashed into his mouth. The painful wound is evident in the photograph, which was taken before he left the service for the final time.

PRIVATE, 5TH NEW JERSEY INFANTRY, MAY 1863

The 5th New Jersey Infantry was formed at Camp Olden, near Trenton, New Jersey, and mustered into U.S. service on August 22, 1861. Almost from the beginning it served with the 3rd Army Corps. When that corps was disbanded in 1864, the regiment was transferred to the 2nd Army Corps, where it remained until the veterans mustered out in November 1865.

In the spring of 1863, the 5th was serving in the 3rd Brigade, 2nd Division, 3rd Corps, commanded by Col. George C. Burling. As the Army of the Potomac began to prepare for the coming campaign, each regiment was ordered to box surplus clothing for storage until needed again the following winter. Because of their weight, blankets and great-coats were generally stored. Brigade commanders often decided what uniform items would be worn and what stored. Though the majority of the regiments of the army elected to wear the four-button fatigue blouse, Burling's men either elected or were ordered to wear the dress frock coat.

The soldier illustrated here represents the 5th New Jersey as it appeared just before the Battle of Chancellorsville. He is armed with the .54-caliber Austrian Lorenz rifle musket. His uniform is army regulation, and he will wear it throughout the coming campaign, which will include the Battle of Chancellorsville, as well as the march to and the Battle of Gettysburg. At Gettysburg, the men of the 5th New Jersey would be sent forward as skirmishers west of the Emmitsburg Road and on July 2 would find themselves temporarily trapped between the Union and Confederate lines, where they would receive numerous casualties.

JOSEPH STAHL

A Simple Souvenir of Battle

We can only wonder what story this tin cup could tell if one could be coaxed from its rusted interior. The 119th Pennsylvania, as part of the 3rd Brigade, 1st Division, 6th Corps, was in the thick of the fighting at Spotsylvania in May 1864. On May 10 at 4:00 P.M. an assaulting column composed of ten regiments, including the 119th Pennsylvania, was formed in three ranks. Charging out of the cover of the woods and across open ground, they attempted to breach the Confederate works. After a desperate struggle, they were forced to fall back. Two days later the 119th was part of the day-long contest for the Rebel works known ever after as the "Bloody Angle." This horrible hand-to-hand struggle ended in a Union victory, with the capture of hundreds of Confederate prisoners and a large quantity of artillery. Pvt. Thomas Ward of Company A was present and took part in the engagements that cost the regiment 215 casualties out of 400 present in seven days. After all of this, it would seem that something more significant than a simple army-issue tin cup would be picked up by a victorious soldier. It may be that the memory of the events just passed was such that the most insignificant item took on a special meaning. Or it could be that a practical man just needed a new cup to enjoy his evening coffee.

The Mark of an Army Pioneer

Army pioneers were handpicked soldiers whose job was to move in front of their regiment or brigade to clear obstructions or to otherwise aid the movement of the army. As armies prepared for battle, infantry pioneers could be rushed forward to throw up low, protective earthen emplacements behind which light artillery pieces could be positioned. To accomplish all of this, the pioneer was armed with a pickax, spade, or shovel. An especially made sling allowed it to be comfortably carried over the shoulder. Most pioneers would also carry a rifle for defense. Within some units, infantry pioneers were issued cavalry carbines with slings that allowed them to be carried much like standard rifle muskets.

It was not until the Civil War had been raging for more than a year that the Federal Army recognized the need to establish organized contingents of pioneers to function with the armies in the field. On March 22, 1863, one regiment, the 148th Pennsylvania Infantry, reported that its "Pioneer Corps" consisted of eleven men equipped as follows:

1—*Corporal*
5—*Pioneers with axes*
1—*Pioneer with a spade*
2—*Pioneers with shovels*
2—*Pioneers with pickaxes*

Not every soldier detailed as an army pioneer wore the crossed ax badge that identified him as such. Most men who served in this capacity were detailed in the field and acted as such for only a comparatively short period of time. For this reason, there seems to have been little effort on the part of the Quartermaster's Department to supply distinctive insignia. Consequently, unless the soldier chose to make or purchase the axes, there would be little other than his equipment to distinguish him from his regimental comrades serving as regular infantry.

The sergeant who wore these chevrons was certainly the exception. It may be that the rank of sergeant placed him in a permanent position within his regiment or brigade and thereby made the addition of the pioneer axes to standard-issue chevrons a requirement. Whatever the reason, these light blue infantry chevrons are topped by cloth axes that appear to be cut from a discarded pair of sky blue trousers.

Pipe of a German Craftsman in Blue

Pvt. Solomon Stern of Company H, 19th U.S. Regular Infantry, was only one of a large number of immigrants who chose to fight for the new country they had adopted. Early in the war, entire Union regiments existed in which English was a second language, if spoken at all. In some volunteer regiments, even the record books the U.S. Army required to be kept were written in German script. This practice was halted in early 1862, when it was found that inspecting officers could not read the books of the units under their charge. In many cases, the regiments made up largely of Germans were looked down upon by other regiments that saw themselves as purely American. This was compounded by the misfortune that befell the Federal 11th Corps at Chancellorsville and Gettysburg. Historians today, removed from the prejudices of the time, can see that in fact many regiments with a high makeup of foreign-born troops fought very well.

The 19th U.S. Regular Infantry was organized by direction of President Lincoln on May 4, 1861, at Indianapolis. Company H was one of two companies detached and sent to Washington, D.C. Its ranks most certainly contained many men of foreign birth who, like Solomon Stern, probably did not feel the regional attachment that would lead them to join a local volunteer regiment. After service as provost guard in the capital, the detached companies were assigned to the 2nd Division, 5th Corps, where they saw action in the Antietam Campaign and at Fredericksburg. Shortly after this, they were ordered to join their parent regiment in Tennessee.

It's not known whether Stern was a craftsman in his home country, but the smoking pipe he skillfully carved and adorned with mother-of-pearl inlays would indicate that he was. The 19th U.S. was part of the 14th Corps in the Atlanta Campaign. Sometime, maybe over the winter of 1864–65, Stern had the time to carve a pipe that in style must have reminded him of his homeland. His devotion to his new country is evident, however. He chose to decorate the sides with inlaid symbols of his service—the Acorn Corps Badge of the 14th Corps and the shield of the United States. Skillfully carved into the body, in his native language, is "Chickamauga" and "37 days fighting for Atlanta." There is a silver cap to keep the precious contents dry, and the bottom ornament is made from part of a Burnside carbine cartridge case.

THE EMMITSBURG ROAD

About 3:00 P.M. on the afternoon of July 3, three divisions of Confederate troops numbering nearly 12,000 men, commanded by Generals Picket, Pettigrew, and Trimble, stepped from the cover of woods that had shielded them from the enemy's view. Under the overall command of Gen. George Picket, they began an advance toward the strongly held waiting line of Union artillery and infantry. To reach their objective, they had to cross nearly a mile of open ground that was bisected by a road bordered by a strong rail fence, with the roadbed several feet below the level of the fields on either side.

Almost immediately they were under fire. As they approached the road, some moved ahead to clear the fence line in their immediate front. With most of its rails down, the Confederates moved into and across the road, only to be met

with the fence line that had not been cleared. As they tore at the rails and climbed over, they were met with a hail of rifle fire from the Federal line. Most men made it over the fence, only to be cut down before crossing the remaining ground necessary to make contact with, and break through, the Union position. Within minutes—which must have seemed like hours—those Confederates who could began to fall back to the shelter of the wooded ridge from which they had come. The charge, which would forever be known as "Pickett's Charge," had covered these brave men with glory but had gained little else.

The scene captured here places the viewer in the ranks of the 7th North Carolina Regiment of Trimble's division, on the left flank of the advancing Confederates, as they move through the downed first fence line. Ahead of them the men

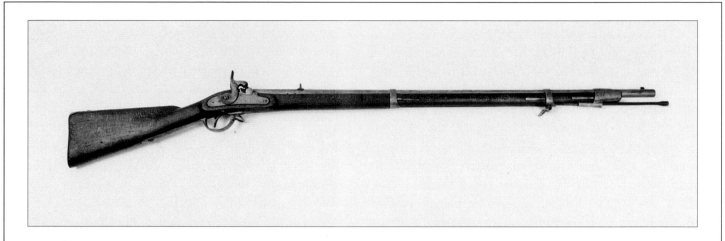

The Model 1854 Austrian Lorenz Rifle Musket

The Austrian Lorenz rifle musket enjoys the distinction of being the second most widely imported and used European arm in the Civil War. Second only to the British Enfield, the Lorenz was carried by both Union and Confederate forces in all theaters of conflict. The arm can be found in both .54 and .58 caliber. It appears that most of the .58-caliber arms saw use in the Union Army; however, some of the early Confederate imports were first sent to Belgium and bored out to .57 caliber to make them compatible with the British Enfield. In both armies, the Lorenz in .54 caliber was by far the most prevalent. The bayonet issued with the Lorenz was also of Austrian manufacture. Although similar in appearance to the socket bayonet of American design, the Lorenz bayonet had a distinctive, quadrangular-shaped blade.

The arm found what may be its greatest use in the western theater by the Confederate Army of Tennessee, with extensive issues to that army in 1863 and 1864. In the east, the Lorenz was used in both the Army of the Potomac and the Army of Northern Virginia. Soldiers armed with the Lorenz carried a sturdy and reliable weapon.

of the 53rd North Carolina are attempting to advance past the second fence line and are receiving the well-directed fire from the Federal infantry of the 2nd Corps.

The men of the 7th Regiment are well uniformed and armed with a mixture of U.S. and Confederate .58-caliber rifle muskets and .54-caliber Austrian rifle muskets. Many had received new uniforms in May and June before leaving Virginia. A typical issue was that distributed in June to Company C, which consisted of 23 jackets, 47 pairs of pants, 35 pairs of drawers, 33 pairs of shoes, 29 pairs of socks, and 22 shirts. The jackets, such as are illustrated here, came from the Richmond Quartermaster Depot and were commonly issued to the Army of Northern Virginia.

During 1862 a large number of caps had been issued as headgear, but early 1863 issues show only a few. Because hats and caps did not tend to wear out as rapidly as jackets, pants, and shoes, it is certain that many of the men of the regiment were wearing the issue Confederate cap on that fateful July afternoon.

The soldier in the left foreground can be seen with a blanket roll consisting of a section of ingrain carpet, which was Confederate issue in lieu of a blanket. Accoutrements are a typical mixture of captured Federal and Confederate manufacture. A close look at the battle flag of the 7th, which is about to move forward onto the Emmitsburg road, will show the numerous battle honors painted on the front side. The 7th North Carolina was a veteran regiment with a record second to none. Soon the name "Gettysburg" would be added.

Corporal Peck's Canteen

The canteen has throughout history been one of the most important pieces of military equipment issued. The water it carries is the very lifeblood of the soldier. On the march, soldiers often cast off almost anything to lighten their loads, but never their canteens. The Federal-issue canteen of the Civil War was no exception.

First adopted by the U.S. Army in 1858, the canteen was stamped from thin sheet iron that was then tin plated. Before issue, the body of the canteen was covered with coarse material, usually wool. Sky blue or gray colors were preferred, but this was not strictly adhered to. As designed, the canteen was to have an adjustable leather sling, but expediency soon saw the substitution of a cloth strap cut to a standard length and sewn together. The straps were held to the canteen body by three iron loops soldered to the sides and bottom edges. A cork stopper, with a wire loop passing through it, kept the contents from spilling. This was in turn secured to the canteen by a cord or chain attached to one of the upper loops.

The general design of the canteen carried from Bull Run to Appomattox remained standard army issue until the early twentieth century. The canteen was to be worn with the strap over the right shoulder, which would allow the canteen body to fall on the left side at about waist level. Civil War soldiers soon discovered that a canteen full of water could stop a bullet. Instances are known of men shortening the cloth sling by tying it in a knot and wearing it slung in the middle of the back.

The canteen carried by Corp. William C. Peck, Company A, 27th Connecticut Infantry, is of the corrugated pattern that was issued heavily to the Army of the Potomac beginning in early 1862. The addition of the badge of the 1st Division, 2nd Corps, was probably done in 1863, as this is the unique shape of the very first die-cut badges issued to soldiers of that famed corps before the Battle of Chancellorsville. The attachment of a corps badge to anything other than the hat or cap was a violation of orders. This tendency to nonconformity may explain why Corporal Peck, who was one of the fortunate few in Company A not captured at Chancellorsville, was later reduced to the ranks.

A Confederate Canteen That Went North

From the Revolution to the present day, the U.S. soldier has been a noted souvenir hunter. The Civil War soldier helped establish this tradition. To this day, homes from New England to Iowa yield relics that were carried home by Yankee volunteers. Sgt. David K. Stannard, Company E, 49th Massachusetts Infantry, was no exception.

Sergeant Stannard, by occupation a mechanic, enlisted in the 49th in September 1862 from his home in New Marlborough. The 49th Massachusetts was one of a number of regiments enlisted in New England for nine months' service that were sent to the area of New Orleans for operations against Confederate strongholds on the Mississippi. The regiment was engaged in the siege of Port Hudson and in the assaults that resulted in that garrison's surrender on July 8, 1863. Sixty-five men of the 49th volunteered for a desperate attempt on the Confederate position on May 27, which resulted in the loss of sixteen officers and men killed. By the time of the final surrender, the term of service of the regiment was almost over.

It is certain that many of the men who saw action were eager to take home a trophy of their service in the South. The Confederate canteen taken by Sergeant Stannard is one of several known today that bear inscriptions relating to their capture at Port Hudson.

During the Civil War, the wooden canteen was unique to Confederate service, which probably accounts for its appeal as a Yankee souvenir. Thousands were issued, the majority of which were manufactured at Confederate government facilities. Most were made of cedar wood with solid sides joined by a series of wooden pieces grooved to fit to the sides and held together by thin iron bands. Iron loops held a cloth sling in place. One of the leading suppliers of the cedar canteen was the Confederate arsenal at Montgomery, Alabama, which fabricated and sent thousands of them to the army. The close proximity of the western Confederate armies may explain the prevalence of this style of canteen in that theater of war. It is likely that the canteen so highly prized by Sergeant Stannard was a product of the Montgomery facility.

UNION INFANTRY DRUMMER, WINTER 1863–64

The infantry spent the winter of 1863–64 largely in camp waiting for the spring campaign, which was sure to be a bloody one. During the months when active service was curtailed by weather, the soldiers of both the Union and Confederate armies were anything but idle. For the cavalry, it was often a period of scouting mixed with drill and parades. For the infantry, it was a time of picket duty, drill, and parades. Within the infantry, the drummer was constantly called upon. His drum beat the cadence while the men were on parade or in drill and was the means of rapid communication within the camp. With the proper command beat on the drum, the colonel could quickly assemble the regiment or call just the sergeants for a meeting.

This drummer is typical of the thousands who served. He is young, as many were, and holds his regulation drum suspended from a white canvas sling close by ready for use. Because it is winter, he is wearing the regular-issue single-breasted overcoat for dismounted men. It is made of the same sky blue kersey material as his trousers. An elbow-length cape is permanently attached for added warmth and has large sleeve cuffs that can be rolled down to cover the hands if necessary. A similar coat for a mounted soldier would feature a cuff-length cape and be double-breasted. On his forage cap is the red diamond corps badge of the soon-to-be-disbanded 1st Division, 3rd Corps.

A U.S. Regulation Regimental Drum

There is no more beautiful piece of Civil War-issue equipment than a regulation regimental drum. The fact that few survive testifies to the hard use they saw. Drummers are often thought of as having been only boys, and it is true that many young men filled the ranks by serving as a "drummer boy." But not all who served in this capacity were youths. Almon Laird served in the regimental drum corps of the 27th Massachusetts Infantry. When he was captured at Drewry's Bluff on May 16, 1864, Laird was forty-eight years old. He had enlisted with the regiment at Springfield in September 1861 as a drummer in Company I and was transferred to the Regimental Drum Corps in 1863.

A photograph of the drum corps of the 27th shows the men in the same uniform as that worn by Hawkins' Zouaves, the 9th New York Infantry. These uniforms were probably received from the U.S. Army Quarter-master Depot in New York City. This depot supplied the initial uniforms to a number of New York regiments and also was responsible for the supply of the Atlantic coastal operations. The 27th Massachusetts spent its entire four years of service in the Tidewater area of Virginia and North Carolina. Almon Laird did not survive his imprisonment; he died of chronic diarrhea. The drum carried by drummer Laird was issued to his regiment after its muster into U.S. service. It is army regulation in every respect.

The Uniform Coat of a Berdan Sharpshooter

The two regiments of Union Sharpshooters raised in 1861 by Col. Hiram Berdan are perhaps the most well known of any on either side in the Civil War. While most recruits had some vague idea that they would be called upon to kill the enemy, those who enlisted in the Sharpshooters knew exactly that this would be their mission. Further, the men they would likely be called on to kill would not be part of an indistinct mass of humanity, but rather a single target with a face and a personality. Be he a brave officer leading his men or a cannoneer manning his gun, he would stand out and would be skillfully and deliberately brought down. To qualify as a member of the Sharpshooters, it was necessary for a recruit, firing from a rest at 200 yards, to be able to place ten consecutive shots in a target, the average distance not to exceed 5 inches from the center of the bull's-eye.

The regiments were made up of companies from several different states, from New England to Wisconsin. They practiced their trade with precision on most of the battlefields of the Army of the Potomac until the very end of the war. Late in 1864 many of the survivors who had joined for three years were mustered out, and the two regiments were consolidated into one. Though there were other sharpshooter units formed during the war, the reputation gained by Berdan's regiments overshadowed all others.

One thing that helped create the image of the Berdan Sharpshooter was the distinctive uniform they were given and that they wore their entire term of service. The first uniforms for the regiments were produced by Martin & Brother of New York City. The original regimental historian, Capt. Charles Stevens of Company G, described the first issue as follows:

> Our uniform was of fine material, consisting of dark green coat and cap with black plume, light blue trowsers, and leather leggings, presenting a striking contrast to the regular blue of the infantry. The knapsack was of hair-covered calfskin, with cooking kit attached. . . . By our dress we were known far and wide and the appellation of "Green Coats" was soon acquired.

No later than May 1862, the blue trousers were replaced by green that matched the coat. The regiment was not always able to keep from mixing parts of the regulation blue uniform with the much-preferred green.

As late as April 1864, objections were registered by men of the 1st Regiment that they were being forced to pay for extra clothing drawn. The men complained that they were compelled to draw green uniforms after being issued blue ones when green was temporarily unavailable.

The buttons on the issue Berdan's uniform were unique to the two regiments. They were made of gutta-percha and were originally black. The button was a small, round cylinder shaped something like a chocolate drop with a brass shank. There was no eagle on them, as found on the regulation brass buttons. The buttons were purchased from Thomas F. Carhart, a New York contractor who would later receive numerous contracts for regulation army uniforms. These are the identical buttons seen on the uniform coat pictured here.

The original material for the Sharpshooters' uniforms had been purchased in Europe and was probably a lighter weight than the material used in regulation uniforms. The Quartermaster's Department was assigned the task of making and supplying all further issues of the uniform. A request for an initial resupply was received at the Philadelphia Depot on April 10, 1862. Since green cloth was not a regular item of purchase, it was necessary to look to the open market. On April 21 the Philadelphia Quartermaster's Depot received the following proposal from Thomas Pilling & Co., which ran Elk Mills, near Newark, Delaware:

> We hereby propose to furnish and deliver to the United States, at the Depot of Army Clothing and Equipage in Philadelphia . . .
> 5250 yards wool dyed, fast color green kersey, 27 inches wide, weighing 11 ounces per yard, all of the Army standard in quality, at 79 cents per yard.

The contract was actually made with Joseph Dean & Co. of Newark, which began delivery on May 10. At the same time, the Philadelphia Depot sent several letters to Thomas Carhart to purchase more of the buttons used on the original-issue coat. Since caps were made of a different material than either coats or trousers, it was necessary to have the yellow cloth on hand dyed green.

The first issue of Sharpshooters' uniforms manufactured by the U.S. Army was finally shipped to the two regiments at the end of May 1862, pursuant to the following order:

Quarter-Master General's Office
Washington City May 29, 1862
Lt. Col. Geo. H. Crosman
Depy' QMG
Phila.

> *Colonel:*
> *The Q M Genl. directs that you will send the clothing ordered on the 10th of April, for "Berdan's Sharpshooters" to the Asst. QM at Fortress Monroe.*
> *Lt. Beebe, QM Berdan's S.S. should be informed when they are sent.*
> *The regiment is with the Army of the Potomac.*
> *Very Respectfully*
> *Yr. Obt. Servt.*
> *By Order of the Q.M.G.*
> *Alex. J. Perry A.Q.M.*

From this time on, the Philadelphia Depot was able, with only minor delays, to maintain the supply of the unique green uniforms to the unique regiments that wore them. By late war, when many of the original Sharpshooters were being mustered out, an ample supply of Berdan's uniforms was on hand. When the new 203rd Pennsylvania Infantry was formed in September 1864, under the name "Birney's Sharpshooters," it was determined to uniform them in Berdan's uniforms. At that time, there were on hand at the advance clothing depot in Washington 878 Berdan's coats, 137 green trousers, and 271 forage caps. The Philadelphia Depot was instructed to manufacture the shortfall to completely uniform the new regiment as sharpshooters. The 203rd was not armed with special rifles, as Berdan's regiments had been, and their service was such that although they bore the name and looked the part, they in fact were not Sharpshooters.

The uniform coat pictured here was the property of Sgt. William F. Tilson of New Hampshire's Company E, 2nd U.S. Sharpshooters. Sergeant Tilson enlisted November 1, 1861, and served with his regiment until he was wounded on May 6, 1864. Later he reenlisted as a lieutenant in the 4th Vermont Infantry, only to be wounded again on April 2, 1865—a wound that cost him a leg. The coat is one of those made for issue by the Federal government at the Philadelphia Depot. It is a very dark forest green with dark green velvet chevrons. The gutta-percha buttons, once black, have turned a dark brown. Except for color, the coat follows exactly the pattern of the standard-issue Union frock coat. It should be noted

here that the government did not issue green chevrons or replacement buttons; it was necessary for the individual to purchase these from the regimental sutler. This may explain some examples of gutta-percha buttons in existence today that appear to have been made in a mold that cast a button of the exact design as the U.S.-issue brass button. It certainly accounts for the extra-rich velvet stripes worn by Sergeant Tilson.

Private, 20th Tennessee Infantry, CSA, Summer 1863

The 20th Tennessee regiment was raised in the summer of 1861 at Camp Trousdale, a few miles south of the Tennessee and Kentucky state line. The regiment was destined to see extensive service with the Confederate Army of Tennessee. Although the 20th was engaged in several small actions in 1861, its first real battle was not until April 6 and 7, 1862, on the field of Shiloh. Fortunately, the men had exchanged their antiquated flintlock muskets for new English Enfield rifle muskets just a few days before. They carried the Enfields for the rest of their term of service.

The soldier of the 20th Tennessee shown here is dressed as he would have been in the summer of 1863. His outfit is based upon Confederate quartermaster and ordnance returns for the regiment. The 20th was issued jackets and hats from the very beginning but, unlike many Confederate regiments, never recorded the issue of the kepi. This soldier's jacket is of the style manufactured by the Columbus, Georgia, clothing depot, which was a major supplier to the Army of Tennessee. His trousers are made of jean cloth, a popular sturdy material of the period that was made with a cotton warp and woolen weft. All of the soldier's equipment is Confederate issue,
including the rectangular "CSA" buckle often seen on soldiers of the western Confederate armies. Although most Confederates wore little or no ornamentation on their caps or hats, the 20th Tennessee sported a small metal badge with the regimental designation in raised letters. The Enfield rifle musket was the standard weapon of the regiment. An ordnance return from the 20th Tennessee that recorded ordnance lost and expended in the Battle of Missionary Ridge on November 25, 1863, showed the following:

> 42 Enfield rifles, .57 cal.
> 42 bayonets
> 23 cartridge boxes
> 51 cartridge box belts
> 53 cap pouches
> 35 bayonet scabbards
> 50 waist belts
> 29 knapsacks
> 57 haversacks
> 82 canteens

A Southern Symbol, and a Prize of War

The rectangular buckle, more properly termed a belt plate, bears the proud letters "CSA," intended to let all know that its wearer was a soldier of the army of the Confederate States of America. It is little wonder that such an article would be highly prized by a Union soldier wishing to take home a souvenir of his time at war. This unusual artifact was part of the war memories of Sgt. Maj. William A. Smith, a Vermonter serving with the 17th Michigan Infantry. It was found on the battlefield of Knoxville, Tennessee, where Smith's 9th Corps regiment had been engaged after being transferred from the eastern to the western theater of the war and where Smith had suffered a wound to the knee.

Had the 17th Michigan not been transferred to the west, chances are that no one in the regiment ever would have encountered a belt plate of a style resembling the one carried home by Sergeant Smith. The eastern Confederate Army of Northern Virginia seldom received an issue of belts with plates bearing the letters "CS" or "CSA." Most of these were manufactured in the Deep South and found their way to the Confederate Army of Tennessee and the armies of the

trans-Mississippi. The fact that this buckle is made of pewter, rather than brass or bronze, is not surprising. Shortages of these materials often led to substitutions being made in areas where use of another material would make no difference. It is certain that the Confederate soldier who wore the plate was pleased to bear the initials of his new nation into battle. His fate, and how the belt plate came into possession of a Yankee sergeant, remains unknown.

A Yankee Enfield

The Enfield might properly be referred to as "the other Springfield." The British rifle musket was imported in tremendous quantity by both the North and South, beginning in 1861 and flowing unabated until the final months of the Civil War. An estimated 900,000 Enfields reached the American shores during that period. A survey of Union infantry regimental arms for the second quarter of 1863 reveals that while 262 regiments were armed with the U.S. model 1861 rifle musket, 431 were armed with the Enfield, and another 60 carried a mixture of the two arms. This figure would change as more contracts for the model 1861 were completed, but it's fair to say that throughout the war there were, at any time, as many Union infantry regiments armed with the Enfield as with American-produced arms.

The Enfield pictured here bears the regimental mark of the 25th Connecticut Infantry. The 25th was recruited in Hartford and Tolland Counties in the fall of 1862. They were one of several nine-month regiments raised at that time that were destined to be sent to the area north of New Orleans for operations against Confederate strongholds on the Mississippi. The regiment's first engagement was at Irish Bend, Louisiana, where they lost ninety-four killed and wounded. This was followed by the siege and capture of Port Hudson and two other, smaller engagements. The regiment returned home and was mustered out at Hartford, on August 26, 1863. During this time, their Enfields served them well.

Enfield Cartridges as Issued in the Field

The caliber of the Enfield was .57 inches, whereas that of the model 1861 was .58 inches. While the slight difference in caliber was initially thought to be a problem in the Union Army, leading to the manufacture of special ammunition, it was soon found that a slight reduction in the caliber of the standard Federal ammunition would work equally well in either arm. The Confederacy faced the same problem, but while they imported large numbers of Enfields, they also imported great quantities of British ammunition.

This package of British-made ammunition for the Enfield was likely part of a shipment bound for a Southern port. Such packets contained 10 individually wrapped cartridges and were packed in wooden crates of 1,000 cartridges. The British-made bullet, like the U.S. bullet, had a conical hollow base that was designed upon firing, to expand into the rifled bore of the musket. The difference, as noted on the packet, was the insertion of a small wooden plug in the base. This was intended to facilitate the expansion of the bullet. Soldiers' cartridge belts were constructed to hold four packs of cartridges; when going into battle, two extra packs were often issued, which the soldiers carried in the jacket pocket.

CORPORAL, COMPANY C, 21ST OHIO VOLUNTEER INFANTRY, SEPTEMBER 1863

The uniform of the 21st Ohio in 1863 is typical of that worn by Federal troops serving in the western theater of the war. The campaigns of the winter and early spring had taken their toll on the uniforms of the regiment, and the men had been issued new ones in August. There is none of the flash or color of the Zouave. Every item from head to toe has a practical value and is standard issue as received from one of the two western quartermaster depots. This soldier's hat is unadorned, and his coat is the plain fatigue blouse of a fighting man ready for action. The round brass plate bearing the U.S. eagle on the sling holding his cartridge box at his side is the only bit of regulation flash present. Even this will eventually be dispensed with as the soldiers move in combat.

If the uniform of the 21st can be considered typical, the arms they carried were anything but commonplace. The men of Company C, like most of the 21st Ohio, were armed with the deadly .56-caliber, five-shot Colt revolving rifle, which they received in May 1863. Many of the rifles carried by the regiment had been turned in by the famed 2nd Regiment U.S. Sharpshooters serving in Virginia, who disliked the complicated mechanism. As with other eastern discards, the rifles were sent west. Here in the hands of farm boys and mechanics of the Buckeye State, they would soon prove their worth.

On September 20 at the bloody Battle of Chickamauga, the men were ordered to hold a position on Horseshoe Ridge, and hold it they did. The rapid-firing Colts of the 21st repulsed repeated Confederate charges and inflicted heavy loss on the enemy. Finally, with the special ammunition required to load the rifles exhausted, they fixed bayonets and continued to fight. During this single day's fight, the 21st Ohio expended over 43,000 rounds of ammunition.

The .56-caliber Colt revolving rifle was one of the most distinctive arms to come out of the Civil War. Those rifles that saw service with the 21st Ohio are particularly important. They represented a piece of both firearm and Civil War history that stands as a monument to American technology and bravery.

EARL J. COATES

A Colt Revolving Rifle of the 4th Michigan Cavalry

The 4th Michigan Cavalry was mustered into Federal service on August 29, 1862, and left for Louisville, Kentucky, a month later. At this time, a concerted effort was being made by the state to provide her sons with the best arms and accoutrements available. The 4th Michigan was armed with the Colt revolving rifle, and the 5th and 6th Michigan with the new Spencer repeating rifle. The 4th also received Colt revolvers in both .44 and .36 caliber.

The Colt revolving rifle has a mixed history. It was either well liked or hated, depending upon which regiment was reporting. In 1863 and '64 the Ordnance Department sent questionnaires to the various officers in the field, asking for comments on arms in use. Of the twenty-nine reporting on the Colt revolving rifle, eleven considered it the best arm in the service, five said it was very good, six just good, five rated it poor, and two worthless. This wide disparity may well have had to do with regimental discipline and the availability of a com-

petent ordnance sergeant within the unit. The Colt was prone to malfunction if not kept clean.

This rifle, serial number 8153, was issued to Corp. John C. Hopkins, Company G, 4th Michigan Cavalry, on December 7, 1862. The 4th had a history second to none, serving with the Army of the Ohio, Army of the Cumberland, and finally, Wilson's Cavalry Corps. Corporal Hopkins was wounded in the arm at Chickamauga in September 1863 but remained with the regiment for its entire length of service. The regiment received Spencer carbines in the summer of 1864 and used these until the end of the war. The 4th Michigan had the distinction of capturing the fleeing Confederate president, Jefferson Davis, at Irwinsville, Georgia, on May 10, 1865. Corporal Hopkins may have been able to retain his Colt rifle, perhaps by outright purchase, when the Spencers were issued. The rifle was found in recent years in his hometown of Adrian, Michigan.

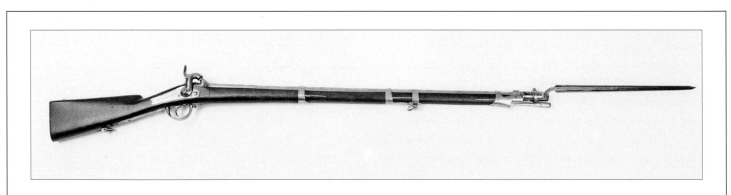

The Double-Band Dresden

One of the most distinctive of the thousands of import weapons used to arm the Civil War volunteer soldier was the model 1857 .58-caliber Saxon rifle musket. The arms were purchased in Dresden, Germany, by agents of the U.S. government and were commonly referred to as the "Dresden rifle." They rank with the best of the foreign imports. Numerous photographs exist

today of volunteers armed with the Dresden, which is immediately recognized by the distinctive double middle band unique to this arm. Many untried foreign arms were sent to equip soldiers in states west of the Allegheny Mountains, accounting for the fact that in 1863, the ordnance returns of only a few regiments from Ohio, Iowa, and Wisconsin list the Dresden as their primary weapon.

The 3rd New Jersey Cavalry

Although numerous regiments of infantry that were raised during the Civil War received Zouave or other special uniforms, only a few mounted regiments were so dressed. One regiment, the 3rd New Jersey Cavalry, carried the exception to the extreme. In European armies, the regiments of Hussars traditionally wore uniforms that were heavily adorned with lace, metallic cord, and brass buttons. In late 1863 and early '64, the 3rd New Jersey was organized and mustered in by companies. As an inducement to enlist, the War Department authorized a "special uniform" that would set them apart from every other mounted regiment in the Union Army. The unit was to take the field as "Hussars." The cost of the uniform was about $3 more than the standard issue for cavalry, but the lure of the braid and buttons it offered was enough to make the men agree to pay the extra out of their own pockets.

The dark blue jacket of the 3rd New Jersey was cut slightly longer than that of the regulation cavalry issue. The front was adorned with a triple row of brass "ball" buttons joined by double rows of yellow cord, and the sleeves with cord design similar to that worn by some officers. The collar had a patch of red and extra yellow cord. The headgear of the regiment consisted of a visorless dark blue cap trimmed in yellow, with brass crossed sabers and the company letter and regimental number. The trousers were the standard sky blue but had a wide, yellow stripe down the side, an adornment usually found on trousers of sergeants. In addition, a Hussar-style short cape or talma with a hood and tassel was issued to each man. Altogether, the men of the 3rd New Jersey must have presented an image that was grand and memorable. When they finally reached the Army of the Potomac in May, the veterans immediately nicknamed them the "butterflies." The name seemed only to deepen the men's pride, as they eventually used a flag embroidered with a butterfly in full color as one of their regimental colors. For all of its show, the 3rd New Jersey developed into a first-class cavalry regiment, its Spencer carbines serving with Sheridan in the Shenandoah Valley. The "butterflies" could sting like a bee.

The jacket shown here belonged to an unidentified member of the 3rd New Jersey. The brass buttons and yellow cord are as bright as when its owner rode off to war with his proud new regiment.

The Sash and Gauntlet of Colonel Ulric Dahlgren

Late on the night of March 2, 1864, a small column of Union cavalry riding within a few miles of the Confederate capital at Richmond ran into trouble. The column, led by twenty-one-year-old Col. Ulric Dahlgren, son of Rear Adm. John Dahlgren, was part of a failed attempt to enter Richmond, free Union prisoners, burn the city, and if possible, kill or capture Jefferson Davis. Now, however, the men were lost. Separated from their main force, they moved ahead into the darkness and into a Confederate ambush. Shots rang out, and the young commander fell from his horse dead. His death was about to touch off one of the great, undying controversies of the Civil War.

Upon his body, the Confederates found papers indicating the intention of the force. The content was published in the Richmond papers. Outraged by what was considered beyond the bounds of warfare, Confederates stripped Dahlgren's body of its uniform, mutilated it, and placed it on public display in the city. Officials in Washington and with the Union Army denied the validity of the papers, saying they were only being used as an excuse to cover the barbarous treatment of the young hero's body.

Those of the column who were not killed and did not manage to escape now ended up on their way to the very prisons they had hoped to empty, probably feeling lucky to avoid public wrath. Due to the intense public feeling, President Davis ordered the colonel's body be buried in a secret location in Richmond's Oakwood Cemetery. Several weeks later, Union agents who were operating in the city discovered the location of the body. On a dark, moonless night, they removed the body from the cemetery and reburied it in a farm outside the city. When the war ended, Colonel Dahlgren's remains were disinterred and sent North. After lying in state in Washington, the metal casket was sent to Philadelphia, and Ulric Dahlgren found his final resting place in Laurel Hill Cemetery.

Some time after the war, parts of the uniform that had been stripped from Ulric Dahlgren's body were returned to the family. Included in the items returned were his blood-stained gauntlet and sash with a hole made by one of the four bullets that hit their mark.

Federal Cavalry Headgear

The military cap, originally copied from the French, with its floppy crown falling forward almost to the visor, is today the most readily recognizable piece of the Civil War soldier's uniform. Even persons with only a passing interest in the war identify this item with the conflict. The cap, properly termed a "forage cap," was adopted by the U.S. Army in 1858. Made of dark blue cloth, it was intended for use on nondress or fatigue duty. The black pattern 1858 army hat, with its tall, stiff crown and wide brim looped up on one side, was to be worn on all other occasions. This was generally adhered to in the regular army, at least until 1861. According to Army General Orders No. 13, regulations were as follows:

> General Orders No. 13
>   War Department
>   Adjutant General's Office
>   Washington, November 30th, 1858
>   The following Regulation has been received from the War Department.
>   Hats with trimmings complete will be issued to enlisted men at the rate of one a year.
>   For Fatigue purposes Forage Caps, of pattern in the Quartermaster General's office, will be issued in addition to hats, at the rate of one a year. Dark blue cloth, with a cord or welt around the crown, of the colors issued to distinguish the several arms of service, and yellow metal letters in front to designate companies. For unassigned recruits dark blue cord or welt around the crown, and without the distinctive badge.
>   Commissioned officers may wear caps of the same pattern with dark blue welt, and the distinctive ornament, in front, of the Corps and regiments.
>   By order of the Secretary of War
>   S. Cooper
>   Adjutant General

The cap, as originally issued, had a colored welt around the edge of the round piece that fell forward to the visor. This welt was made in the usual colors of red for artillery, yellow for cavalry, and light blue for infantry. This feature was discontinued in the early months of the war as an economic measure, to make the same cap usable by all regiments. Also, the use of only the company letter on the cap changed quickly, as many volunteer regiments did not receive the dress hat, on which the regimental designator and branch insignia were intended to be placed.

The three pieces of headgear illustrated here were all worn by Union cavalrymen. The two caps belonged to volunteers and the hat to a Regular. Both caps clearly illustrate the usage of the issue brass insignia as came to be common practice on the forage cap. The cap of Charles Bent of the 1st Massachusetts Cavalry shows him to be a member of Company C. The cap worn by William H. Hosford, Company F, 15th New York Cavalry, identifies him as a member of that unit. The 1st Massachusetts served with the cavalry corps of the Army of the Potomac from the Battle of Antietam to the end of the war. It saw action in nearly every engagement of the famed eastern army. The 15th New York spent most of its service in the northern Virginia and Shenandoah Valley area but joined the Army of the Potomac in time for the Appomattox Campaign.

The hat shown here belonged to a trooper of the 4th U.S. Cavalry. It is without a doubt the hat of a veteran. It is a regulation pattern 1858 army hat that was modified by the soldier to a more rakish appearance by crushing in the top and adding a silver "4" and "US," both of which are nonregulation and were most likely purchased from a sutler. He also adorned the hat with an officer's hat cord and a plume that is held to the hat by a silver cockade. In the prewar regular army, such modification probably would not have been tolerated, but war has a way of changing things.

HAMPTON'S DUEL

For nearly a month, beginning June 9, 1863, the cavalry forces of the Army of Northern Virginia and the Army of the Potomac had engaged in a series of battles, taking them from the fields of Brandy Station, Virginia, to the little town of Gettysburg, Pennsylvania. During this time the Southern cavalry, under such leaders as Jeb Stuart and Wade Hampton, had gained a new respect for their Yankee opponents, who had given them little trouble in 1861 and '62. On July 3, just east of Gettysburg the two forces would clash again. On this day, in a desperate hand-to-hand struggle with troopers of the 1st New Jersey Cavalry, General Hampton came close to losing his life. It would be apparent to any who witnessed the Jersey men in action that day that they had taken to heart an order that had been circulated in the division the previous March, reading in part:

> It is time that the officers and men of this Division begin to appreciate the ineffable shame of a disgraceful and dastardly surrender. The spectacle of men with superior arms

and equipments unresistingly, without a struggle, surrendering to a gang of yelling rebels with old shotguns and horse pistols is too revolting to contemplate. . . . [T]he men of this Division must come to the understanding that it is their business to fight, and if necessary die, whenever they meet the enemy.

Although shotguns and horse pistols may have indeed been common issue in the cavalry of the Army of Northern Virginia early in the war, by the Gettysburg campaign, most troopers carried a rifle or carbine, a revolver, and a saber. At this same time the cavalry regiments of the Army of the Potomac, with two notable exceptions, were universally equipped with a breech-loading carbine, revolver, and saber. The exceptions were the 5th and 6th Michigan, who carried the new Spencer repeating rifle. The 1st New Jersey was armed with the Burnside carbine, the Colt Army revolver, and a mixture of model 1840 and 1860 cavalry sabers.

General Hampton wields his distinctively heavy straight-blade saber while several Southern troopers rush forward to rescue their hard-pressed leader. Within seconds Hampton is severely wounded by a saber thrust to the head, and at least two of his attackers are dead, as are two of those who came to his defense. Covered by others who have come to his aid, the general spurs his horse forward and leaps a nearby fence just as a Yankee bullet strikes him in the hip. He will live to fight another day, but many who entered the maelstrom that day on East Cavalry Field did not.

On that hot July day most of the Union cavalrymen were dressed in the close-fitting dress jacket with its high collar. Following the battle many of these would be replaced by the more comfortable fatigue blouse. Most, if not all, Confederate troopers were outfitted in the short jacket issued by the Richmond Quartermaster Depot.

Custom-Made Jacket, Sergeant of Cavalry

Not all enlisted men were content to wear the uniform as issued by the Federal government. Embellishments were often made, depending on the wealth of the individuals. Some would purchase items from sutlers intended for sale to officers, such as hat cords and insignia woven of gold metallic thread. Others, particularly regular army soldiers, would requisition uniforms in a size too large for them and then give them to a company or regimental tailor to alter to a custom fit.

All of these practices were sure to excite the wrath of some officer, either within the regiment or somewhere on up the chain of command. A May 27, 1863, order from General Zook, who commanded a brigade in the 2nd Corps, forbade the wearing of any piece of non-regulation dress by enlisted men. It did not, however, address the wearing of custom-tailored or tailor-made uniforms that generally conformed to army regulations. Such uniforms continued to be worn in the army by those who took extra pride in their personal appearance.

Because of its unique cuff trim, this meticulously tailored jacket is believed to have been worn by a sergeant of the 11th New York cavalry. It is made of officer's-quality material and is adorned with officer's buttons. It obviously belonged to a sergeant with money to spare. The attachments for the brass shoulder scales remain in place on the shoulders. The 11th New York, also known as "Scott's 900," began its service by spending nearly two years in the defenses of Washington, with numerous scouts and expeditions as far west as Harpers Ferry. The chances for a young sergeant to acquire a finely fitted jacket, sure to attract the ladies of the capital city, were many. We can only wonder if the expense paid off. In March 1864, the 11th was transferred to the Department of the Gulf and from that point on saw active service in Mississippi, Louisiana, and Tennessee.

Two Carbines That Rode to War

The variety of firearms used in the Civil War can stagger the imagination. Two of the many types that were issued to the Union cavalry were the Burnside (top) and the Smith. Prior to the Civil War, the Federal government was testing a variety of arms with a view to rearming the dragoons and cavalry with a new breech-loading weapon to replace the Sharps carbine then in general use. The possibility of lucrative sales to the army had spurred many inventors and would-be inventors to bring forward their ideas. Two of the arms tested were the Burnside and Smith. Although the army considered the Smith the better arm for mounted troops, both were destined to see extensive service in the conflict that was about to engulf the nation.

The Burnside carbine was the brainchild of Ambrose Everett Burnside, a West Point graduate who had resigned his commission in 1853 to pursue the manufacture of the arm that was to bear his name. Before the war, his company, the Bristol Firearms Company of Bristol, Rhode Island, had been successful in selling several hundred carbines to the government for trial use in the field. Two companies of the 1st Cavalry had been armed with them.

The Burnside used a metallic, cone-shaped cartridge. The arm employed a breech system that would allow easy loading of the cartridge into a rectangular steel block housed in the breech. The block would tilt upward when the loading lever, which also served as a trigger guard, was lowered. A slight problem developed in actual field service during the war. It was found that repeated firing could cause fouling to build up in the cartridge cavity, making the empty cartridge casing hard to remove. Troopers found that this could be remedied by forcing a previously fired cartridge case inside the one remaining in the chamber, thereby giving an extra amount of exposed surface to grab hold. In recent years, relic hunters have found numerous Burnside cartridge cases stuck one inside the other. Before the war's end, the

U.S. Army had purchased and issued over 53,000 Burnside carbines.

The Smith carbine employed a simple, effective method of loading that impressed the army officers who examined the weapon in 1860. To open the breech, the soldier pressed upward on a brass pin located in front of the trigger. This action raised a leaf spring, which allowed the barrel and loading chamber to pivot forward. The soldier would then simply (in theory) remove the spent cartridge and drop in another. Trouble developed during the war, however, which made one regiment, the 1st Massachusetts Cavalry, very happy to exchange their Smiths for Sharps carbines in the spring of 1863. Two types of cartridges were issued for the Smith carbine. One type employed a case of brass foil, the other a case of hard rubber. While the brass cases worked well, the rubber ones began to stick in the breech during rapid firing. Apparently the 1st Massachusetts had the misfortune of being issued rubber cartridges.

Both the Burnside and Smith carbines belonged to a generation of arms that bridged the gap between muzzle-loading and magazine rapid-firing breechloaders. While both did in fact load from the breech and used a metallic cartridge that sealed and protected the powder charge, they still required an external primer in the form of a percussion cap. The true arms revolution would come when cartridges containing their own primer came on the scene. When the war began, weapons employing this system existed. By 1863 they made an appearance on the battlefield, and by 1864 they began to dominate the field.

Burnside and Smith carbines were both popular with the Confederate cavalryman, who received his from the same source as the Union trooper: the U.S. government. This issue was not intended, however. Extensive captures, particularly during the first year of the war, when Rebel troopers ruled the field, placed an ample supply of these arms in Southern hands.

A Historic McClellan Saddle

The McClellan saddle took its name from its inventor, Capt. George B. McClellan. Captain McClellan's idea for an ideal military saddle was based on his observations while traveling in Europe and serving on the U.S. western frontier. His greatest influence in the design came from the saddle used by the Prussian Army. The captain's invention was submitted for examination and trial in 1859 and was adopted for general use by the army in that year, making it officially the model 1859.

Both the saddle and its inventor were destined to gain fame in the Civil War. Nearly every mounted soldier in the Union Army would become intimately acquainted with the saddle. General McClellan's army career ended in 1864, but the saddle that bore his name continued in use in the U.S. Army, with only minor changes until tanks and machine guns made the mounted trooper obsolete just prior to World War II.

The McClellan saddle pictured here is the regulation model 1859. With one exception—the leather valise that is strapped to the cantel (rear) of the saddle   it is exactly as used by the enlisted Union cavalryman. The enlisted trooper was expected to carry his extra clothing and necessary small items in issued saddlebags. October 9, 1863, orders to the 14th Pennsylvania cavalry stated, "The men will carry in their saddle bags the following articles viz.— 1 shirt, 1 pair drawers, 2 pair stockings, soap, towel and comb." Officers often purchased a cylindrical valise to serve this purpose. This valise also gave them a little extra room for a few additional luxuries.

Officers also often purchased more finely finished saddles with extra padding and trim. This saddle was the property of an enlisted man who received an officer's commission. Sgt. Egbert Clapp was likely issued this saddle when the 31st Massachusetts Infantry, in which he was serving, was mounted and designated the 6th Massachusetts Cavalry in December 1863. After receiving his commission, the new second lieutenant probably added an officer's valise to set himself apart from the men he now commanded. The 6th Massachusetts spent its entire service in the area of Mississippi and Louisiana. A note that remains with Lieutenant Clapp's saddle testifies that he was using this saddle when he was injured by his horse falling on him while carrying dispatches.

The Jacket of a Cavalry Bugler

Military musicians have a long history of receiving uniforms with distinctive trim or colors that clearly identify their status as different from the ordinary soldier. The uniform of the musician in the U.S. Army of the Civil War era carried on this tradition. The uniform adopted in 1858 required the coat or jacket of the musician to have an arrangement of ³/₈-inch wool lace extending down the front, from the neck to the waist, "in something called the herring-bone form." The trim would be of the color of the facing of the corps: red for artillery, yellow for cavalry, and light blue for infantry. By this means, the infantry or heavy artillery commander could quickly identify his drummer and the light artillery or cavalry officer his bugler.

This was important, for within the ranks of the fighting regiments of all branches of the army, the musician held an important and responsible position. Musical instruments were the surest and quickest means of communicating the commander's orders during the roar of battle. While in camp, they could quickly and effectively let an entire regiment know that the routine was being interrupted by some special requirement. The cavalry bugler rode close to the regimental or company commander. At the command of the officer, the calls of the bugle could send the regiment charging toward the enemy or recall them from a difficult or dangerous position.

This jacket adheres exactly to the government regulation. Its yellow braid stands out as well today as it did during the tumultuous days of the Civil War. Inside the jacket, the letters "SA" indicate that it was made for, and inspected at, the main quartermaster depot Schuylkill Arsenal, located in Philadelphia. The receipt of substandard articles of clothing purchased on contract in the early months of the war caused the imposition of regulations that, after early 1862, required uniforms made for issue to the army be indelibly marked inside to make the origin of the garment readily known.

Garments produced directly under the authority of the Schuylkill Arsenal were hand-sewn by women working in their homes. These women, usually the wives, mothers, or often widows of soldiers, would receive the cutout, unassembled garment at the arsenal and return it to that facility when completed. Each garment was then individually inspected by a quartermaster department inspector, and if satisfactory, the women would then be paid. It was by this means that several thousand women in Philadelphia, and those fortunate enough to live near other similar government facilities, made the money necessary to augment the $13-a-month pay of a private soldier or the small pension the woman might receive upon his death.

The Spencer and the Sharps

When the Civil War began, the U.S. Cavalry was almost entirely armed with the famous Sharps carbine. By 1865, when the last shots were fired, the Sharps had been replaced by the rapid-firing Spencer, which, with its self-contained metallic cartridge and magazine-fed lever action, had begun to revolutionize warfare.

Throughout the war, the Sharps had remained a workhorse. It fired a bullet with its powder charge encased in a paper- or linen-wrapped cartridge. The case would disintegrate upon firing, making it no longer necessary to remove a spent metal casing. The Sharps required the soldier to use the same type of musket cap and cocking mechanism found on the muzzle-loading arms. Overall, the carbine's chief advantages were its reliability and the ease and relative quickness of loading the weapon. Like the cartridges for the muzzle loaders, which were similar in construction, the Sharps cartridge could not survive exposure to moisture or rough handling.

The Confederates favored the Sharps above all other carbines. The arm existed in the hands of militia units and in state arsenals and was available to equip the early volunteers. During the war, captured Sharps helped supplement the Confederate supply, but this barely offset combat losses. The decision was made in Richmond to produce a Southern copy of the Sharps. After some difficulty with machinery, the arms were produced and issued beginning late 1862.

Problems arose almost immediately. The arm was not produced to the same tolerances as the Federal weapon, nor was the material used of the same quality. As early as May 1863, Col. W. Leroy Brown, Confederate chief of armories, reported that he knew of thirty or forty of the arms that had burst on firing. He recommended the substitution of a muzzle-loading arm with a swivel similar to the Enfield carbine. He felt that such an arm would be "cheaper, simpler, more durable and quite as efficient as the breech loaders." There were estimated to have been only about 5,000 Confederate Sharps produced, as compared to well over 100,000 of the original U.S. Sharps.

In every major war, some bit of technology comes along that changes the way things have been done and opens the door to a new level of killing. In the spring of 1863 the first products of the Spencer Repeating Rifle Company were placed in the hands of Union troops. The arm was a seven-shot repeater that used a metallic cartridge with a self-contained primer. By activating a lever that also served as a trigger guard, the soldier could in two quick motions eject a spent cartridge and load a fresh one. He then had only to cock the hammer mounted on the side of the receiver, aim, and shoot. Warfare would never be the same.

The Spencer was an immediate success. Its operation was nearly flawless, the ammunition waterproof, and even a new recruit could be quickly trained in its use. The first Spencers delivered went to the 5th and 6th Michigan Cavalry. These arms were not carbines but had the barrel length of a rifle. This slight inconvenience was more than made up for by the arm itself. On East Cavalry field at Gettysburg on July 3, 1863, the Michigan men made good use of the weapon. Federal ordnance officers had already been convinced of the importance of the arm and were quick to order more. These, too, were rifle length, but by October 1863 orders were placed for Spencer carbines. The conversion was easy; all the factory had to do was shorten the barrel and forestock and add a ring for the cavalryman's carbine sling hook. As the war progressed, the government bought the entire output of the factory and began the process of rearming the Federal cavalry. The war ended before the process was anywhere near complete, but the die had been cast. Repeating arms were the wave of the future.

ROCK OF ERIN

The gallant stand of the 69th Pennsylvania Volunteers on July 3, 1863 at Gettysburg has long been over-shadowed by the fighting at the "Bloody Angle" a few hundred feet away. In what can only be described as a classic "last stand," this hardy band of Philadelphia Irishmen held onto the center of the Federal line, regardless of being flanked, and suffered horrendous casualties. Facing the full brunt of Pickett's division, Colonel O'Kane ordered his men to hold their fire *"until they came so close to us, that we could distinguish the whites of their eyes."* Nearly overwhelmed by the Southern onslaught, the men fought so fiercely that musket butts were swung in the close-quarter turmoil. In a war where courage was common, there were few examples of tenacity to parallel the doggedness of the 69th. Had they not

stood, the entire Union line might have collapsed, with dire results. By battle's end, Colonel O'Kane lay mortally wounded, Lieutenant Colonel Tschudy was slain, Major Duffy was shot through the hip, and half the regiment was lost to casualties.

The soldiers shown here are typical of the Federal infantry during mid-1863. Most are dressed in the sack coat and sky blue kersey trousers, as prescribed by regulations. Their forage caps are adorned with the early form of the badge of the 2nd Division, 2nd Corps.

Although most Pennsylvania regiments carried a single state color, the 69th carried two. The Pennsylvania flag was a U.S. National Pattern, with the state seal painted in the canton and a green Presentation Irish color.

A Glimpse at a Soldier's Life

While he was on campaign, the solder's knapsack was his home. In it he carried the personal items that made his life more comfortable and allowed him to retain some amount of privacy. During the first two years of war, the Union soldier was allowed more leeway on the contents of his knapsack than he would find if he remained in service for the blood-and-guts campaigns of 1864 and 1865. Modern historians occasionally find the listing of what was in a soldier's knapsack. These were usually done up as a "statement of effects" if the soldier died while in camp or in a hospital. Although such written documents are a valuable resource, they leave much to the imagination. Like a time capsule, the knapsack of Edgar S. Yergason of Company A, 22nd Connecticut Infantry, lay in storage for more than 125 years. The items that Yergason had placed there were waiting to be rediscovered to give us a glimpse of soldier life.

The knapsack itself is a rare example of white gutta-percha-coated canvas. Similar knapsacks were known to have been issued to volunteer troops in the early months of the war. As late as June 1863, the Gutta Percha Manufacturing Company of New York was offering "gray gutta percha knapsacks" for sale to the Quartermaster's Department, promising to deliver 7,000 or 8,000 at once. The company had already delivered waterproof blankets and talmas (raincoats) beginning in 1861.

To a great extent, the contents of Yergason's knapsack are typical of the items that would have been found in the possession of a volunteer of 1862. Gone are the totally unnecessary trinkets that overburdened the volunteer of 1861, yet the contents are not quite down to the totally no-nonsense level of 1864. At a later date it is unlikely you would find the tarred linen hat cover or the nonregulation shirt. While the writing kit might still be found, it is more likely that there would be only a few envelopes and some paper. The small sewing kit containing needles, thread, and spare buttons, known as a "housewife," would remain, as would the Bible. For the summer campaign of 1863 or '64, the wool blanket would likely give way to a shelter tent and a rubber blanket. (The army wool blanket weighed 5 pounds and didn't keep the soldier dry.) The combination knife, fork, and spoon, as well as the small candle holder, were considered necessary by most soldiers. The almanac, though not indispensable, was nice to have and added no noticeable weight. Several items found in the average knapsack are not included here. Soap, towel, and a razor were carried by most soldiers, as were extra socks and an extra pair of underwear.

Two Rifles That Delivered

The decade prior to the Civil War saw numerous advances in small-arms technology. Perhaps the most important single innovation was the successful production of a metallic case cartridge with a self-contained priming system. The cartridge was patented by Smith & Wesson in 1854. The design of the cartridge led to the production of the first of many famous revolvers by the firm of Smith & Wesson.

The cartridge also lent itself to use in arms other than revolvers. One of these was the rifle, and later the carbine, invented by Christopher Miner Spencer. Spencer was nineteen when he was issued the patent dated March 6, 1860, for the seven-shot, tubular magazine-fed, lever-action rifle that was to bear his name. He had barely gone into production of the arm when Fort Sumter was fired on in April 1861, and the nation was plunged into war. Spencer was able to have the weapon tested by both the army and the navy and received contracts from both services, even though the army chief of ordnance, Gen. J. W. Ripley, did not like the breech-loading arms. The first 700 Spencer arms to reach the armed forces went to the navy; the next order was sent to Michigan to arm the newly formed 5th Michigan cavalry.

It would not be until June 24, 1863, that the rifle would receive its first real test in battle. On that date, at an obscure site known as Hoover's Gap, Tennessee, in the hands of a brigade of mounted infantry, the Spencer rifle would begin to change warfare. The brigade, known later as the Lightning Brigade, consisted of the 98th and 123rd

Illinois Infantry as well as the 17th and 72nd Indiana Infantry and Lilly's Indiana battery of artillery. The infantry had been armed with the Spencer for just over a month, when circumstances placed them in front of the army and responsible for holding an important mountain gap that controlled the road on which the main Union force was advancing. The Lightning Brigade fought all day against an entire Confederate division, repulsing numerous charges with volley after volley from their fast-firing rifles. The story told on that day was not lost on the army, which placed orders for the entire future production of Spencer arms.

It cannot be claimed that the Spencer made the telling difference in the ultimate Union victory. The total purchase of the weapon both as rifle and carbine by the U.S. government during the war was just over 107,000 arms. It can be claimed, however, that the age of repeating arms was born.

Spencer rifle serial number 4619, pictured here, was issued to Pvt. Martin Ingersoll, Company D, 72nd Indiana Mounted Infantry. There is no doubt that the arm was at Hoover's Gap and was carried through the many campaigns that the regiment participated in until the end of the war. Ingersoll, a schoolteacher from Crawfordsville, Indiana, served until mustered out on June 26, 1863. We can only wonder what stories his future students heard of his years with the Lightning Brigade.

Though the significance of the Sharps rifle is overshadowed by the Spencer, its fame as a weapon of the Civil War is certainly not. The Sharps was in production well before the war, and U.S. Regular Dragoons and Cavalry were armed with the carbine version of the arm while serving on the western frontier. The Sharps rifle, like the Spencer, differed significantly from the carbine version of the army only in the length of the barrel. Although the Sharps was a breechloader, it fired a linen case cartridge that required the use of a standard musket cap for ignition. The cartridge was vulnerable to all of the hazards of the paper-wrapped cartridge used in the musket. Still, in comparison with the musket, the Sharps was a rapid-fire arm. The most famous regiment to use the Sharps rifle was without doubt Berdan's Sharpshooters. Other regiments and parts of regiments, however, also made good use of the famous rifle. One of these was the 9th Regiment Pennsylvania Reserves. Company A of this regiment purchased its own Sharps rifles and put them to good use in its service with the Army of the Potomac.

This Sharps rifle, serial number 39678, has a silver plaque set into the stock showing it to be the property of "Thomas Campbell, Co. A, 9th P.R.V.C." Here, too, is an arm that saw real battle. Campbell served with the regiment its entire term of service and was present at every battle it fought in, including Antietam and Gettysburg.

Together the Spencer and the Sharps could have tipped the scales of battle, had they been employed in significant numbers. In what is almost a postscript to the war, Gen. W. S. Hancock was authorized in the final days of 1864 to raise a "corps" to be made up of all veteran soldiers armed with breech-loading rifles. As an inducement to enlistment, these men were all to be allowed to retain their arms upon completion of their enlistment. In all, nine infantry regiments were mustered as U.S. Veteran Volunteers. Several of these regiments were armed exclusively with the Sharps rifle. The "corps" was not fully organized before the war ended, and none of the regiments saw combat. What such an organization of battle-hardened infantry, armed with breechloaders, might have done in battle can only be guessed.

1ST COMPANY, RICHMOND HOWITZERS, 1863

VAL FORGETT

One of the better-known batteries of artillery to serve the Confederacy from the state of Virginia was the 1st Company of Richmond Howitzers. The company had its origin in 1859 and was first called out in response to the perceived threat to the state following the John Brown raid on Harpers Ferry. The unit was hastily equipped for the emergency and armed with muskets but was given little in the way of uniform dress.

As war clouds gathered, the company began a serious regimen of drill and ordered gray uniforms made. By the time they joined the Confederate Army at Manassas, they had come a long way. Two other companies of Richmond

Howitzers were formed in May 1861, but the three never served together.

The corporal shown here leaning against one of the battery's howitzers is wearing the uniform that was typical of the Army of Northern Virginia in 1863. His jacket is the second pattern produced by the Richmond Quartermaster Depot, which is piped in artillery red. His headgear is a cap also trimmed in red for the artillery. His boots are of fine quality and may have been English in origin, as is the belt visible under his jacket. The overcoat draped over the gun barrel came to him courtesy of the Yankees.

The Jenifer Saddle

The second most widely used saddle in the Civil War was patented just prior to the war by Lt. Walter H. Jenifer of the 2nd Cavalry. Lieutenant Jenifer received his patent in June 1860; ten months later he resigned his U.S. Army commission to join the Confederacy. During the coming war, Jenifer, a Maryland native, would command the 8th Virginia Cavalry.

The Jenifer saddle differed from the McClellan in several ways. The most significant was its solid seat, as opposed to the open-center seat of the McClellan. The Jenifer also had a noticeably higher cantle and pommel. The design of the saddle was well liked in the Southern cavalry, and it was produced both on government contract and in government-run depots.

This example of a Confederate Jenifer was produced by C. A. Farwell of Mobile, Alabama. It has a brass shield on the pommel, with the letters "CS." Farwell was a contractor with the South for harnesses and saddles.

One of the most important facilities for making saddles and harnesses for the Confederacy was located at Clarksville, Virginia. During 1863 the shop was run by Capt. Henry Pride. For most of that year, his shop produced saddle trees of both the Jenifer and McClellan patterns and sent them in large quantity to the ordnance shops in Richmond and Charleston, South Carolina, to be finished. In March 1863 the shop received orders from Richmond to stop making the Jenifer trees, but research has shown that the demand for the saddle was such that they continued its manufacture at least through September of that year. On May 7, 1863, 6,000 Jenifer saddle trees were sent to Richmond, and June 4 the facility completed and sent on special order a "full quilted" Jenifer saddle to Gen. Fitzhugh Lee. In September Captain Pride received a request to send 2,000 "skeleton saddle of Jenifer pattern" to Col. J. R. Waddy at the Charleston facility. At least part of this order was filled.

The Clarksville Depot is only one example of Southern saddle production, but the brief look at that

facility should give today's student of the war some idea of the extent of usage of the Jenifer saddle by the troopers who rode for the South. The Jenifer was indeed "the other McClellan."

Confederate Artillery Jacket

This fine example of a Confederate light artillery jacket was taken at the battle of Labadieville, Louisiana, on October 27, 1862, by a Haverhill, Massachusetts, soldier. At this battle, Battery H, 1st Mississippi Light Artillery, was overrun by Massachusetts troops, and though there is no identification with the jacket, it likely belonged to a soldier from that unit. The jacket is now a medium gray color but was originally a dark blue-gray. It is trimmed with red cord and has a pair of cloth crossed cannons on the standing collar. The sleeves each have an inverted chevron of yellow, believed to indicate that the wearer had prior service in the cavalry. The buttons are of U.S. issue and may have been from a captured garment.

Battery H was organized at Natchez, Mississippi, on April 30, 1862, by Capt. George Ralson, a planter from Adams County. The battery was armed with both 6-pound smoothbore guns and 12-pound howitzers. Although part of the 1st Mississippi Artillery Regiment was commanded by Col. William Temple Withers, himself a wealthy plantation owner, Battery H was detached and did not serve directly under Wither's command.

UNION ARMY SURGEON 1861–65

The Civil War soldier had a great deal better chance of dying from disease or wounds than he did of being killed outright in battle. With this reality in mind, the army surgeon could be either his best friend or his worst enemy. Like the soldiers and volunteer officers of the line, the experience and expertise of those who came to serve as military doctors varied widely. For the most part, they were sincere and dedicated, but service as small-town doctors in Ohio or rural Georgia could not prepare them for the diarrhea and measles that would sweep through the camps in epidemic proportions. Nor could the daily routine of a doctor, in even a large city, prepare any man for the carnage of a battle such as Shiloh or Antietam, where a surgeon may be called upon to perform more amputations in a day than he would do in a decade of civilian practice.

An example of the conditions facing the Civil War surgeon can be found in the report made by the medical director of the 2nd Division, 1st Corps, on November 13, 1862, after completing an inspection of the 16th Maine Infantry:

I this day made a thorough inspection as to the sanitary conditions of the 16th Maine. . . .

I find the mean strength of the regiment to be 693 men, 181 of which were under treatment by the regimental surgeon of which number I find

Sick & unfit for duty 56
Convalescent (not yet fit for duty) 79
Shirks 46
Total 181

The prevalent diseases are Diarrhea, Dysentery, Bronchitis, Rheumative affections & a few cases of intermittent fever.

The surgeon attributed the problems largely to unsanitary conditions in camp. He found that the men were generally not in the habit of bathing and that those who had underclothes had not washed them in two and a half months.

The military surgeon at any level of service, from regiment to army corps, was considered a member of the headquarters staff. For this reason, his uniform is, with three exceptions, that of a staff officer. By regulations, an officer of the staff was required to wear the frock coat appropriate to his rank, single-breasted for company-grade officers—lieutenants or captains—and double-breasted for field-grade officers, which included majors and above. The surgeon's shoulder straps, like those of other staff officers, denoted his standing in the normal fashion, with the rank-indicating devices placed on a regulation dark blue or black background within the borders of the strap. A variation much

favored by medical officers placed the letters "MS" (for medical staff) in old English in the middle of the strap between the rank devices.

At a distance, however, the surgeon without his sword and sash would be indistinguishable from a staff officer or any other discipline. It was these badges of office that truly set him apart. Army regulations called for a sash of "medium or emer-ald green" for medical officers. The same regulations pre-scribed a small sword of a pattern on deposit in the surgeon general's office. The sword most commonly worn was adopted in 1840. It had a thin, straight blade and a guard of two grace-ful quillions on either side of a small shield, which, like the shoulder straps, bore the letters "MS." Like the surgeon him-self, his sword was not intended to be involved in combat.

The Tools of a Military Surgeon

For a Civil War regimental surgeon, the necessity to perform the amputation of a wounded soldier's arm or leg was accepted as an almost routine part of the job. The standard projectile used in infantry combat, the .58-caliber minié ball, would impact the bone of a human limb with such devastating force that reconstruction was impossible, under even ideal nineteenth-century condi-tions. The doctor's kit shown here was designed specifi-cally for the amputation of arms and legs. The various tools, all made of the finest steel with black gutta-percha handles, were made for the U.S. Army by H. Hernstein of New York City. The red velvet lining of the case can-not soften the menacing appearance of the bone saw and other instruments.

This kit was the property of Dr. Thomas Morton Hills, the regimental surgeon of the 27th Connecticut Infantry. Dr. Hills was from Willimantic, Connecticut,

and was descended from one of the oldest families of the state, with a history dating back to 1632. His qualifica-tions as a surgeon were among the best, as he had stud-ied medicine at Yale. At the Battle of Fredericksburg, Virginia, in December, he was one of three surgeons working in a hospital near the battlefield. For over sixty hours, the three manned the operating table, where this set of instruments certainly saw more than ample use. Following the Union defeat, the doctors were among the very last to cross the Rappahannock River before the pontoon bridge was destroyed.

Despite his devotion, Dr. Hills was dismissed from the service for having left equipment behind. No longer an army surgeon, Dr. Hills returned to the field in 1864 as chief surgeon for Drs. Brown and Alexander, govern-ment embalmers. After the war, Dr. Hills returned to Willimantic to practice medicine.

Chevrons of a Hospital Steward, 1st Maine Heavy Artillery

The hospital steward of any regiment was an important link to the well-being of that command. Working as an assistant to the regimental surgeon, the hospital steward took on many of the duties of a nurse and a modern-day medical corpsman. The rank of this soldier was indicated by a half chevron of emerald green cloth, upon which was embroidered a yellow caduceus. The chevron was adopted by the army in 1851 and worn with little change until 1887. The hospital steward served as part of the regimental staff and received the pay of a sergeant.

The chevrons of Hospital Steward Benjamin C. Frost of the renowned 1st Maine Heavy Artillery appear to have been privately purchased. They are of generally higher quality than the standard issue, with a forest green velvet background and a heavy gold embroidered caduceus and edging. The eyes and tongues of the snakes are done in red silk.

The 1st Maine was enlisted as the 18th Maine Infantry in August 1862. The regiment was sent immediately to Washington, D.C., where the men were put to work building some of the defensive earthwork forts that eventually encircled the city. In January 1863 the regimental designator was changed to heavy artillery, and they were assigned to duty principally in Fort Sumner, on the western defenses near the Potomac River. At this time they added two new companies, bringing the total to twelve, which was the required strength of a heavy artillery regiment. They would continue to serve in the defenses until the following May. It was probably during this period that the elegant chevrons were purchased somewhere in the city.

On March 12, 1864, Hospital Steward Frost was commissioned as a lieutenant in Company M. Two months later, the 1st Maine was ordered to join the Army of the Potomac, then engaged in the first battle of the summer campaign of 1864. The proud regiment had been continually drilled as both infantry and heavy artillery for two years. Leaving their heavy guns behind, they marched with flags flying and polished brass to join the veteran army as infantry. It is certain that none could have imagined the fate that awaited them. Within just over a month, the regiment would be nearly wiped out, having sustained unbelievable casualties at Spotsylvania and in the June 18 assault on the Confederate trenches at Petersburg. By the time the regiment was finally mustered out in September 1865, a total of 23 officers and 400 enlisted men had been killed and mortally wounded, the highest loss of any regiment in the entire war. Lieutenant Frost was one of the fortunate few to return home, to Bangor, Maine.

CONFEDERATE STATES MEDICAL SERVICE

By twentieth-century standards, medicine as practiced during the Civil War was primitive at best. Most military doctors came from small-town practices where farm accidents and childbirth were the common emergencies. To be suddenly thrown into the trauma of caring for the human wreckage of a major battle was likely beyond the imagination of many who donned the uniform of the Union or Confederacy to serve as an army surgeon.

As the war progressed, efforts were made to establish a Medical Service, which would include regularly detailed enlisted men to assist in caring for the wounded. This was found necessary to put a stop to the problem of able-bodied fighting men leaving the ranks to assist wounded comrades to the rear. Often musicians from regimental bands were assigned to this duty, and frequently it was given to men who for one reason or another could not perform front-line duty. Contrary to common belief, most field surgeons, as well as those in the larger hospitals, were usually well supplied with the proper medicines, and few amputations were performed without the benefit of anesthetics.

Disease was in reality a far greater problem for the Medical Service. Wounds, no matter how severe, could usually be divided into categories of treatable or untreatable. Disease, on the other hand, could respond to available medicine or mysteriously defy all treatment. It could spread quickly, and its origin was often unknown. Efforts were continually made to control or prevent disease. On August 6, 1864, the Confederate Surgeon General's Office directed Surgeon Joseph Jones to "institute an extended investigation upon the causes, Pathology and treatment of Fevers and the relation of climate and soil to disease." The results of this study were to be deposited in the Surgeon General's Office for the use of the Medical Department of the Confederate Army. It is an interesting note that this same Surgeon Jones had, in March 1863, submitted plans for the development of poison gas for use

against ironclad vessels and to be placed in artillery shells for use against troops. Fortunately, his obvious knowledge was turned to more humane fields of endeavor.

For the Confederate Army, large hospital complexes were established in most of the major cities. Richmond, being close to the major struggle in the East, at times must have seemed to be one vast hospital. Early in the war, Nashville served the same purpose for the western Confederate armies. Most hospitals were run with efficiency, and convalescent soldiers were adequately supervised and returned to duty as soon as possible, but it seems that things in Tennessee got somewhat out of hand. Maj. A. J. Lindsay, a former U.S. Army officer who was serving as a Confederate ordnance officer in Nashville, reported on December 17, 1861, that "three of the hospitals are flooded with filth from the overflow of the water closets. The plumbers refuse to work because they cannot be paid." Not surprisingly, a week later he reported a near mutiny in one of the hospitals. To further emphasize the conditions in the city, on January 6, 1862, Lindsay observed that "the convalescent sick are running about the streets, filling the Grog shops and houses of prostitution and utterly set at defiance of the police." Not all was well in Nashville, but in the early months of the war there was a lot to learn.

The soldiers and the surgeon depicted here represent a Confederate Medical Service that had profited from experience. The surgeon, a lieutenant colonel, wears a uniform trimmed in black to indicate his position as a staff officer. The enlisted stretcher bearers are wearing red bands on their hats, with the badge of the Ambulance Corps clearly visible on the front to distinguish them from others who may be leaving the battlefront without proper authority. The temporary hospital has been set up in close proximity to the battlefield so that the wounded soldier will receive immediate assistance. If necessary, he will then be transferred to a large general hospital.

The Distinctive Marks of a Union Army Surgeon

The sword of Dr. J. W. Hotaling, surgeon of the 121st New York Infantry, was presented to him on March 28, 1863, "by his friends," as the inscription reads. The sash and shoulder straps on which it rests belonged to surgeon Ambrose Pratt of the 22nd Connecticut. Such tokens of respect as this sword were often presented to officers who had endeared themselves to their regiment or community. Not all surgeons were so highly thought of. One, the surgeon of the 115th Pennsylvania Infantry, was described in a letter dated October 20, 1862, as "simply an ignoramus, an illiterate quack and a positive swindle on the government."

A Visit to a Soldier's Quarters

It is not often that twentieth-century students of the Civil War are given the opportunity to "visit" the living quarters of a soldier of that war. Those who attend reenactments or some of our battlefield parks can be treated to a modern idea of soldier life but are left to wonder if that's really the way it was. A few Civil War soldiers left written accounts of where they lived, but even these leave much to the imagination. One member of the 169th New York Infantry chose to use his obvious skill as a model maker to give us an actual look into the place where he and two of his comrades saw some of their service time. This "folk art" model of a soldier's hut is a unique gift to us today. The mess area with cups and plates is located outside. Inside, life has been made as much like home as possible. Three miniature muskets, along with their accoutrements, are a reminder of the reality of the situation. But aside from these, the tiny

bunks, pictures on the wall, pots and pans, and even tasseled sleeping camps could belong to a fishing camp in the Finger Lakes region.

The 169th was one of the many regiments that served with the Union forces operating against the Confederate ports and fortifications along the Atlantic coast of the Carolinas and Florida. Though they spent time camped on Folly Island, South Carolina, they were constantly on the move with operations that took them away from the island. In 1864 the regiment returned to Virginia, where they were assigned to the 10th Army Corps for the operations south of the James River and opposite Petersburg. They would return to the coast again for the taking of Fort Fisher, but never to the island where they passed some pleasant hours in the comfort of their hut.

Soldier's Mittens

The need for mittens or gloves to protect soldiers during long hours on picket duty or on winter marches was only partially addressed by the army supply system. Limited contracts for gloves or one-finger mittens were let with such companies as Jordan Marsh of Boston. But general issue of such items never occurred. Popular ladies books such as *Godey's* occasionally contained patterns for knitting or making items for soldiers. Loving gifts such as scarves, suspenders, and mittens were often included in packages sent to men serving with the armies.

These light blue and white speckled mittens, lined with white flannel for extra protection, were woven with a trigger finger and may well have seen use on a cold picket post somewhere in Virginia or Tennessee. There is no marking to indicate their origin, be it issue, purchase, or a gift from a loved one.

Officer's Rank Insignia, 1864

As early as December 1862, a few commanders within the Union Army had realized the impracticality of officers going to battle wearing a uniform and insignia that clearly identified them as such. Such readily recognizable marks as officers' shoulder straps stood out at a distance and marked the wearer as a target for Confederate marksmen.

The practice of officers shunning the wearing of obvious rank insignia had begun to take hold in the Army of the Potomac. On September 1, 1863, the following order was issued in response:

> *2nd Division, 12th Corps*
>
> *A number of officers in this command, it has been observed, wear the designation of their rank in places not prescribed in the Regulations.*
>
> *As deviation from the rules regulating the uniform of the Army are direct violations of Orders, all officers will be required to wear the insignia of their rank in the proper places, only and failures to comply with this order will be noted by all inspectors of the command in every inspection hereafter made.*
>
> *Officers insignia may be readily obtained by Express or through any of the sutlers attached to the Division.*
>
> *By Command*
> *John W. Geary*

Even so, photographic evidence clearly shows that by 1864, the practice of wearing nonobvious rank insignia was becoming widespread in the Union Army. This metal disk was sold by the famous New York military outfitters Schuyler, Hartley and Graham. It is stamped of gilded brass, with two bars and a yellow enamel background, indicating the wearer to be a captain of cavalry. The device has a pin back and was usually worn pinned to the breast of the officer's fatigue coat or jacket. In a similar light, some officers are known to have had borderless single-rank devices sewn or pinned to the shoulder of the coat. It can be presumed that the wisdom of making less of a target of oneself had become clearly evident as 1864 approached.

CORPORAL, 8TH REGIMENT, THE VETERAN RESERVE CORPS, MARCH 1864

The Veteran Reserve Corps was one of the better ideas to come out of Washington during the Civil War. The corps, which was instituted in April 1863, eventually consisted of twenty-four regiments and a number of independent companies. The idea was to allow disabled soldiers, who were no longer able to serve in the front-line regiments but who still wanted to serve their country, to do so. When first formed, the corps was appropriately named the "Invalid Corps." This name, however, became the object of a number of jokes and at least one popular song, which hinted that this was a place for able-bodied malingerers to serve with no danger of being in combat. All of this resulted in the name of the corps being changed to the Veteran Reserve Corps in March 1864.

The soldiers of the Veteran Reserve Corps performed duties that freed the truly able-bodied to be moved to the front. Those still able to handle a musket were used as guards for railroad bridges, at government installations, and also at prisons for captured Confederates. Those unable to perform this duty were assigned to work in hospitals, as clerks in offices, or even as cooks. For the most part, they served honorably and well. The jokes eventually died out, and those who wore the unique uniform of the Veteran Reserve Corps were proud to do so.

Except for the jacket, the uniform of the various Veteran Reserve Corps regiments was the same as that worn by the soldiers serving in the combat forces. The jacket was adopted in May 1863 and was described by U.S. Army quartermaster regulations as being "of sky blue kersey, with dark blue trimmings, cut like the jacket of cavalry, to come well down on the loins and abdomen." Although the jacket, because of its cut, appears much longer than those issued to the cavalry, it was in fact only about 1 inch longer. It was also made with a slit in the side and shoulder loops, which are not found in the issue cavalry jacket. Chevrons for noncommissioned officers corps were made of the same dark blue worsted lace as the jacket trim.

The soldier pictured here is a corporal of the 8th Regiment who has suffered the loss of part of his right hand. This regiment, along with the 15th Regiment, supplied guards for the Confederate prisoner-of-war camp called Camp Douglas, near Chicago.

The arms for the various Veteran Reserve Corps regiments were initially those that had been turned in as front-line regiments were rearmed with the model 1861 Springfield or the Enfield rifle muskets. In most cases, the muskets carried, at least until mid-1864, were smoothbores. The 8th Regiment was armed with muskets listed on

WILLIAM RODEN

ordnance returns as "Austrian, Prussian, and French caliber .69 to .72." Later in 1864 they received Enfield rifle muskets. The arm carried by this soldier is one of the early Prussian imports. His cartridge box is the standard pre-Civil War U.S. box designed to hold the .69-caliber cartridge. It is likely that guards were issued buckshot cartridges, which would, in fact, make the large-caliber smoothbore musket an ideal weapon for this duty.

Officers of the corps were originally intended to wear a sky blue frock coat. This uniform was not popular, and though some officers did wear a sky blue jacket of the refined cut for an officer, most tended to wear the regulation army dark blue. Another factor that may have influenced this decision was the unlikelihood that private tailors who were regularly supplying uniforms for officers would have had the proper sky blue material on hand to make this garment.

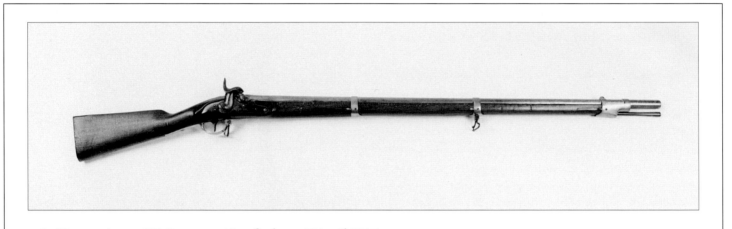

A Prussian "Veteran" of the Civil War

Among the multitude of arms purchased in Europe were thousands of French, Belgian, and Prussian muskets that dated from the first decades of the nineteenth century. Many of these arms had begun life as flintlocks, all had been altered to the more modern percussion cap ignition system. For the most part, the American volunteer would have been better off if these arms had remained in their country of origin. Many a young volunteer of 1861 had his dreams of glory dampened when he received a heavy, outdated arm that was obviously a European castoff. It's a bit of irony that most of these substandard arms ended up in the hands of Union volunteers. Southern soldiers at early battles such as Shiloh in 1862, were often better armed than the men who fought under the flag of the Federal government. By 1863 most of these arms had disappeared from service and were sitting in reserve in Federal and state armories. When the war ended, many of them were purchased at bargain prices from the Federal government by the same brokers who had imported them in 1861. The arms were shipped back to Europe and then sold or used for trade in such areas as Africa, India, and the Orient.

The Gauntlets and Shoulder Straps of a Hero, Major General Joshua L. Chamberlain

For many of today's students of the Civil War, no man stands taller than Maj. Gen. Joshua L. Chamberlain. Chamberlain possessed all the attributes that make a military hero. As a volunteer officer, he was courageous in battle, respected—even loved—by his men, and he always seemed to be in the right place at the right time. To top this off, he was highly literate and wrote several books and reminiscences dealing with his wartime experiences. Perhaps more important, he has attracted the attention of no less then three competent biographers.

Chamberlain's star rose quickly at Gettysburg on July 2, 1863. His regiment, the 20th Maine, held the Union right flank on Little Round Top. After repulsing several determined Confederate attacks, he ordered a bayonet charge, which drove back the Rebels and ended the threat to that critical position. For his action at Gettysburg, he received the Medal of Honor. He was promoted to brigadier by General Grant for gallantry in the early actions against Petersburg, Virginia, and breveted major general for his conduct at the Battle of Five Forks. General Chamberlain was given the honor of receiving the formal surrender of the Army of Northern Virginia at Appomattox. In the postwar years, he was elected governor of Maine three times and served as president of Bowdoin College.

General Chamberlain's gauntlets and shoulder straps remained in his family until 1996, when they were purchased along with his wartime letters. The black background on his shoulder straps clearly shows the modification made for him in the field when he received the second star of a major general. A photograph of General Chamberlain taken at the end of the war, part of the collection of the Maine State Archives, shows him wearing these exact straps.

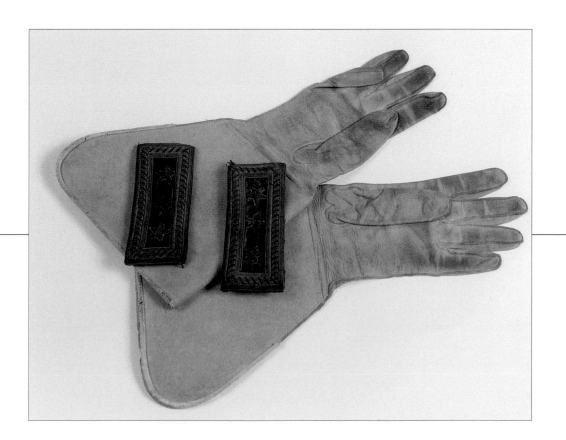

A Simple Wooden Marker for a Fallen Soldier

For the soldier who fell in battle, the erection of even a simple wooden marker was often impossible. It would be left to those who took up his remains for reburial to attempt to place a name with the bones and bits of clothing and equipment they found. For thousands more, death came in the form of disease. These men often died in camp or in a hospital erected near the army's place of encampment. Those whom fate had robbed of a hero's death facing the enemy would at least have their resting places temporarily marked so that friends and family could find them. It is an unfortunate fact, however, that even these markers often did not serve their intended purpose. If left unattended, the effects of weather would cause them to become illegible.

Wyman D. Jacobs of Haverhill, Massachusetts, was one of over 100 of the 50th Massachusetts who would succumb to disease and die far from home. His regiment was one of a number of those enlisted for nine months' service who were sent to the area of New Orleans. In nearly every case, these units reported shocking losses to sickness. This wooden marker, one of the few surviving today of the many thousands erected, identified Jacobs's place of burial near Port Hudson, Louisiana. It was possibly sent home with his remains. During the campaign to take Port Hudson, the 50th Massachusetts reported 103 dead; however, only two men were killed in battle.

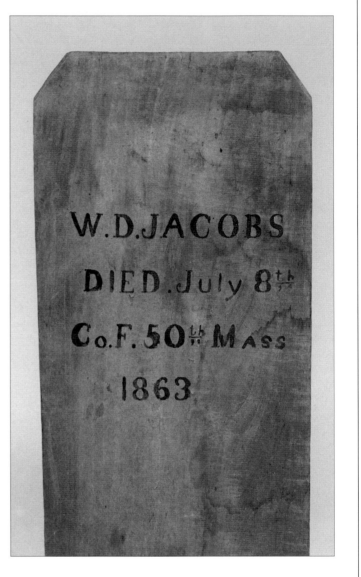